Word Map

Word Map

What words are used where in Australia

builder's smile

Written by Kel Richards

Research by The Macquarie Dictionary and ABC Online

ABC
Books

First published by ABC Books for the
AUSTRALIAN BROADCASTING CORPORATION
GPO Box 9994 Sydney NSW 2001

First published in February 2005

National Library of Australia
Cataloguing-in-publication data:
Richards, Kel, 1946- .
Word map : what words are used where in Australia.

ISBN 0 7333 1540 2.

1. English language - Australia - Terms and phrases.
I. Australian Broadcasting Corporation.
II. Title : Macquarie dictionary.

427.994

Cover design by Christabella Designs
Cover cartoons by Alan Moir
Internals set in 10.5/12.5pt Minion by Kirby Jones
Printed and bound in Australia by Griffin Press, Adelaide

5 4 3 2 1

Introduction

by Susan Butler

Australian Word Map, the corner of the ABC website devoted to Australian regionalisms, is the result of the synthesis of the special aptitudes of Macquarie Dictionary and the ABC. Macquarie does the lexicography behind the scenes. The ABC picks up our small voice and amplifies it across Australia, then follows up by providing the mechanism by which people from around the country can reply.

The idea of collecting regionalisms appealed to the ABC because its role as a national broadcaster requires it to provide services to the regions. It appealed to us because we were tired of the well-worn examples of regionalism that made up our sum of knowledge to date. After *devon*, *fritz*, *polony* etc., what was there to say? The dreadful thought had occurred to us that perhaps regionalism was part of a colonial past and no longer existed under the barrage of national communications and standardisation.

To our delight, the response from the website was immediate and encouraging. At the time of the publication of the *Macquarie ABC Dictionary* we had selected 6000 contributions to go on the site from about twice that number of unedited offerings, and another 6000 people had commented on the listed items. At the time of publication of the dictionary the website was being accessed at the rate of 20,000 hits a week.

The reason for the introduction of an editorial filter was that the response, though enthusiastic, was somewhat undisciplined. We were getting general colloquialisms as well as regionalisms which, if included, would have blurred the focus of the site. We felt that it was better to keep people attuned to the notion of regionalism.

Of course, publication on the site was one thing, but publication in the dictionary was another. For that we needed evidence that an item had some kind of general currency, even if that currency was limited to a small region.

The comments from contributors helped to corroborate offerings which we might otherwise have decided were one-off eccentricities.

In addition we researched other available resources and were able to track down items and in some instances account for their presence in the region. Finally, we compiled a national email list from the addresses helpfully provided by contributors willing to be part of a follow-up campaign. These people were surveyed on a number of items to provide verification for their regions.

The fact that there were words and phrases appearing on Word Map which were new to the editors of the dictionary tells us, I think, that the spoken language is still primary and has a range of expression and a lexicon that goes beyond what might appear in print.

There are phrases that seem to run around the countryside as a national shared joke. Each community develops its own version of the joke which makes it even more delicious. Take, for example, the range of humorous names for a cask of wine – *red handbag, Dapto briefcase* etc. And the collection of words for Speedos – *budgie-smugglers, ballhuggers, nylon disgusters, dick-pokers* or *dick stickers, dick togs* or *DTs*.

Just as the key items of Australian English identify us as a community separate from those communities which speak British English or American English, so too do these regionalisms in their smaller sphere identify a person from one part of the country as distinct from another. Often it is when we move out of the area in which we grew up to another part of the country that we notice the identifying features of our regional dialect. With time, that keen observation blurs and we begin to adopt the local expressions of the new community to which we belong, while retaining a distinct sense of nostalgia about the words we have left behind. Language and identity, even at this local level, are entwined.

Historically there have been two major causes of regional variation – the make-up of the original settlement community with its various language influences, and the imposition of items by state governments setting standards in matters of housing, roads, transport and education.

The original patterns of settlement made different dialects of British English influential in different parts of the country. Victorians may well ask for a *piece* instead of a sandwich, thus revealing a Scottish presence in their community. The Tasmanians refer to a spoiled or troublesome child as a *nointer* betraying a Northern British dialect. How the South Australians acquired the term *gent* for a maggot, a shortening of *gentleman*, which dates back to the jargon of anglers in England in the 1500s, is a mystery.

Background languages had their influence too. So, for example, the German community in the Barossa has given rise to a number of distinct items of English in South Australia, such as *fritz* (a luncheon meat), *schnitter* (a sandwich) and *streusel cake* (a cake with a topping of nuts, sugar and spices).

In some cases regional items from the early days of settlement have become fossilised in a particular community. Thus the *badger box* bears witness still to the fact that colonial Tasmanians referred to *wombats* as *badgers*. There are still rural areas where *echidnas* are known as *porcupines*. Queenslanders will have a *duchesse* in their bedrooms rather than a dressing table, the *duchesse* in mid-nineteenth-century England being a particular kind of dressing table with a swing glass.

The other strongly discernible influence is the statewide standard imposed in some areas of language. Sometimes these jargons are actually set by state governments, as in education and the infrastructure of roads and railways. Sometimes they simply operate within a state by custom and convenience and the influence of statewide media, as in the jargon of real estate.

Thus a *kindergarten* in New South Wales is a *prep class* in Victoria and Tasmania, and a *reception class* in South Australia. A power pole is a *Stobie pole* in South Australia, an *SEC pole* in Victoria, and a *hydro pole* in Tasmania.

A semi-detached house is in South Australia called a *maisonette*. A *sleep-out* is in most of Australia a partially enclosed porch or veranda, but in Victoria it is a building separate from the main house. This building is in Tasmania called a *chalet*.

The nature of particular localities also imposes itself on the language of the community that lives there. Darwin claims the *build-up* because of its tropical weather patterns. Coastal Queensland where sugar cane is grown experiences *black snow*, sometimes called *Burdekin snow*. Plants and animals go by different names in different places, the *crayfish* being a *rock lobster*, a *crawfish*, a *yabby*, a *koonac*, a *marron* or a *gilgie*, depending on where you are.

In the past, collecting evidence of regionalism was a laborious exercise, carried out in the old way, with questionnaires and field research. It is just as well that new technology has given us the means to tap into this aspect of Australian English and move past *devon*, *fritz, polony* ...

Susan Butler
Publisher of the *Macquarie Dictionary*

Introduction

by Kel Richards

Australians are world-renowned for their amusing and inventive colloquialisms. In compiling this book of words I have tried to echo the whimsical and unique tone of Aussie English. The result is a dictionary that should be read while wearing a T-shirt, shorts and thongs rather than a suit, collar and tie. I hope you'll find the *Word Map* to be an enjoyable book that you can dip in and out of, and that belongs as much at the beach or in the bush as it does on the bookshelf. If I should happen to make a surprise visit to your house I don't want to find your copy of the book in immaculate condition, sandwiched between *The Complete Works of William Shakespeare* and Plato's *Republic*. I'd much rather find it lying on the kitchen table, bent and heavily thumbed, with beer and tomato sauce stains on every page.

The aim has been to give you a book that is accurate, but not too serious. This is the first national dictionary of Australian regionalisms, and the first dictionary sourced and compiled from a website. As with all pioneering efforts there will be errors and omissions. Blood, sweat and tears have been expended to minimise errors and omissions – but some will inevitably remain.

For this reason your feedback is absolutely vital. We need to hear from you on entries that are missing, misunderstood or mis-located.

Please send your feedback to the *Macquarie Dictionary* at the following address:

Macquarie Dictionary
Macquarie University
NSW 2109
Australia

And, in the meantime, enjoy the astonishing verbal inventiveness of your fellow Aussies!

Australian Regional Map

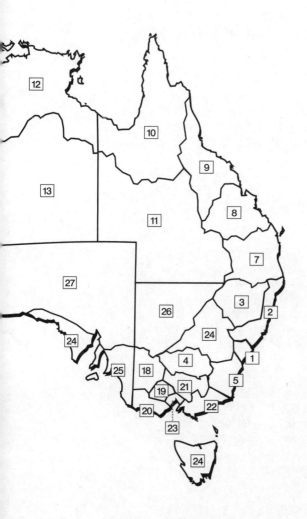

A

acker[1] a large playing marble. The game of marbles has been an extremely popular game with Aussie kids for many years. As a result there's an extraordinary list of names for particular marbles but with wide regional variations. What is an acker in one place is an **alley**, a **doog**, a **cat's eye** or a **tombola** elsewhere. (If a group of adults who grew up in different regions ever tried to play marbles they'd never get past the argument over what to call them!)

[TASMANIA, WIMMERA AND MALLEE, MELBOURNE REGION, EYRE AND YORKE PENINSULAS, ADELAIDE REGION]

acker[2] a pimple (what an American, or American-influenced Aussie, would call a "zit"). Is this related to acker[1]? Was a spectacular pimple ("as big as a marble") called an acker? See also **gumby** and **zots**.

[SYDNEY REGION, MELBOURNE REGION]

ackers testicles. If the cricket ball slammed into your testicles while playing a match on King Island the call for the physio would be: "This bloke's been hit in the ackers!" Elsewhere in Tasmania your injury would have been to the **aggles**. See also **coods**, **goolies**, **nuggets** and **nurries**. [TASMANIA]

ACTION acronym for the "ACT Internal Omnibus Network". It would appeal to the Australian sense of irony to call catching the bus "taking ACTION". [SOUTH COAST AND SOUTHERN TABLELANDS]

afters childcare provided at the school after school hours. See also **BASC** and **oosh**. [MELBOURNE REGION]

aggles marbles. Some contributors reported knowing these marbles as "aggies". However, in Tasmania aggles means "testicles" (except for King Island where the same anatomic items are known as **ackers**). Hence, when visiting Tasmania, and admiring someone's marbles, it's probably best not to say "Nice aggles!"

[MELBOURNE REGION, TASMANIA]

A-grouper anyone born in Broken Hill. "In the old days," wrote one contributor, "you had to be an A-grouper, or married to one, to get a job in the mines." Another suggested being born or educated in the West Darling region made you an A-grouper. See also **B-grouper**.

[FAR WEST NSW]

AJ army personnel. This seems to have born in Townsville (site of a major military base) as the derogatory term "army jerks". But, like all useful expressions, it then spread.

[BRISBANE REGION, CENTRAL COAST QLD, NORTH COAST QLD]

Albany doctor a cooling afternoon sea breeze which arrives in Kalgoorlie. There are several of these winds providing medical attention on hot days. See also **Canberra doctor**; **doctor, the**; **Esperance doctor** and **Fremantle doctor**. [CENTRAL WEST AUSTRALIA]

alleys both the name of the game "marbles" and a name for individual marbles. The alley became (in the 1940s, 1950s and 1960s) a common synonym for the word "marbles" itself. The game you played was alleys and what you played with were also alleys. See also **dibs**[1] and **doogs**.

[BRISBANE REGION, PERTH REGION, TASMANIA, GIPPSLAND, MELBOURNE REGION, ADELAIDE REGION, FAR WEST NSW]

American in suburban Melbourne in the 1950s and 1960s some marbles were named after their patterns: there were **birdcages** (with an internal net pattern) and Americans (opaque with three colours). [MELBOURNE REGION]

apple scroll a rolled sweet bun containing diced apple. Typical school **tuck shop** fare. See also **London bun**.

[MELBOURNE REGION, ADELAIDE REGION]

aqua bog a **bogan** who wears surf shirts with black jeans and black ripple sole desert boots. This sort of dress sense was also rewarded with the labels "surfs", "surfies", "skegs" or "skeg heads". [PERTH REGION]

arcing up 1. crying. 2. launching a verbal attack. 3. an angry reaction (perhaps parallel to the expression "bridle up"). One contributor suggests the expression comes from welders starting to weld steel: the cry "arcing up" was a warning to look away.

[SYDNEY REGION, NORTH COAST QLD, TASMANIA, NORTHERN VICTORIA, MELBOURNE REGION]

area school a state school in a rural area providing both primary and secondary education. See also **central school**, **consolidated school**, **district school**, **high top** and **secondary tops**.

[EYRE AND YORKE PENINSULAS, ADELAIDE REGION, NORTHERN SOUTH AUSTRALIA, TASMANIA]

arftie a SA abbreviation of "afternoon". See also **arvey**, **arvo**[1], **sarvey** and **sarvo**.

[EYRE AND YORKE PENINSULAS, ADELAIDE REGION, NORTHERN SOUTH AUSTRALIA]

arrester bed an area on the side of a road filled with soft sand and gravel in which a vehicle can be brought to a halt if the brakes fail. Also called a "vehicle arrester bed" or "truck arrester bed". See **safety ramp.** [CENTRAL WEST AUSTRALIA, PERTH REGION]

arvey another Australian diminutive for "afternoon". See also **arftie**, **arvo**[1], **sarvey** and **sarvo**. [SYDNEY REGION]

arvo[1] perhaps the most common of the many abbreviations of "afternoon" in Australia. See also **arftie**, **sarvey** and **sarvo**.

[SYDNEY REGION, TASMANIA, BRISBANE REGION, NORTH COAST QLD, FAR NORTH QLD, MELBOURNE REGION, PERTH REGION]

arvo[2] afternoon detention at high school. [SYDNEY REGION]

Ascotian (rhymes with "lotion") a resident of the Brisbane suburb of Ascot. [BRISBANE REGION]

as dry as a blacksmith's apron thirsty; very thirsty; or perhaps very *very* thirsty! [HUNTER VALLEY AND NORTH COAST]

Ashgrovian(s) 1. women's high-heeled boots reaching to just under the knee. (The name reportedly comes from the Brisbane suburb of Ashgrove.) 2. residents of the suburb of Ashgrove. 3. a domestic architectural style associated with the Brisbane suburb of Ashgrove (typically a multi-gabled house with a wide front veranda or portico). [BRISBANE REGION]

assembly a weekly gathering of the entire school. Commonly held outside with pupils lined up rank and file. See also **parade.**

[ADELAIDE REGION, SYDNEY REGION, MELBOURNE REGION, BRISBANE REGION, SOUTH COAST AND SOUTHERN TABLELANDS, HUNTER VALLEY AND NORTH COAST]

attack of the flying axe handles severe and sudden diarrhoea.

[TASMANIA]

aunty arms the flabby triceps of an overweight woman. See also **bingo wings**, **by nows**, **good-bye muscle**, **nannas**, **piano arms**, **reverse biceps**, **ta-ta flaps**, **tuckshop arm** and **widow's curtain.**

[NORTH COAST QLD]

Australia used by Tasmanians when referring to the mainland. See also **big island; mainland, the; northern island** and **other side, the**. [TASMANIA]

autotray (or "autotrolley") a tea trolley; a small table on castors for carrying dishes when serving food, tea, coffee etc. See also **traymobile**.

[WIMMERA AND MALLEE, CENTRAL HIGHLANDS VICTORIA, WESTERN DISTRICT, NORTHERN VICTORIA, GIPPSLAND, MELBOURNE REGION, TASMANIA]

away where people who are not born in Broken Hill come from. Also used in the same way on King Island. (You're either from "here" or from "away".) [TASMANIA, FAR WEST NSW, CENTRAL WEST NSW]

axle grease Vegemite. See also **blacka butter**.

[CENTRAL HIGHLANDS VICTORIA]

B

backpacker an elderly person occupying a room in an aged care hostel on a respite care basis. [THE RIVERINA]

back sack the Melbourne name for what is elsewhere called a "back pack" or "ruck sack". [MELBOURNE REGION]

back-seat bogan a kid sitting in the back seat of the school bus (where you'd expect to find a **bogan** sitting). Also "back seat **bevan**" or "back seat toughie".
[PERTH REGION, MELBOURNE REGION, BRISBANE REGION]

badger wombat. (Hence the Tasmanian placenames that include "badger" as a component.) [TASMANIA]

badger! an expression uttered by schoolboys after breaking wind. It's followed quickly by a whistling noise. This ritual prevents other schoolboys from pummelling the perpetrator for his antisocial offence. See also **vince**.
[PERTH REGION, MELBOURNE REGION, ADELAIDE REGION, WIMMERA AND MALLEE]

badger box a shack or poorly built house. This term was used by workers felling Huon pine trees on the west coast of Tasmania in the 19th century for the small, temporary huts they built. Conditions in these huts were poor, prone to flooding and constantly leaking due to the metres of annual rainfall in the area. See also **humpy**. [TASMANIA]

badlands the rural area surrounding Darwin. (Possibly a melodramatic media coinage.) [DARWIN AND NORTH COAST NT]

bag schoolgirls' slang for a good-looking young man. [SYDNEY REGION]

bag it drive fast. See also **fang**. [SYDNEY REGION]

bag of death a cask of cheap wine, usually red. See also **Balga handbag**, **Bellambi handbag**, **boxie**, **box monster**, **Broadmeadows briefcase**, **cardboard handbag**, **Coraki handbag**, **death bag**, **Dubbo handbag**, **gin's handbag**, **goon**, **goonbag**, **goonbox**, **goonie**, **goonsack**, **lady in the boat**, **red handbag**, **sack** and **vino collapso**. [TASMANIA]

bag of doughnuts a fat person. [PERTH REGION]

bags (something) to lay claim to (something). (More commonly used by children than adults.)
[PERTH REGION, SYDNEY REGION, ADELAIDE REGION]

Baillie in need of psychiatric care. (From Baillie Henderson Psychiatric Hospital in Toowoomba) See also **crackadog**, **Richmond Clinic**, **ward eight**, **ward twenty** and **womba**.
[BRISBANE REGION]

baldie a white-headed pigeon (also sometimes applied to Poll Hereford cattle). [HUNTER VALLEY AND NORTH COAST]

Balga Bog a **bogan** from Balga. [PERTH REGION]

Balga by the sea the northern suburbs of Perth (such as Merriwa, Clarkson etc.), site of numerous housing commission homes.
[PERTH REGION]

Balga handbag a cask of wine See also **bag of death**, **Bellambi handbag**, **boxie**, **box monster**, **Broadmeadows briefcase**, **cardboard handbag**, **Coraki handbag**, **death bag**, **Dubbo handbag**, **gin's handbag**, **goon**, **goonbag**, **goonbox**, **goonie**, **goonsack**, **lady in the boat**, **red handbag**, **sack** and **vino collapso**.
[PERTH REGION]

ballhuggers see **Speedos**. See also **boasters**, **budgie-huggers**, **budgie-smugglers**, **cluster busters**, **cockchokers**, **cock jocks**, **codjocks**, **dick bathers**, **dick-pointers**, **dick-pokers**, **dick stickers**, **dick togs**, **dikdaks**, **dipsticks**, **fish frighteners**, **jammers**, **Jimmy clingers**, **knobbies**, **lolly-baggers**, **lolly bags**, **meat-hangers**, **nut huggers**, **nylon disgusters**, **racers**, **racing bathers**, **scungies**[2], **sluggers**, **sluggos**, **slug huggers**, **tights**, **toolies**, **trunks** and **wog togs.** [PERTH REGION, MELBOURNE REGION]

Balmain basket weavers pathetically politically correct greenies who choose to live in the concrete and brick of expensive inner Sydney. (Coined by former prime minister Paul Keating.)
[SYDNEY REGION]

Balmain bulldozer a four-wheel drive that never sees the bush (but sits in a neatly cemented driveway pining for the feel of dirt and mud beneath its tyres). See also **Bronte buggy**, **Burnside bus**,

Kenmore tractor, **North Shore tank**, **Rose Bay shopping trolley**, **Toorak tractor** and **Turramurra tractor**. [SYDNEY REGION]

banana[1] one strongly opposed to development of any kind. (From "Build Absolutely Nothing Anywhere Near Anybody"). An extreme case of the "Nimby" ("Not in My Backyard"). [MELBOURNE REGION]

banana[2] a splash-generating leap into the swimming pool with one leg tucked up under the arms and the other extended. See also **can-opener**, **horsey** and **peg leg**. [MELBOURNE REGION]

bandicoot to steal potatoes from a field or garden by digging under the plant without disturbing its top. (Can be used on other fruit and veg obtained in a similarly secretive fashion.) [GIPPSLAND, TASMANIA]

bandy to waste time. Also spelled "bandie". [WESTERN DISTRICT]

bandy abbreviation of "bandicoot" (small marsupials belonging to the *Peramelidae* and *Thylacomyidae* families). [TASMANIA]

banger an idiot (not worth bothering with). See also **minda**, **nuff nuff**, **oxygen thief**, **random** and **roo**. [PERTH REGION]

bar[1] 1. an exclamation used to gain a respite from the rules during a children's game. 2. a designated place where such safety is found during a game. From **barley** which has been used in this way by children (reports folklorist June Factor) since the 14th century (possibly originally from the French *parlez*, in English "parley" – a place of truce, safe quarters). There is some evidence that this outcry used in children's play continued in Australia after it had died out in Britain (although this is not certain). Sometimes as **bars**[1], **barley** or **barleys**, or spelled out as B-A-R. (Not an Australian term as such, but used with regional variations around Australia.) See also **var lese**. [SYDNEY REGION, HUNTER VALLEY AND NORTH COAST, NEW ENGLAND DISTRICT, THE RIVERINA, SOUTH COAST AND SOUTHERN TABLELANDS, CENTRAL WEST NSW, BRISBANE REGION, CENTRAL COAST QLD, NORTH COAST QLD]

bar[2] 1. to carry a second person on a horse, bicycle or motorcycle. 2. a ride as a secondary passenger. See also **dink**, **dinky**[1], **dinky-double**, **donkey**[1], **double**, **dub** and **pug**. [HUNTER VALLEY AND NORTH COAST]

bar[3] 1. to lay claim to. (See also **bags** and **dibs**[1].) 2. to rule out a person or possibility (as in "Jimmy you're barred from the next game").

[BRISBANE REGION, CENTRAL COAST QLD, NORTH COAST QLD]

Barcy abbreviation for Barcaldine (western Queensland).

[BRISBANE REGION, WEST CENTRAL QLD]

barie to give someone a ride on the bar of your pushbike. Also spelled "barrie". (Note: pronounced bar-ee.) See also **dink**, **dinky**[1], **dinky-double**, **donkey**[1], **double**, **dub** and **pug**.

[HUNTER VALLEY AND NORTH COAST]

barkada a group of friends, mates or regular companions.

[WIMMERA AND MALLEE]

barkers woollen socks. [SOUTH COAST AND SOUTHERN TABLELANDS]

barker's egg canine faecal matter (usually adhering to the sole of your shoe, because you didn't look where you trod, did you, eh?) See also **barker's nest**.

[SOUTH COAST AND SOUTHERN TABLELANDS, MELBOURNE REGION, PERTH REGION, GIPPSLAND, ADELAIDE REGION, EYRE AND YORKE PENINSULAS]

barker's nest see **barker's egg**. [MELBOURNE REGION, TASMANIA]

barley an outcry claiming safety or immunity during a children's game. Often the place of safety would be decided before the game began. Sometimes it was not a place, but a colour (such as touching or holding anything green, in which case the cry might be: "barley green!"). See also **bar**[1], **barleys**, **bars** and **var lese**. (For a suggestion as to the source see **bar**[1].)

[CENTRAL HIGHLANDS VICTORIA, GIPPSLAND, MELBOURNE REGION, NORTHERN VICTORIA, WESTERN DISTRICT, WIMMERA AND MALLEE]

barleys see **bar**[1], **barley**, **bars**. (Some contributors reported using this expression, or a variation of it, as adults to mean "let's not touch that subject".)

[ADELAIDE REGION, NORTHERN SOUTH AUSTRALIA, WIMMERA AND MALLEE, EYRE AND YORKE PENINSULAS, PERTH REGION, CENTRAL WEST AUSTRALIA, MELBOURNE REGION, WESTERN DISTRICT]

barmy as a bandicoot sub-clinically neurotic. [TASMANIA]

Barney box an esky bulging with beer. [BRISBANE REGION]

barnie a lie, a tall tale, an exaggerated story. [SYDNEY REGION]

baron sausage see **beef Belgium**, **Belgium sausage**, **bung fritz**, **Byron sausage**, **devon**, **Empire sausage**, **fritz**, **German sausage**, **luncheon sausage**, **mystery meat**, **polony**, **pork German**, **Strasburg** and **Windsor sausage**. [HUNTER VALLEY AND NORTH COAST]

barouche operating theatre trolley.
[EYRE AND YORKE PENINSULAS, ADELAIDE REGION, NORTHERN SOUTH AUSTRALIA]

barred excluded. [SOUTH COAST AND SOUTHERN TABLELANDS, SYDNEY REGION]

barry 1. a young **bogan** or the younger brother of a **bogan**. 2. a bad experience, or a bad joke, a "real shocker" (rhyming slang, from Barry Crocker).
[PERTH REGION, TASMANIA, BRISBANE REGION, SYDNEY REGION, HUNTER VALLEY AND NORTH COAST]

bars[1] see **bar**[1], **barley**, **barleys** and **var lese**.
[ADELAIDE REGION, WIMMERA AND MALLEE, EYRE AND YORKE PENINSULAS]

bars[2] to lay claim to. See also **bags** and **dibs**[1].
[ADELAIDE REGION, SOUTH COAST AND SOUTHERN TABLELANDS]

Barwell's bull a type of railcar introduced on South Australian country lines in the 1920s. From the name of the premier at the time, the Honourable Sir H.N. Barwell, KCMG (premier of South Australia 1920-24), and the horn of these railcars, described as being "a loud and not very melodious bellow". (One is preserved and still operates on the Pichi Richi Railway.) The last of these 75 class railcars was retired in 1971. See also **blue bird**, **Brill car** and **red hen**. (Sometimes known as "a Barwell Bull", or just "Bull".)
[ADELAIDE REGION, EYRE AND YORKE PENINSULAS, NORTHERN SOUTH AUSTRALIA]

BASC acronym for "Before and After School Care". See also **afters** and **oosh**. [SYDNEY REGION]

baso a style of haircut that looks as though a basin has been placed over the victim's head, and all the hair remaining visible trimmed off. Also known as a "basin haircut". Later, a nickname for all bad haircuts. [ADELAIDE REGION, FAR WEST NSW]

bathers a swimming costume. Non-users of this term regard it as either old fashioned or a bit "proper", perhaps on the grounds that it's a long time since the activity of swimming has been called "bathing" (although one Sydney contributor reported wearing a "cossie" when he went to swim at the Bankstown **baths**). See also **clubbies**[1], **cossie**, **costume**, **swimmers**, **swimsuit**, **togs** and **trunks**.

[ADELAIDE REGION, PERTH REGION, MELBOURNE REGION, TASMANIA, WIMMERA AND MALLEE, BRISBANE REGION, FAR WEST NSW, SOUTH COAST AND SOUTHERN TABLELANDS, THE RIVERINA, DARWIN AND NORTH COAST NT, THE CENTRE]

bathing box a small privately owned structure erected on a beach, particularly those of Port Phillip, to provide shelter for those enjoying beach activities. See also **beach box** and **boat shed**. (Those that still survive are now regarded as a valuable asset.)

[MELBOURNE REGION]

baths public swimming pools. Some Melbournian contributors remember "baths" as fenced or supervised sea water swimming areas (in contrast to the municipal swimming pool); and some country contributors remember "baths" as referring to fenced-in pools on rivers (in both cases the reference is to something other than an Olympic-length facility). See also **pools**.

[MELBOURNE REGION, BRISBANE REGION, SOUTH COAST AND SOUTHERN TABLELANDS]

batter the high wall of an open-pit mine. [PERTH REGION]

battered sav a saveloy deep fried in thick batter then dipped in tomato sauce; also called a **dagwood dog**, **death stick**, **dippy dog**, or **pluto pup**. (Basically, cholesterol on a stick.) [SYDNEY REGION]

Baulko the Sydney suburb of Baulkham Hills. [SYDNEY REGION]

the bay 1. Byron Bay [HUNTER VALLEY AND NORTH COAST]. 2. Glenelg [ADELAIDE REGION]. 3. Nelson Bay or Shoal Bay at Port Stephens [HUNTER VALLEY AND NORTH COAST] 4. Port Phillip Bay [MELBOURNE REGION].

bay trout another name for Australian salmon.

[WIMMERA AND MALLEE, CENTRAL HIGHLANDS VICTORIA, WESTERN DISTRICT, NORTHERN VICTORIA, GIPPSLAND, MELBOURNE REGION]

bazman an extension of **barry** (meaning "shocker"); something worse than shocking (a bazman is a barry with bells on!)
[HUNTER VALLEY AND NORTH COAST]

beamie a handball game that involves bouncing the ball against a wooden building beam (often played underneath the old high-set high school buildings of Queensland).
[NORTH COAST QLD, CENTRAL COAST QLD, WEST CENTRAL QLD]

beanie brigade people who wear checked flannelette shirts and knitted hats (not a good fashion statement). [SYDNEY REGION]

bed a group of trees, usually of the same type, growing together (now largely obsolete). [TASMANIA]

bedlam a playground game. According to some contributors similar to hide-and-seek, according to others closer to **cockylora**. See also **British bulldog**, **bullrush**, **hipstick** and **red rover**.
[BRISBANE REGION, NORTH COAST QLD]

beef Belgium processed meat. See also **baron sausage**, **Belgium sausage**, **Byron sausage**, **bung fritz**, **devon**, **Empire sausage**, **fritz**, **German sausage**, **luncheon sausage**, **mystery meat**, **polony**, **pork German**, **Strasburg** and **Windsor sausage**. [TASMANIA]

beer coat an invisible garment, donned by consuming numerous beers, which miraculously protects the "wearer" from the cold.
[SYDNEY REGION]

bee's whisker an informal unit of measurement; an extremely small distance. [ADELAIDE REGION]

beetle crushers the feet. [PERTH REGION]

befores 1. before-school childcare (contrasts with **afters**).
[MELBOURNE REGION] 2. a party held before setting off to a school ball or formal. [PERTH REGION]

Belco the Canberra suburb of Belconnen.
[SOUTH COAST AND SOUTHERN TABLELANDS]

Belgium sausage processed smallgoods that had once been meat in a previous existence (sometimes just "Belgium" for short). See also **baron sausage**, **beef Belgium**, **Byron sausage**, **bung fritz**,

devon, **Empire sausage**, **fritz**, **German sausage**, **luncheon sausage**, **mystery meat**, **polony**, **pork German**, **Strasburg**, **wheel meat** and **Windsor sausage**. [TASMANIA, CENTRAL COAST QLD]

Bellambi handbag a cask of wine (especially that favoured by teenagers for drinking in a park or at the beach). See also **bag of death**, **Balga handbag**, **boxie**, **box monster**, **Broadmeadows briefcase**, **cardboard handbag**, **Coraki handbag**, **death bag**, **Dubbo handbag**, **gin's handbag**, **goon**, **goonbag**, **goonbox**, **goonie**, **goonsack**, **lady in the boat**, **red handbag**, **sack** and **vino collapso**. [SOUTH COAST AND SOUTHERN TABLELANDS]

belly buster a poorly executed and painful dive in which one hits the water stomach first. See also **belly flop** and **belly whacker**. [SYDNEY REGION]

belly flop see **belly buster** and **belly whacker**. [HUNTER VALLEY AND NORTH COAST, FAR WEST NSW, MELBOURNE REGION]

belly whacker see **belly buster** and **belly flop**. [GIPPSLAND, SYDNEY REGION, MELBOURNE REGION]

below-ground pool a domestic swimming pool set into the ground. Elsewhere an **in-ground pool**. [WEST AUSTRALIA, CENTRAL WEST AUSTRALIA, PERTH REGION]

bennie see **bevan**. See also **bethan**, **bog**[2], **bogan**, **booner**, **boonie**, **chigger**, **chookie**, **cogger**[1], **garry**, **scozzer** and **westie**. [TASMANIA]

berliner a jam-filled doughnut (sometimes also containing cream filling, and sometimes iced). [ADELAIDE REGION]

berm the grassy verge in front of the house. (Of New Zealand origin; unclear why it caught on in Perth and not elsewhere.) [PERTH REGION]

Bermuda jacket a sports jacket (usually navy blue) with silver buttons. See also **reefer jacket**. [ADELAIDE REGION, SYDNEY REGION]

Berrimah line an imaginary line separating Darwin from the rest of the Northern Territory. From Berrimah, a suburb on the southern edge of Darwin, on the Stuart Highway (supposedly the limit of Territorian politicians' interest). [DARWIN AND NORTH COAST NT]

best and fairest an award for the football player who has displayed the greatest skill and fairest play during a season. See also **fairest and best**.

[SYDNEY REGION, HUNTER VALLEY AND NORTH COAST, NEW ENGLAND DISTRICT, THE RIVERINA, SOUTH COAST AND SOUTHERN TABLELANDS, CENTRAL WEST NSW, FAR WEST NSW, BRISBANE REGION, CENTRAL COAST QLD, NORTH COAST QLD, FAR NORTH QLD, WEST CENTRAL QLD, TASMANIA, WIMMERA AND MALLEE, CENTRAL HIGHLANDS VICTORIA, WESTERN DISTRICT, NORTHERN VICTORIA, GIPPSLAND, MELBOURNE REGION]

bethan similar to **westie**, **bevan** and **bogan** (from the Adelaide suburb of Elizabeth). See also **bennie**, **bog**², **booner**, **boonie**, **chigger**, **garry** and **scozzer**. [ADELAIDE REGION]

bevan a young man who is uncool, a dag (from the male name Bevan). See also **bennie**, **bethan**, **bog**², **bogan**, **booner**, **boonie**, **chigger**, **chookie**, **cogger**¹, **feral**, **garry**, **scozza** and **westie**.

[BRISBANE REGION, CENTRAL COAST QLD, NORTH COAST QLD, FAR NORTH QLD, WEST CENTRAL QLD, NEW ENGLAND DISTRICT, SYDNEY REGION, MELBOURNE REGION]

bev-chick the girlfriend of a **bevan**. [NORTH COAST QLD]

B-grouper someone not born in Broken Hill who has the unmitigated gall to live there (a caste system determining the order in which people are laid off during employment downturns). See also **A-grouper**. [FAR WEST NSW]

Bidgee abbreviation of Murrumbidgee. [THE RIVERINA]

big bot a 750 ml bottle of beer. See also **big bud**, **Corinna stubby**, **longie**, **long neck** and **tallie**. [NEW ENGLAND DISTRICT]

big bud a large bottle of beer also known as a **long neck**. See also **big bot**, **Corinna stubby**, **longie** and **tallie**.

[EYRE AND YORKE PENINSULAS]

big dipper a steep section of the F3 freeway at Wahroonga.

[SYDNEY REGION]

big henry a large bottle of beer. See also **depth charger**.

[NORTHERN SOUTH AUSTRALIA]

big island the Australian **mainland**. See also **Australia, the mainland, north island** and **the other side**. [TASMANIA]

big lunch 1. the midday break at school. 2. the meal eaten during this break. See also **little lunch**, **little play**, **play lunch**, **playtime**, **recess** and **snack**. (Contributors' comments suggest this term, and its collateral **little lunch**, may have been born in Queensland and then, like the cane toad, migrated south.)
[SYDNEY REGION, HUNTER VALLEY AND NORTH COAST, NEW ENGLAND DISTRICT, THE RIVERINA, SOUTH COAST AND SOUTHERN TABLELANDS, CENTRAL WEST NSW, BRISBANE REGION, CENTRAL COAST QLD, NORTH COAST QLD, TASMANIA, CENTRAL WEST]

big mob lots. Used of any group that can come in large numbers (cattle, people etc.).
[DARWIN AND NORTH COAST NT, FAR NORTH QLD, WEST CENTRAL QLD, CENTRAL WEST AUSTRALIA, NORTHERN SOUTH AUSTRALIA, THE CENTRE]

big school primary school (in contrast to preschool).
[SOUTH COAST AND SOUTHERN TABLELANDS]

big wet, the monsoon season in tropical north Queensland.
[NORTH COAST QLD]

biggest mob lots more; bigger than a **big mob**.
[DARWIN AND NORTH COAST NT, FAR NORTH QLD, WEST CENTRAL QLD, CENTRAL WEST AUSTRALIA, NORTHERN SOUTH AUSTRALIA, THE CENTRE]

bilby a person of poor or uneducated background; local equivalent of the American "hayseed" or "hillbilly". See also **charnie bum**.
[HUNTER VALLEY AND NORTH COAST]

Bill Lawry a bottle opener or corkscrew (from one of Australian cricket's most famous opening batsmen). [PERTH REGION]

billy a surfer from Bankstown (i.e. someone who surfs badly). In full a "Billy Bankstowner". [SOUTH COAST AND SOUTHERN TABLELANDS]

billy bot a greenish glass marble (originally a stopper in an old-fashioned bottle). [THE RIVERINA]

billy boulder a large rock. (Much sought after in the sapphire areas of Queensland as an indicator of the possible presence of sapphires.) [WEST CENTRAL QLD]

billy cart a small, homemade cart used by children as a downhill racer (propelled by gravity, and stopped, as a rule, by steering into the nearest large object). At one time the standard billy cart consisted of a fruit box on pram wheels (although ball-bearings made a better noise and were, possibly, faster). Also spelled "billie cart". The name (possibly) comes from their resemblance to small carts drawn by billygoats (in the days before motor cars became common). One contributor wrote: "Pram wheels, a drink crate, a plank, a steering bolt, a rope and a few nails and the hill was yours!" See also **go-cart**, **hill trolley** and **soapbox**.

[SYDNEY REGION, MELBOURNE REGION, PERTH REGION, CENTRAL HIGHLANDS VICTORIA, NORTHERN SOUTH AUSTRALIA]

billy-cart hill a steep, straight stretch of road, perfect for billy carts.

[CENTRAL HIGHLANDS VICTORIA]

Billy Dunn nails (or "Billy Boulders") rocks used to hold a corrugated-iron roof in place. [WEST CENTRAL QLD]

billy grips a utensil for picking up a hot billy. Sometimes "billy lifters" or "billy tongs". [MELBOURNE REGION]

billy lids kids (rhyming slang). [MELBOURNE REGION]

billy longleg a spider. (Elsewhere a "daddy longlegs".)

[WEST CENTRAL QLD]

BIN acronym "born in Narrogin". (Derogatory, implying stupidity.) From the small town south-east of Perth. [PERTH REGION]

bindi-eye 1. a low-growing plant (*Soliva pterosperma*) often found in lawns, with small spiky burrs which cannot penetrate footwear but are painful for bare feet. 2. one of the burrs from this plant. 3. a daisy-like flower (*Calotis cuneiflora*) found in the dry areas of central and eastern Australia. 4. also loosely applied to a range of weedy plants with sharp spines. Also spelled "bindii" and "bindi-I". From the Kamilaroi and Yuwaalarraay Aboriginal languages. See also **bindy**, **joey**, **jo-jo** and **prickle**.

[SYDNEY REGION, BRISBANE REGION, WIMMERA AND MALLEE, FAR NORTH QLD, CENTRAL WEST AUSTRALIA, MELBOURNE REGION]

bindy an abbreviation of **bindi-eye**. Also spelled "bindi". See also **joey**, **jo-jo** and **prickle**.

[PERTH REGION, CENTRAL WEST AUSTRALIA, SYDNEY REGION, BRISBANE REGION, MELBOURNE REGION, NEW ENGLAND DISTRICT, SOUTH COAST AND SOUTHERN TABLELANDS]

binghi an Aboriginal person. [NORTHERN WEST AUSTRALIA]

bingo wings the flabby triceps (upper arms) of an overweight woman. Sometimes "bingo arms". See also **aunty arms**, **good-bye muscle**, **nannas**, **piano arm**, **reverse biceps**, **ta-ta flaps**, **tuckshop arm** and **widow's curtain**. [PERTH REGION, SYDNEY REGION]

binji stomach (Aboriginal word). See also **binny**[1]. [SOUTH COAST AND SOUTHERN TABLELANDS]

Binjour bear a legendary creature living in the Binjour Plateau area; possibly a type of yowie, or an ape or bear escaped from a circus. See also **Pilliga yowie**. [BRISBANE REGION]

bin man a council worker who collects garbage bins; a "garbage man" See also **garbo** and **rubbish collector**. [PERTH REGION, SYDNEY REGION]

binny[1] stomach (an infantile term, like "tummy"). [MELBOURNE REGION]

binny[2] unappealing; belongs in the rubbish bin. [MELBOURNE REGION]

birdcages marbles with an internal net pattern. [MELBOURNE REGION]

biscuit when feeding a horse the hay bale is broken into parts and each part is called a biscuit. [EYRE AND YORKE PENINSULAS, ADELAIDE REGION, NORTHERN SOUTH AUSTRALIA]

biscuit factory the men's toilet. (From the Adelaide-based biscuit manufacturer W. Menz & Co.) [MELBOURNE REGION]

bitamin sealed road (the "bitumen"). [ADELAIDE REGION, TASMANIA]

BJ iced coffee ("**bogan** juice"). [ADELAIDE REGION]

blacka butter Vegemite. See also **axle grease**. [MELBOURNE REGION]

black aspirin cola, used as a hangover cure. [HUNTER VALLEY AND NORTH COAST]

black bob an inbred rural yokel (symptoms: receding chin and low IQ). [CENTRAL COAST QLD, TASMANIA]

black death any brand of cola soft drink. Sometimes abbreviated to "death". See also **black aspirin** and **black doctor**. [SOUTH COAST AND SOUTHERN TABLELANDS]

black doctor any brand of cola soft drink. See also **black aspirin** and **black death**. [CENTRAL WEST NSW]

Blackers the Sydney suburb of Blacktown. Sometimes spelled "Blackas". [SYDNEY REGION]

blackfella's spear the tall stalk on which the seed pod of a grasstree grows. [HUNTER VALLEY AND NORTH COAST]

Blackheathens residents of Blackheath (Blue Mountains, NSW). [SYDNEY REGION]

blackies large yabbies. Apparently yabbies change colour as they grow in size and age – from **greenies** to **blueys** to **blackies**. [MELBOURNE REGION]

black over Bill's mother's, it's dark storm clouds on the horizon. [NEW ENGLAND DISTRICT]

black prince a type of cicada, black in colour. See also **brown baker**, **brown bomber**[2], **cicada**, **cherrynose**, **floury baker**, **greengrocer**[2], **tick tock** and **yellow Monday**. [SYDNEY REGION]

black rat a can of rum and cola. [NORTH COAST QLD, DARWIN AND NORTH COAST NT]

blacks an unrestricted driver's licence; the progression being from L plates to P plates to blacks. [SYDNEY REGION]

black snake a crowbar. [WEST CENTRAL QLD]

black snake it to go to bed in your work clothes (without the benefit of a bath or shower). One step worse is to **king cobra**. [PERTH REGION, FAR NORTH QLD, NORTH COAST QLD]

black snow embers from sugarcane fires drifting through the air (and settling on the washing you've just hung out to dry). [BRISBANE REGION]

blind man an exclamation of understanding, of comprehension; short for "'I see!' said the blind man". [PERTH REGION]

blind mullet untreated faecal matter released into waterways. See also **blind trout**, **Bondi cigar**, **brown trout**, **pollywaffle** and **Werribee trout**. [SOUTH COAST AND SOUTHERN TABLELANDS]

blind trout see **blind mullet**. [TASMANIA]

block a carton of beer. See also **box**, **carton**, **case**[2] and **slab**.
[PERTH REGION]

block bombing driving a car continuously around the CBD of west coast Tasmanian towns, usually looking for girls. [TASMANIA]

blocker 1. the occupier of a small block of rural land.
2. one who owns a **fruit block** (a small orchard or vineyard). See also **blockie**[1].
[ADELAIDE REGION, CENTRAL HIGHLANDS VICTORIA, EYRE AND YORKE PENINSULAS, GIPPSLAND, MELBOURNE REGION, NORTHERN VICTORIA, TASMANIA, WESTERN DISTRICT, WIMMERA AND MALLEE]

blockie[1] a horticulturist; owner of a **fruit block**.
[WIMMERA AND MALLEE, THE RIVERINA]

blockie[2] to drive around a block doing only left-hand turns (usually in a fast, noisy car – small things amusing small minds).
[NORTHERN VICTORIA, TASMANIA]

blockie[3] a person who buys a (usually agriculturally unviable) block of land from a developer, moving from city to country.
[BRISBANE REGION]

blocko a schoolyard game. Several contributors kindly sent us the rules for blocko which turn out to be more complicated than chess and more confusing than Gaelic football (hence they are not reproduced here – they may, however, be published separately in six large volumes as *The Blocko Book*). [ADELAIDE REGION]

block rat a cadet at Duntroon or the Australian Defence Force Academy military colleges who stays in on weekends and doesn't socialise. See also **cordie**[2]. [SOUTH COAST AND SOUTHERN TABLELANDS]

bloke of … a person having the name of … (as in "That bloke of Smith …") See also **girl of …**
[SOUTH COAST AND SOUTHERN TABLELANDS, HUNTER VALLEY AND NORTH COAST, CENTRAL WEST NSW]

blood blister sister. [MELBOURNE REGION]

blood-eye a white marble with a red streak. [PERTH REGION]

blood nose bleeding from the nose. Some contributors distinguished between these terms, rather than seeing them as synonyms; as in, "One has a **nosebleed** for medical reasons, but is given a blood nose by a blow". Others, however, did not see this distinction. It's suggested that blood nose is a bowdlerised version of **bloody nose**. See also **bloody nose** and **nosebleed**.
[ADELAIDE REGION, CENTRAL HIGHLANDS VICTORIA, EYRE AND YORKE PENINSULAS, GIPPSLAND, MELBOURNE REGION, NORTHERN VICTORIA, PERTH REGION, TASMANIA, WESTERN DISTRICT, WIMMERA AND MALLEE]

blood nut a person with red hair. See also **copper-top** and **ranga**.
[CENTRAL WEST NSW, PERTH REGION, SOUTH COAST AND SOUTHERN TABLELANDS]

bloody nose bleeding from the nose. See also **blood nose** and **nosebleed**. [ADELAIDE REGION, TASMANIA, CENTRAL WEST NSW]

bloomers sports briefs worn by girls under their skirts but over their underwear. See also **bum shorts**, **runners** and **scungies**[1].
[BRISBANE REGION, PERTH REGION]

blue bird diesel railcars used on country lines (principally the Mount Gambier line); painted blue and silver, each bore the name of a native bird. See also **Barwell's bull**, **Brill car** and **red hen**.
[ADELAIDE REGION, NORTHERN SOUTH AUSTRALIA]

blue bomber a parking inspector (from the colour of their uniform). See also **brown bomber**, **grey ghost**, **grey meanie** and **sticker licker**. [ADELAIDE REGION]

bluebottle[1] a large, noisy, annoying blue-black blowfly. See also **butcher-shop canary**, **canary**[2] and **dunny budgie**.
[MELBOURNE REGION, PERTH REGION]

bluebottle[2] a marine stinger of the genus *Physalia*.
[SYDNEY REGION, BRISBANE REGION]

bluebottle[3] a policeman. [PERTH REGION]

blue can a can of Foster's beer. See also **green can**, **red can**, **white can** and **yellow can**. [MELBOURNE REGION]

blue crab a blue swimmer crab (*Portunus pelagicus*); of blue-green colour and capable of powerful sustained swimming. See also **bluey, blue swimmer, blue manna crab** and **blue manna**.
[EYRE AND YORKE PENINSULAS, ADELAIDE REGION]

blue kangaroo a traffic policeman. [FAR WEST NSW]

blue manna see **blue crab**, **blue swimmer crab**, **blue swimmer**, **blue manna crab** and **bluey**.
[CENTRAL WEST AUSTRALIA, NORTHERN WEST AUSTRALIA, PERTH REGION]

blue manna crab see **blue crab**, **blue swimmer crab**, **blue swimmer** and **blue manna**.
[CENTRAL WEST AUSTRALIA, NORTHERN WEST AUSTRALIA, PERTH REGION]

blue rattler a suburban railway carriage. The 1950s Harris trains were blue rattlers, while the 1970s Hitachi/Silver trains have been called **silver rattlers**. See also **red rattler**. [MELBOURNE REGION]

blue swimmer[1] see **blue crab**, **blue manna** and **blue swimmer crab**.
[CENTRAL WEST NSW, FAR WEST NSW, HUNTER VALLEY AND NORTH COAST, NEW ENGLAND DISTRICT, SOUTH COAST AND SOUTHERN TABLELANDS, SYDNEY REGION, THE RIVERINA, BRISBANE REGION, ADELAIDE REGION, PERTH REGION, NORTHERN WEST AUSTRALIA, CENTRAL WEST AUSTRALIA]

blue swimmer[2] a ten dollar note (from the colour of the note).
[SYDNEY REGION]

blue swimmer crab see **blue crab**, **blue manna crab** and **blue swimmer**.
[CENTRAL WEST NSW, FAR WEST NSW, HUNTER VALLEY AND NORTH COAST, NEW ENGLAND DISTRICT, SOUTH COAST AND SOUTHERN TABLELANDS, SYDNEY REGION, THE RIVERINA]

bluetongue[1] a small child (being close to the ground, about at eye-level with bluetongue lizards). See also **little tacker** and **passion killers**. [TASMANIA]

bluetongue[2] a roustabout who works for a specific shearer.
[WEST CENTRAL QLD]

blue weed the herb *Echium plantagineum*. See also **Lachlan lilac**, **Murrumbidgee sweet pea**, **Paterson's curse**, **Riverina bluebell** and **Salvation Jane**. [PERTH REGION]

bluey[1] a summons issued for a traffic or parking offence.
[CENTRAL WEST NSW, FAR WEST NSW, HUNTER VALLEY AND NORTH COAST, NEW ENGLAND DISTRICT, SOUTH COAST AND SOUTHERN TABLELANDS, SYDNEY REGION, EYRE AND YORKE PENINSULAS, ADELAIDE REGION, NORTHERN SOUTH AUSTRALIA, THE RIVERINA, TASMANIA]

bluey[2] see **bluebottle**[2]. [SYDNEY REGION, BRISBANE REGION]

bluey[3] a large grey-blue woollen coat or jacket used in cold, wet weather, first designed by Robert Marriott (an early pioneer of the Derwent Valley, Tasmania) and marketed with the words: "Put your bluey on if you're going out in this weather."
[NORTHERN VICTORIA, TASMANIA]

boasters see **Speedos**. See also **ballhuggers**, **budgie-huggers**, **budgie-smugglers**, **cluster busters**, **cockchokers**, **cock jocks**, **codjocks**, **dick bathers**, **dick-pointers**, **dick-pokers**, **dick stickers**, **dick togs**, **dikdaks**, **dipsticks**, **fish frighteners**, **jammers**, **Jimmy clingers**, **knobbies**, **lolly-baggers**, **lolly bags**, **meat-hangers**, **nut huggers**, **nylon disgusters**, **racers**, **racing bathers**, **scungies**[2], **sluggers**, **sluggos**, **slug huggers**, **tights**, **toolies**, **trunks** and **wog togs**. [WESTERN DISTRICT]

bobtail a small lizard, a skink. (Sometimes mistakenly spoken of as a "bobtail goanna".) [PERTH REGION]

bocka[1] a haircut (usually a short haircut).
[CENTRAL HIGHLANDS VICTORIA, MELBOURNE REGION]

bocka[2] a punch to the upper arm, inflicted by schoolboys on each other, either playfully or as revenge. [BRISBANE REGION]

bodgie the largest size of marble (in the game of marbles).
[SYDNEY REGION]

bodgies pyjamas. [HUNTER VALLEY AND NORTH COAST]

bog[1] to shovel, especially underground.
[CENTRAL WEST AUSTRALIA, NORTHERN WEST AUSTRALIA, PERTH REGION]

bog[2] a **bogan**, especially a rough one. (While the full word is pronounced so as to rhyme with "Logan", this abbreviation is pronounced so as to rhyme with "log".) See also **bennie**, **bethan**, **bevan**, **booner**, **boonie**, **chigger**, **chookie**, **cogger**[1], **garry**, **scozzer** and **westie**. [CENTRAL WEST AUSTRALIA, PERTH REGION]

bog a duck in wellies, it'd description of very muddy conditions. Sometimes as "it'd bog a duck in boots." [DARWIN AND NORTH COAST NT]

bogan a young man so desperately unfashionable (and so unaware) as to think it cool to dress in black jeans, black T-shirt (with checked flannelette shirt over the top) and either (a) moccasins, (b) ugg boots, or (c) desert boots. This entire ensemble is often completed by a mullet haircut, a taste for heavy metal music, and an old bomb car with a noisy muffler. (Derogatory; now that surprises you, doesn't it?) See also **bennie, bethan, bevan, bog**[2], **booner, boonie, chigger, chookie, cogger**[1], **feral, garry, scozzer** and **westie**.

[MELBOURNE REGION, TASMANIA, PERTH REGION, BRISBANE REGION, ADELAIDE REGION, NEW ENGLAND DISTRICT, SYDNEY REGION, SOUTH COAST AND SOUTHERN TABLELANDS]

bogan bag a brightly coloured carry bag. After the town of Nyngan was flooded in 1990 the locals were allowed back to clean their houses. They were bussed from Dubbo for the day, returning each evening. To bring washing, personal effects etc. back to Dubbo they purchased cheap zip-up bags which became known as bogan bags (from the Bogan River that flooded the town).

[CENTRAL WEST NSW]

bogan gate a temporary farm gate, consisting of several strands of fencing wire for the horizontals and a few pieces of timber for the verticals. (From the western NSW town of Bogan.) See also **COD gate, Methodist gate** and **wire gate**.

[HUNTER VALLEY AND NORTH COAST, NEW ENGLAND DISTRICT, THE RIVERINA, SOUTH COAST AND SOUTHERN TABLELANDS, CENTRAL WEST NSW, FAR WEST NSW, CENTRAL COAST QLD, NORTH COAST QLD, FAR NORTH QLD, WEST CENTRAL QLD]

bogan navy a **bogan** who surfs or hangs out at the beach. See also **aqua bog**[1]. [PERTH REGION]

bogey 1. a bath or swim (in the Northern Territory this would normally be in a station dam). See also **dhobi**. [DARWIN AND NORTH COAST NT, THE CENTRE, FAR NORTH QLD, NORTHERN WEST AUSTRALIA] 2. a rock pool for swimming or bathing in. [HUNTER VALLEY AND NORTH COAST, SYDNEY REGION] Also spelled "bogie". (From the Dharug Aboriginal language.)

bogger 1. a person who shovels away waste material, especially in underground mining. [CENTRAL WEST AUSTRALIA, NORTHERN WEST AUSTRALIA, PERTH REGION, FAR NORTH QLD, WEST CENTRAL QLD, NORTHERN SOUTH AUSTRALIA] 2. a machine that performs the same task; a type of front-end loader for removing "bog" (or waste) underground. [CENTRAL WEST AUSTRALIA, NORTHERN WEST AUSTRALIA, PERTH REGION]

bog lap driving around the same street a number of times. [PERTH REGION]

bog locks long locks of hair as worn by a **bog**². [PERTH REGION]

bogo 1. a layabout who lives off the dole. 2. those council workers who lean on their shovels watching others work. (A contraction of **bog rat**.) [SYDNEY REGION]

BOGOF acronym "Buy One Get One Free". [BRISBANE REGION]

bog out to clean out. Coming from the mining industry, this expression was extended to other walks of life (including domestic life). [CENTRAL WEST AUSTRALIA]

bogox both good and bad at the same time. (Can apply to a place, event or thing.) [PERTH REGION]

bog rat a road or council worker. (Possibly from their employment in the construction of the sewerage system.) See also **bogo**. [SYDNEY REGION]

Boheena beauty a burr that embeds itself in clothing and is difficult to remove. (Boheena is the name of a creek in the Pilliga Scrub.) [NEW ENGLAND DISTRICT]

boing boing surfers' rash (produced by wet board shorts rubbing on thighs). [BRISBANE REGION]

bokka see **bocka**². [MELBOURNE REGION, WIMMERA AND MALLEE]

bomb black sapphire (a large but valueless piece of corundum: hard crystallised alumina). [WEST CENTRAL QLD]

bommy knocker the seed pod of the liquidambar tree. From a children's book featuring a giant's spiked club that resembled

these seed pods. (In case you'd like to check it out, the book in question is *The Hungry Giant* by Joy Cowley, 1980.) See also **castor oil**.
[NEW ENGLAND DISTRICT, HUNTER VALLEY AND NORTH COAST, SYDNEY REGION, CENTRAL WEST NSW]

Bondi chest an insult addressed to a skinny male. The full phrase is: "Bondi chest – far from Manly". [SYDNEY REGION]

Bondi cigar solid faecal matter in the surf. See also **blind mullet**, **blind trout**, **brown trout**, **King River prawn**, **pollywaffle** and **Werribee trout**. [SYDNEY REGION]

book a popular magazine (such as *Woman's Day*, *New Idea*, *Women's Weekly* or *TV Week)*. [BRISBANE REGION]

boomer a young male in a car with a powerful sound system, the booming base notes of which can be heard at traffic lights (where they attract attention by making the road vibrate). [PERTH REGION]

boon[1] strong disagreement (from a verbal slanging match to fisticuffs). [BRISBANE REGION]

boon[2] contraction of **booner**. [SOUTH COAST AND SOUTHERN TABLELANDS]

boondie[1] a lump of damp, yellow sand serving as a missile in children's games. Also spelled "boondy"; sometimes referred to as a "sand boondie" to distinguish it from **boondie**[2]. (Possibly from a WA Aboriginal language.) See also **coondie**.
[CENTRAL WEST AUSTRALIA, PERTH REGION]

boondie[2] a medium to large stone or rock. Also spelled "boondy" or "bundy". (Possibly from a WA Aboriginal language.) One contributor suggests this term was born in the mining industry and first used of rocks too big to go through a crusher. Several contributors suggest a smaller stone was a **coondie**. See also **brinnie**, **connie**[2], **gibber**, **gonnie**, **goolie**, **ronnie** and **yonnie**.
[CENTRAL WEST AUSTRALIA, PERTH REGION]

Boondoktown nickname for any isolated rural town. Also spelled "Bundocktown". [WIMMERA AND MALLEE]

booner the ACT equivalent of **bevan**, **bog**^{2}, **bogan**, **chigger**, **boonie**, **feral**, **westie**. One contributor suggests this is more about fashion than class when employed in the relatively flat socioeconomic landscape of Canberra. [SOUTH COAST AND SOUTHERN TABLELANDS]

boonie an untrendy fashion tragic, out of touch and from the outer suburbs. See also **bennie**, **bethan**, **bevan**, **bog**^{2}, **bogan**, **booner**, **chigger**, **chookie**, **feral mocca**, **scozzer** and **westie**.
[ADELAIDE REGION, BRISBANE REGION]

boonies the outer suburbs or country areas. (Possibly a contraction of the American term "boondocks".) [BRISBANE REGION]

boonted messed up or broken. [CENTRAL WEST AUSTRALIA]

bopple macadamia nut. (A corruption of "bauple" from Mt Bauple, near Maryborough.) Also as "bopple nut" or "bauple nut". See also **macca** and **Queensland nut**.
[CENTRAL COAST QLD, FAR NORTH QLD, NORTH COAST QLD, WEST CENTRAL QLD, BRISBANE REGION]

borerunner a person who starts and repairs bores and windmills (mostly on cattle stations in the Great Artesian Basin in northern and central Australia).
[CENTRAL WEST AUSTRALIA, NORTHERN WEST AUSTRALIA, DARWIN AND NORTH COAST NT, THE CENTRE, FAR NORTH QLD]

Boston bun an iced raisin loaf (a popular school **tuck shop** item).
[CENTRAL HIGHLANDS VICTORIA, GIPPSLAND, MELBOURNE REGION, NORTHERN VICTORIA, WESTERN DISTRICT, BRISBANE REGION, WIMMERA AND MALLEE, TASMANIA]

bot a glass marble of smoky green colour (highly prized in the game of marbles). Originally recycled glass stoppers from the necks of glass bottles (bot being an abbreviation of "bottle").
[SYDNEY REGION, GIPPSLAND, THE RIVERINA]

bottle to tip over a sailing boat. [MELBOURNE REGION]

bottlo a bottle shop. [BRISBANE REGION, SYDNEY REGION]

bounce down the action that starts an Australian Rules game in Western Australia. The equivalent of Victoria's "ball up".
[PERTH REGION]

bowgee to have a shower (or, in cattle country, to have a cooling swim in the station dam or the nearest stock watering place). [NORTHERN WEST AUSTRALIA, CENTRAL WEST NSW, WEST CENTRAL QLD]

bowl bath a wash in a bowl or bucket when no bath is available (or water is scarce). [PERTH REGION]

bowlo bowling club. [SOUTH COAST AND SOUTHERN TABLELANDS, SYDNEY REGION]

box carton of beer. See also **block**^{2}, **carton**, **case**^{2} and **slab**. [THE CENTRE]

boxie a cask of wine. (Abbreviation of **box monster**.) See also **bag of death**, **Balga handbag**, **Bellambi handbag**, **Broadmeadows briefcase**, **cardboard handbag**, **Coraki handbag**, **death bag**, **Dubbo handbag**, **gin's handbag**, **goon**, **goonbag**, **goonbox**, **goonie**, **goonsack**, **lady in the boat**, **red handbag**, **sack** and **vino collapso**. [TASMANIA]

box monster see also **bag of death**, **Balga handbag**, **Bellambi handbag**, **boxie**, **Broadmeadows briefcase**, **cardboard handbag**, **Coraki handbag**, **death bag**, **Dubbo handbag**, **gin's handbag**, **goon**, **goonbag**, **goonbox**, **goonie**, **goonsack**, **lady in the boat**, **red handbag**, **sack** and **vino collapso**. [TASMANIA, CENTRAL WEST AUSTRALIA]

Bra boy a Maroubra lad. [SYDNEY REGION]

brand 'em bunny a schoolyard game that involved evading tennis balls thrown with great force by the other players. (One contributor noted that wetting the tennis ball increased the impact – and the thrower's delight.) See also **brandies**, **brandings** and **brandy**. [CENTRAL WEST NSW]

brandies see also **brand 'em bunny**, **brandings** and **brandy**. [NEW ENGLAND DISTRICT, CENTRAL WEST NSW]

brandings see also **brand 'em bunny**, **brandies** and **brandy**. [SYDNEY REGION]

brandy a schoolyard game that involved evading tennis balls thrown with great force by the other players. See also **brand 'em bunny**, **brandies** and **brandings**. [CENTRAL HIGHLANDS VICTORIA, GIPPSLAND, MELBOURNE REGION, NORTHERN VICTORIA, WESTERN DISTRICT, WIMMERA AND MALLEE, ADELAIDE REGION, CENTRAL WEST AUSTRALIA, CENTRAL COAST QLD, SYDNEY REGION, PERTH REGION, BRISBANE REGION, THE RIVERINA]

brapping driving around the streets and doing various mildly illegal things. [SOUTH COAST AND SOUTHERN TABLELANDS]

breakie a breakwater at a harbour entrance.
[HUNTER VALLEY AND NORTH COAST]

breeze air an evaporative air cooling unit. (Originally a brand name, later applied generically to all air coolers and air conditioners.) [FAR WEST NSW, NORTHERN SOUTH AUSTRALIA]

breezer boy an effeminate male. [ADELAIDE REGION]

Brekky Creek the Breakfast Creek Hotel (Brisbane). [BRISBANE REGION]

Breville a toasted sandwich of the type formerly called a jaffle. (From the brand name of the appliance in which they are made.)
[HUNTER VALLEY AND NORTH COAST]

brickfielder a **southerly buster** which stirs up the dust (obsolete); from Brickfield Hill at the southern end of the Sydney CBD, formerly the site of a brick-pit – southerly winds would cloak the city with dust from this site. [SYDNEY REGION]

Bridgewater Jerry a dense, compact stream of fog which rolls down the western shore of the Derwent River into parts of Hobart (from its presumed place of origin, Bridgewater). Sometimes referred to simply as "jerry"; also spelled "gerry". [TASMANIA]

Brighton-le-wog (derogatory) term supposedly describing the dominant ethnicity of the suburb of Brighton-le-Sands.
[SYDNEY REGION]

Brill car type of railcar introduced by the South Australian Railways in the 1920s. (Probably from the name of the American manufacturer Brill Co.) See also **Barwell's bull**, **blue bird** and **red hen**. [ADELAIDE REGION, EYRE AND YORKE PENINSULAS, NORTHERN SOUTH AUSTRALIA]

brinnie a small stone. Also spelled "brinny". (Possibly from an Aboriginal source word.) According to some contributors brinnie and **yonnie** are interchangeable, while others insist that a **yonnie** was always bigger than a brinnie. See also **boondie**[2], **connie**[2], **gibber**, **gonnie**, **goolie**, **ronnie** and **yonnie**.
[WIMMERA AND MALLEE, CENTRAL HIGHLANDS VICTORIA, WESTERN DISTRICT, NORTHERN VICTORIA, GIPPSLAND, MELBOURNE REGION, TASMANIA]

Bristol hut once the local official name for a demountable school building. See also **demountable**, **dogbox**, **hot box**, **musset hut**, **portable**, **pre-fab**, **relocatable**, **silver bullet**[1], **terrapin unit** and **transportable**. [NORTHERN VICTORIA]

Bris-Vegas Brisbane. Also spelled "Briz-Vegas" or just "The Vegas". (Used affectionately by the locals for the air of rakish glamour it sheds over their home town.) See also **Brizzy**. [BRISBANE REGION]

British bulldog a schoolyard game in which groups of children run across the playground trying to avoid being caught by designated catcher(s). See also **bedlam**, **bullrush**, **cockylora**, **hipstick** and **red rover**.
[PERTH REGION, SYDNEY REGION, MELBOURNE REGION, BRISBANE REGION, ADELAIDE REGION, TASMANIA]

Brizzy Brisbane. See also **Bris-Vegas**. [BRISBANE REGION]

Broadie Broadmeadows. Also spelled "Broady". [MELBOURNE REGION]

Broadmeadows briefcase 1. cheap red, white and blue striped bag ($2 at your nearest bargain bin). 2. cask of cheap wine. See also **bag of death**, **Balga handbag**, **Bellambi handbag**, **boxie**, **box monster**, **cardboard handbag**, **Coraki handbag**, **death bag**, **Dubbo handbag**, **gin's handbag**, **goon**, **goonbag**, **goonbox**, **goonie**, **goonsack**, **lady in the boat**, **red handbag**, **sack** and **vino collapso**.
[MELBOURNE REGION]

Broadmeadows wedding shoes moccasins. See also **Corio work boots**, **moccas**, **Ringwood Reeboks** and **Sunshine stilettos**.
[MELBOURNE REGION]

broady to drive a motor vehicle in a sweeping broadside (skidding the vehicle sideways out of a turn). Also spelled "broadie". See also **broggie**. [MELBOURNE REGION]

broggie to slide a car or bike around a corner (preferably leaving skid marks on the road or in the dust, and providing a spectacular performance). See also **broady**.
[DARWIN AND NORTH COAST NT, PERTH REGION, SOUTH COAST AND SOUTHERN TABLELANDS]

Bronte buggy a four-wheel drive driven only in the city, belonging in the same quiet suburban garage as the **Balmain bulldozer**, **Burnside**

bus, **Kenmore tractor**, **North Shore tank**, **Rose Bay shopping trolley**, **Toorak tractor** and **Turramurra tractor**. [SYDNEY REGION]

brown baker a type of cicada. See also **black prince**, **brown bomber**[2], **cherrynose**, **cicada**, **floury baker**, **greengrocer**[2], **pisswhacker**, **tick tock** and **yellow Monday**. [SYDNEY REGION]

brown bomber[1] a parking inspector (now obsolete). See also **blue bomber**, **grey ghost**, **grey meanie** and **sticker licker**.
[SYDNEY REGION, HUNTER VALLEY AND NORTH COAST, NEW ENGLAND DISTRICT, THE RIVERINA, SOUTH COAST AND SOUTHERN TABLELANDS, CENTRAL WEST NSW, FAR WEST NSW, ADELAIDE REGION]

brown bomber[2] a type of cicada. See also **black prince**, **brown baker**, **cherrynose**, **cicada**, **floury baker**, **greengrocer**[2], **pisswhacker**, **tick tock** and **yellow Monday**. [SYDNEY REGION]

brown cows currently students at Ivanhoe Girls' Grammar School; previously students at the Catholic Ladies College, Eltham (from the colour of the uniforms worn). [MELBOURNE REGION]

brown sandwich a bottle of beer. See also **malt sandwich**.
[BRISBANE REGION]

brown trout untreated faecal matter in waterways. See also **blind mullet**, **blind trout**, **Bondi cigar**, **King River prawn**, **pollywaffle** and **Werribee trout**. [TASMANIA]

brumby a faulty item (appliance, toy, car etc.).
[BRISBANE REGION, CENTRAL COAST QLD, NORTH COAST QLD, FAR NORTH QLD, WEST CENTRAL QLD]

bubbler source of cool drinking water on a hot day (very necessary in the days before bottled water). See also **bubble tap**, **drinking fountain**, **drinking tap**, **drink tap**, **fountain** and **water fountain**. There was some disagreement among contributors as to the regions in which **bubbler** is used. However, a survey of capital city respondents locates this term most strongly in Sydney, followed by Brisbane, with Melbourne and Perth further back, and Adelaide and Hobart trailing the field. This suggests a term spread by an itinerant population from the one or two centres in which it began.
[SYDNEY REGION, HUNTER VALLEY AND NORTH COAST, NEW ENGLAND DISTRICT, THE RIVERINA, SOUTH COAST AND SOUTHERN TABLELANDS, CENTRAL WEST NSW, BRISBANE REGION, CENTRAL COAST QLD, NORTH COAST QLD, DARWIN AND NORTH COAST NT, FAR WEST NSW]

bubble tap see **bubbler, drinking fountain, drinking tap, drink tap, fountain** and **water fountain**.
[WIMMERA AND MALLEE, CENTRAL HIGHLANDS VICTORIA, WESTERN DISTRICT, NORTHERN VICTORIA, GIPPSLAND, MELBOURNE REGION, TASMANIA]

bubs the first year of school. See also **infants, kindergarten, kindy** and **prep**.
[MELBOURNE REGION, CENTRAL HIGHLANDS VICTORIA, PERTH REGION, WESTERN DISTRICT, GIPPSLAND]

buckboard a utility (now obsolete). See also **tilly**.
[ADELAIDE REGION, EYRE AND YORKE PENINSULAS, NORTHERN SOUTH AUSTRALIA]

bucket a small container of ice-cream (approximately 100 ml). See also **dandy** and **dixie**.
[BRISBANE REGION, CENTRAL COAST QLD, CENTRAL WEST NSW, HUNTER VALLEY AND NORTH COAST, NEW ENGLAND DISTRICT, NORTH COAST QLD, SOUTH COAST AND SOUTHERN TABLELANDS, SYDNEY REGION, THE RIVERINA]

Budd car air-conditioned fast railcars operated by the Commonwealth Railways from the 1950s to the 1980s, based in Port Augusta. (Also used by NSW railways for the rail motor services south from Sydney.) From the name of the manufacturer Budd Corporation (USA).
[NORTHERN SOUTH AUSTRALIA, SOUTH COAST AND SOUTHERN TABLELANDS]

budget footy information booklet (South Australian National Football League list of competition games).
[EYRE AND YORKE PENINSULAS, ADELAIDE REGION, NORTHERN SOUTH AUSTRALIA]

budgie-huggers see **Speedos**. See also **ballhuggers, boasters, budgie-smugglers, cluster busters, cockchokers, cock jocks, codjocks, dick bathers, dick-pointers, dick-pokers, dick stickers, dick togs, dikdaks, dipsticks, fish frighteners, jammers, Jimmy clingers, knobbies, lolly-baggers, lolly bags, meat-hangers, nut huggers, nylon disgusters, racers, racing bathers, scungies**[2]**, sluggers, sluggos, slug huggers, tights, toolies, trunks** and **wog togs**. [BRISBANE REGION]

budgie-smugglers see **Speedos**. When it became profitable for criminals to smuggle exotic Australian birds overseas (where they would fetch high prices from collectors), someone dreamed up this witty description of men's snug-fitting swimmers. (And the joke hasn't quite worn out yet.) See also **ballhuggers, boasters, budgie-huggers, cluster busters, cockchokers, cock jocks, codjocks, dick bathers, dick-pointers, dick-pokers, dick stickers, dick togs, dikdaks, dipsticks, fish frighteners, jammers, Jimmy clingers, knobbies, lolly-baggers, lolly bags, meat-hangers, nut huggers, nylon disgusters, racers, racing bathers, scungies**[2]**, sluggers, sluggos, slug huggers, tights, toolies, trunks** and **wog togs**. [PERTH REGION, SYDNEY REGION, MELBOURNE REGION, BRISBANE REGION, SOUTH COAST AND SOUTHERN TABLELANDS]

budjo poorly made; of low quality. [PERTH REGION]

bug an edible crustacean; Moreton Bay bug. [NORTH COAST QLD]

builder's smile the cleavage that creeps coyly above the belt of the builder's shorts. See also **coin slot, council man's cleavage** and **worker's crack.** [MELBOURNE REGION]

build-up the period just before the wet season when there is a gradual increase in heat, humidity and irritability. See also **suicide season**. [DARWIN AND NORTH COAST NT, THE CENTRE, NORTHERN WEST AUSTRALIA]

buju a good-looking person, male or female. Also spelled "budju". (Possibly from an Aboriginal word.)
[DARWIN AND NORTH COAST NT, NORTH COAST QLD, ADELAIDE REGION]

bulb electric light bulb. See also **globe**.
[BRISBANE REGION, CENTRAL COAST QLD, FAR NORTH QLD, NORTH COAST QLD, WEST CENTRAL QLD, HUNTER VALLEY AND NORTH COAST]

bulk! an exclamation of approval. [MELBOURNE REGION, ADELAIDE REGION]

bullaburra blue sky (especially a patch of blue sky on a cloudy day).
[BRISBANE REGION]

bull bar a protective metal grille extending from the front of a vehicle. See also **roo bar**. [TASMANIA]

bullboar a thick, spicy sausage (generally made of beef).
[CENTRAL HIGHLANDS VICTORIA]

bullhead 1. a low-growing plant (*Emex australis*) having many hard, spiny seeds (which will sometimes even puncture shoe soles). 2. one of the seeds of this plant. See also **California puncture weed**, caltrop, cat head[1], cat's eye[1], double-gee, goat's head and three-corner jack.

[BRISBANE REGION, CENTRAL COAST QLD, FAR NORTH QLD, NORTH COAST QLD, WEST CENTRAL QLD]

bullies a boys' game (played with quandong seeds threaded on string – the object being to smash the opponent's quandong or "bullie"). [FAR WEST NSW, THE RIVERINA, NORTHERN SOUTH AUSTRALIA]

bullrush a schoolyard game. See also **bedlam**, **British bulldog**, **cockylora**, **hipstick** and **red rover**.

[NEW ENGLAND DISTRICT, SYDNEY REGION]

bull's hoof rhyming slang: "poof" (gay male). [MELBOURNE REGION]

bulltwang! an exclamation of disbelief; used by schoolboys and sometimes abbreviated to "twang". See also **bunnies to that!; chowoon; eh; gammon; hells, bells and bootlaces; Himmel** and **strike me roan!** [SYDNEY REGION, FAR WEST NSW]

bull wagon a police van. See also **bun wagon**, **divvy van** and **paddy wagon**. [SYDNEY REGION]

bulyu a cigarette. From an Aboriginal word meaning "smoke". Marijuana is "nunta bulyu", literally "crazy smoke". See also **bunger, busta, dar, darb** and **racehorse**[2]. [EYRE AND YORKE PENINSULAS]

bum nuts eggs.

[PERTH REGION, NORTHERN SOUTH AUSTRALIA, SOUTH COAST AND SOUTHERN TABLELANDS, NEW ENGLAND DISTRICT]

bum shorts sports briefs worn by girls under their skirts but over their underwear. See also **bloomers, runners** and **scungies**[1].

[NORTH COAST QLD]

bum-stinger the small cone of the *Cupressus macrocarpa* used as a projectile in children's battles. To turn one's back on an incoming missile was to risk a stinging blow. [TASMANIA]

Bundaberg snow the ash that rises from the sugarcane fires common along the Queensland coast. "It settles", writes one contributor, "into every nook and cranny in the house and garden." Sometimes known as "Bundy snow". See also **Burdekin snow**. [BRISBANE REGION, CENTRAL COAST QLD]

Bundiwallop a mythical remote outback town. (Belongs on the same map as **Kickastickalong**, **Oodnagalahby** and **Wheelyabarraback**.)

[SYDNEY REGION, TASMANIA]

bung railway slang: a "please explain" from the boss for alleged misdemeanours. [SYDNEY REGION]

bungalow[1] a small self-contained dwelling in the grounds of a house. Although this is not a word of Australian origin, it is a regionalism in that it's used differently in different parts of the country. (The word is of Hindustani origin, coming from the days of the British Raj.) Also **bungalow**[2], **chalet** and **granny flat**.

[CENTRAL HIGHLANDS VICTORIA, GIPPSLAND, MELBOURNE REGION, NORTHERN VICTORIA, WESTERN DISTRICT, WIMMERA AND MALLEE]

bungalow[2] a small house or cottage of one storey. Also **bungalow**[1], **chalet** and **granny flat**.

[CENTRAL WEST NSW, FAR WEST NSW, HUNTER VALLEY AND NORTH COAST, NEW ENGLAND DISTRICT, SOUTH COAST AND SOUTHERN TABLELANDS, SYDNEY REGION, THE RIVERINA]

bungarra a large goanna, brownish in colour, commonly called "Gould's goanna". Sometimes also called "barney".

[CENTRAL WEST AUSTRALIA, NORTHERN WEST AUSTRALIA, PERTH REGION]

bunge mate or friend. An abbreviation of **bungee**. (Probably of Aboriginal origin.)

[CENTRAL COAST QLD, WEST CENTRAL QLD, MELBOURNE REGION]

bungee mate, friend. See also **bunge**. [FAR NORTH QLD, NORTH COAST QLD]

bunger a cigarette. See also **bulyu**, **busta**, **dar**, **darb** and **racehorse**[2].

[BRISBANE REGION]

bung fritz a type of processed sausage. Sometimes just **fritz**. Some contributors insist that **bung fritz** has a natural casing (orange in colour), while **fritz** is a plastic-wrapped supermarket sausage. See also **baron sausage**, **beef Belgium**, **Belgium sausage**, **Byron sausage**, **devon**, **Empire sausage**, **fritz**, **German sausage**, **luncheon sausage**, **mystery meat**, **polony**, **pork German**, **Strasburg**, **wheel meat** and **Windsor sausage**.

[EYRE AND YORKE PENINSULAS, ADELAIDE REGION, NORTHERN SOUTH AUSTRALIA]

bungum worm a beachworm found on the southern and eastern coasts of Australia; also called a "slimy".

[EYRE AND YORKE PENINSULAS, ADELAIDE REGION, NORTHERN SOUTH AUSTRALIA]

bun loaf a loaf of raisin bread.

[BRISBANE REGION, SOUTH COAST AND SOUTHERN TABLELANDS]

bunnies to that! an exclamation of disbelief and/or irritation. See also **bulltwang!; chowoon; eh; gammon; hells, bells and bootlaces; Himmel** and **strike me roan!**

[GIPPSLAND, MELBOURNE REGION, PERTH REGION, ADELAIDE REGION]

bunny chop a blow to the back of the neck with the side of the hand. See also **rabbit killer.** [NORTHERN SOUTH AUSTRALIA]

bunta madly enthusiastic cheering or applause.

[EYRE AND YORKE PENINSULAS, ADELAIDE REGION, NORTHERN SOUTH AUSTRALIA, CENTRAL HIGHLANDS VICTORIA]

bun wagon a police van. See also **bull wagon**, **divvy van** and **paddy wagon.** [THE RIVERINA]

Burdekin duck corned beef. (Sometimes restricted to corned beef fritters – corned beef cooked in batter.) See also **desert chicken**.

[BRISBANE REGION, CENTRAL COAST QLD, NORTH COAST QLD, FAR NORTH QLD, WEST CENTRAL QLD, DARWIN AND NORTH COAST NT]

Burdekin mud chocolate blanc-mange. [NORTH COAST QLD]

Burdekin snow the ash that rises from the sugarcane fires common along the Queensland coast. [NORTH COAST QLD]

burn a reddie to burn a dead red gum tree. (A contributor writes: "When the pub was about to close on a Saturday night and there were no parties to go to, folk would set fire to a red gum tree on someone's farm. The tree had probably been ringbarked long ago. It was a great event to sit around an enormous fire and tell yarns and consume large quantities of alcohol.") [WESTERN DISTRICT]

Burnside bus a city-only four-wheel drive. See also **Balmain bulldozer**, **Bronte buggy**, **Kenmore tractor**, **North Shore tank**, **Rose Bay shopping trolley** and **Turramurra tractor**.

[ADELAIDE REGION]

burnt[1] foolish. [NORTHERN SOUTH AUSTRALIA]

burnt[2] being made fun of. [PERTH REGION]

Burra abbreviation of Muttaburra, a Queensland town.
[WEST CENTRAL QLD]

burr up to become annoyed, to "flare up". [BRISBANE REGION]

bus any motor vehicle. [TASMANIA]

bush blow clearing one's nose without the use of a handkerchief.
[PERTH REGION, ADELAIDE REGION]

bush chook[1] an emu.
[SYDNEY REGION, WEST CENTRAL QLD, NORTHERN WEST AUSTRALIA, CENTRAL WEST
AUSTRALIA, PERTH REGION]

bush chook[2] a Tasmanian native hen. [TASMANIA]

bush foal a child born out of wedlock. [WEST CENTRAL QLD]

bushman a chainsaw operator in a team of logging contractors.
[TASMANIA]

bushpig a girl of unkempt appearance and rough manners
(derogatory). [HUNTER VALLEY AND NORTH COAST, SYDNEY REGION]

bushy campfire. [ADELAIDE REGION]

busta cigarette (short for "lung buster"). See also **bulyu**, **bunger**,
dar, **darb** and **racehorse**[2]. [MELBOURNE REGION]

busy-bee voluntary community work done in a team. See also
working bee. [PERTH REGION, SYDNEY REGION]

but employed not as a conjunction (or disjunction) but shifted to
the terminal position in a sentence, where it can play a number of
roles. 1. it can be a terminator, a spoken full stop: "It's a big job
but." 2. it can seek agreement, in the manner of "isn't it?" (or *n'est-
ce pas*): "It's a hot day, but?" 3. it can perform its usual function in
an unusual place in the sentence: "But I didn't do it" can become
"I didn't do it but". 4. it can be little more than an unconsciously
employed verbal tic. (As a linguist would put it: "It's an interesting
bit of syntax but.") See also **eh; eh, but!** and **well.**
[CENTRAL WEST NSW, FAR WEST NSW, HUNTER VALLEY AND NORTH COAST, NEW
ENGLAND DISTRICT, SOUTH COAST AND SOUTHERN TABLELANDS, SYDNEY REGION,
THE RIVERINA, MELBOURNE REGION, BRISBANE REGION, FAR NORTH QLD]

butcher a small glass of beer (approximately 200 ml). From German *becher*: a drinking vessel. See also **glass**, **handle**, **middy**, **pony**, **pot**, **schooner**[1], **schooner**[2] and **seven**.
[EYRE AND YORKE PENINSULAS, ADELAIDE REGION, NORTHERN SOUTH AUSTRALIA]

butcher boy a small insect that rolls itself into a ball.
[MELBOURNE REGION]

butcher shop canary a blowfly. Sometimes as "butcher's canary". See also **bluebottle**, **canary**[2] and **dunny budgie**.
[WIMMERA AND MALLEE, CENTRAL HIGHLANDS VICTORIA]

butterfish a type of fish, commonly sold in fish and chip shops.
[ADELAIDE REGION]

buzz box originally a cheap, shoddy car, now (sometimes) a small, inexpensive car (especially if it's been hotted up). [BRISBANE REGION]

buzzy 1. a grass seed that clings to the legs or clothing. 2. a low-growing herb which grows in eastern Australia; bidgee widgee. Also spelled "buzzie". [TASMANIA]

bye nows the flabby triceps (upper arms) of an overweight woman. (From the flap of flesh that wobbles while waving good-bye.) See also **aunty arms**, **bingo wings**, **good-bye muscle**, **nannas**, **piano arm**, **reverse biceps**, **ta-ta flaps**, **tuckshop arm** and **widow's curtain**. [SYDNEY REGION]

by jingo iceblock on a stick. Also spelled "bi jingo", "bye jingo", "bigingo". See also **iceblock**, **icy pole** and **Paddle-pop**.
[FAR NORTH QLD, NORTH COAST QLD]

Byron sausage one of the many names for this precooked sausage, usually sliced thinly and eaten cold. (May have originated as a brand name.) See also **baron sausage**, **beef Belgium**, **Belgium sausage**, **bung fritz**, **devon**, **Empire sausage**, **fritz**, **German sausage**, **luncheon sausage**, **mystery meat**, **polony**, **pork German**, **Strasburg**, **wheel meat** and **Windsor sausage**.
[HUNTER VALLEY AND NORTH COAST]

C

cabana a local name for cabanossi (a pre-cooked, mildly spiced beef sausage of European origin). In the US a cabana is a hut or shelter at a beach or swimming pool (from the Spanish for "cabin").
[MELBOURNE REGION, ADELAIDE REGION, TASMANIA]

cabaret not, as you might expect, a nightclub or restaurant with a floorshow, but a local dance at which alcoholic drink is available (possibly held in a hotel lounge, with a band to provide music). In some places the local annual cabaret was a bit of a legend – as is the case at Gordonvale in far north Queensland where the highlight of the evening was the cabaret act performed by a group of local men, described by one local as "highly choreographed and hugely funny".
[BRISBANE REGION, CENTRAL COAST QLD, FAR NORTH QLD, NORTH COAST QLD, WEST CENTRAL QLD, NORTHERN SOUTH AUSTRALIA, TASMANIA]

cack to laugh (probably from "cackle" – making a chuckling noise like a chook that's laid an egg – yet another Aussie diminutive).
[SYDNEY REGION, MELBOURNE REGION, BRISBANE REGION]

cacker an undersized crayfish, crab or marron (also spelled "kakka"). [CENTRAL WEST AUSTRALIA]

cadbury someone who can't hold their alcohol, and gets drunk easily. From an old advertising campaign for Cadbury's which claimed that each block of chocolate contained "a glass and a half" of milk. So anyone who gets tiddly on a glass and a half is a **cadbury** (also known as a "two pot screamer"). By extension it can mean someone who gets very silly after smoking a small amount of dope. See also **omo**.
[PERTH REGION, ADELAIDE REGION, NEW ENGLAND DISTRICT, SYDNEY REGION, BRISBANE REGION]

Calaglese a hybrid Italian-Australian dialect derived from the Calabrian migrant group. A combination of conversational Calabrian (from southern Italy) and English that developed from an attempt to linguistically assimilate during the wave of 1950s and 1960s immigration. Only understood by Calabrian migrants in Australia. One contributor reported that in Calaglese "see you

in the garden" would probably sound like "di vidiamo te la backyarda", and to "go bush" in Calaglese would be "vai busho".
[SOUTH COAST AND SOUTHERN TABLELANDS]

California puncture weed the spiny seeds of a low-growing plant (*Emex australis*) – extremely painful to step on and which will sometimes even puncture through shoe soles (also known simply as "puncture weed"). One contributor grumbles: "They are a real menace. You can't go barefoot even indoors, because they come in with your shoes and get stuck in the carpet, and then in your feet." See also **bullhead**, **caltrop**, **cat head**[1], **cat's eye**[1], **double-gee**, **goat's head** and **three-corner jack**.
[ADELAIDE REGION, WIMMERA AND MALLEE, EYRE AND YORKE PENINSULAS]

Callaghan Parks, **the** if you've "got the Callaghan Parks" you've got "the trots" (or "the runs" or diarrhoea). From the name of the local race track at Rockhampton. [CENTRAL COAST QLD]

call on to pick on someone, to verbally attack them, humiliate them. As in, "I didn't do my homework so my teacher called on me." [TASMANIA]

caltrop see **California puncture weed**. See also **bullhead**, **cat's eye**[1], **double-gee**, **goat's head** and **three-corner jack**.
[NORTHERN SOUTH AUSTRALIA]

camel bite a sharp blow to the skin (usually someone's bare legs) with a cupped hand. In Sydney called a "horse" or "horsey" bite. (Schoolboys find inflicting pain on each other a source of great hilarity.) See also **crow peck**, **horse bite** and **monkey shine**.
[ADELAIDE REGION, PERTH REGION]

camel melon the fruit of a South African vine now growing in Australia. Confusingly, also sometimes called a "paddymelon" – which was originally the name given to a small, compact-bodied wallaby. (If someone offers you a slice of "paddymelon" just be quite clear about what they're offering!)
[THE RIVERINA, SOUTH COAST AND SOUTHERN TABLELANDS]

can[1] the distance travelled while drinking a can of beer (a strictly informal unit of linear measurement). As in, "Grassy is four and a half cans from Currie". [TASMANIA, BUT RESTRICTED TO KING ISLAND]

can[2] an expression acknowledging that something is possible, or something can be done, as in: "Got time for a drink down at the pub?" "Can." (Meaning "sure can" or "yes, that's okay".) From the Asian influence in the multicultural community on Christmas Island – from where it's been exported to Perth. This is mainly used by the Malay and Chinese communities, but tends to be picked up by many in the wider community as they become accustomed to it. [PERTH REGION]

Canadian passport another name for a mullet (a trendy haircut). A high school student seen with a mullet might be pointed out with a cry of: "Hey, he's got a Canadian passport!" (Why the Canadians are blamed for bad hairstyles is not clear.)
[SOUTH COAST AND SOUTHERN TABLELANDS]

canary[1] a notice, in the form of a yellow sticker attached to the windscreen of a vehicle, issued by police identifying the vehicle as unroadworthy and requiring that it be repaired within a specified period of time. (Basically a noble attempt to prevent some aging rust bucket from leaking oil in your driveway.) See also **yellow sticker**.
[NORTHERN WEST AUSTRALIA, CENTRAL WEST AUSTRALIA, PERTH REGION, WIMMERA AND MALLEE, CENTRAL HIGHLANDS VICTORIA, WESTERN DISTRICT, NORTHERN VICTORIA, GIPPSLAND, MELBOURNE REGION]

canary[2] a blowfly, as in: "Shut the door, ya mug! We don't want another canary in the kitchen!" See also **bluebottle**[1], **butcher-shop canary** and **dunny budgie**. [ADELAIDE REGION]

Canberra doctor an easterly evening wind from the coast that helps to cool Canberra (if it reaches Canberra, that is – it often runs out of breath around Braidwood or Bungendore). This is one of a number of medically qualified zephyrs around Australia. See also **Albany doctor**; **doctor, the**; **Esperance doctor** and **Fremantle doctor**. [SOUTH COAST AND SOUTHERN TABLELANDS]

Candy car 1980s nickname for Victoria Police yellow highway patrol cars (used in special operations and as chaser patrol cars).
[MELBOURNE REGION]

can'een an idiomatic way of saying "canteen". (What happened to the missing "T" is unclear, but several people are assisting police with their inquiries.) [HUNTER VALLEY AND NORTH COAST]

cankles fat ankles, a combination of "calves" and "ankles" (the rolls of fat making it impossible to tell where the ankles end and the calves begin). [CENTRAL WEST AUSTRALIA]

can-opener a type of "bomb" dive that involves jumping into the water with one leg tucked under the arms against the chest and the other extended straight out. Note: a full "bomb" requires both legs to be so tucked. The intention is to create the maximum splash and inconvenience to others. This loutish behaviour is known by different names in different places. See also **banana**, **horsey** and **peg leg**. (One contributor suggests that this term can-opener may have been imported from America, while the other labels may be the local inventions.) [SOUTH COAST AND SOUTHERN TABLELANDS]

cantaloupe a foreign name for the rockmelon. It came into English from Italian via French in the 18th century. But in some Australian regions it is now the more common name for the fruit. Some contributors suggest this name has come into wider use only in recent years (perhaps as part of an attempt to gentrify Aussie English).
[WIMMERA AND MALLEE, CENTRAL HIGHLANDS VICTORIA, WESTERN DISTRICT, NORTHERN VICTORIA, GIPPSLAND, MELBOURNE REGION, TASMANIA]

canteen there appears to be no distinctively Australian name for the shop at school which sells food. In some regions canteen is used, in others **tuck shop** – both are of English origin (from the 18th and 19th centuries respectively).
[ADELAIDE REGION, WIMMERA AND MALLEE, SOUTH COAST AND SOUTHERN TABLELANDS, SYDNEY REGION, THE RIVERINA, MELBOURNE REGION]

Cape Barren Islander the name widely used in Tasmania to describe the descendants of Aboriginal women and the sealers (and sailors) who visited Cape Barren Island (in Bass Strait). Also applied to others of Aboriginal appearance. (Probably offensive.)
[TASMANIA]

cardboard handbag wine cask. See also **bag of death**, **Balga handbag**, **Bellambi handbag**, **boxie**, **box monster**, **Broadmeadows briefcase**, **Coraki handbag**, **Dapto briefcase**, **death bag**, **Dubbo handbag**, **gin's handbag**, **goon**, **goonbag**,

goonbox, **goonie**, **goonsack**, **lady in the boat**, **red handbag**, **sack** and **vino collapso**.
[MELBOURNE REGION]

Carrara koalas nickname for the AFL team currently called the Brisbane Lions but formerly known as the Brisbane Bears – Carrara being their home ground. (Yes, I know koalas are not bears, but you can see the connection, can't you?) [BRISBANE REGION]

car shed a garage or carport. One contributor writes: "We always had a car shed. Only snobs called it a garage." However, railwaymen call carriages "cars", and so the place where railway carriages are maintained and stored is also called a "car shed".
[HUNTER VALLEY AND NORTH COAST, BRISBANE REGION, SYDNEY REGION]

carton a cardboard case of 24 cans or stubbies of beer. This is one of those common items that has various regional names. See also **block**², **box**, **case**² and **slab**.
[SYDNEY REGION, ADELAIDE REGION, EYRE AND YORKE PENINSULAS, NORTHERN SOUTH AUSTRALIA, TASMANIA, MELBOURNE REGION, BRISBANE REGION, NORTHERN WEST AUSTRALIA, CENTRAL WEST AUSTRALIA, SOUTH COAST AND SOUTHERN TABLELANDS, PERTH REGION, NEW ENGLAND DISTRICT]

Cascade country Tasmania is a divided state – the dividing line being drawn by which of the state's two major beers you drink. Southern Tasmania is **Cascade country**. (In the north they drink Boags, but this hasn't created a territorial title.) [TASMANIA]

case¹ the sort of box or container that in other areas is called a **port**. For example, depending on where you are, you pack either a case or a port to go on holidays.
[CENTRAL HIGHLANDS VICTORIA, GIPPSLAND, MELBOURNE REGION, NORTHERN VICTORIA, WESTERN DISTRICT, WIMMERA AND MALLEE]

case² see **carton**, **block**², **box** and **slab**.
[SYDNEY REGION, SOUTH COAST AND SOUTHERN TABLELANDS]

cash to borrow and/or lend something. As in "I cashed his pen" or "I'll cash you my car". See also **scab**.
[SOUTH COAST AND SOUTHERN TABLELANDS]

castor oil a seed pod of a liquidambar tree. See also **bommy knocker**. [HUNTER VALLEY AND NORTH COAST]

casual day a day on which uniforms and suits can be discarded in favour of casual clothes. See also **free dress day**, **mufti day** and **out of uniform day**. [ADELAIDE REGION]

catch and kiss a derogatory name for soccer. "Because," writes one contributor, "when they score a goal they run around hugging and kissing each other." Typical of the abuse heaped by the followers of one football code upon another. (Also a primary school game in which boys pursued girls.) See also **catch me kiss me**.
[BRISBANE REGION]

catch me kiss me a derogatory name for all rugby football codes. Standard Melbournian response to the charge that AFL is "aerial ping pong". [MELBOURNE REGION]

cat head[1] see **California puncture weed**. See also **bullhead**, **caltrop**, **cat's eye**[1], **double-gee**, **goat's head** and **three-corner jack**. Sometimes mistakenly called a **bindi eye** (which is actually a different plant).
[HUNTER VALLEY AND NORTH COAST, NEW ENGLAND DISTRICT, THE RIVERINA, SOUTH COAST AND SOUTHERN TABLELANDS, CENTRAL WEST NSW, FAR WEST NSW]

cat head[2] small ferns of various species growing in the understorey of temperate rainforests. [TASMANIA]

cathedral underpants tight underpants (because, in the famous schoolboy joke, in a cathedral there is no ballroom).
[MELBOURNE REGION]

cat's eye[1] see **California puncture weed**. See also **bullhead**, **caltrop**, **cat head**, **double-gee**, **goat's head** and **three-corner jack**.
[CENTRAL WEST NSW, FAR WEST NSW, HUNTER VALLEY AND NORTH COAST, NEW ENGLAND DISTRICT, SOUTH COAST AND SOUTHERN TABLELANDS, SYDNEY REGION, THE RIVERINA]

cat's eye[2] a type of marble resembling a cat's eye.
[SOUTH COAST AND SOUTHERN TABLELANDS, FAR WEST NSW]

cat's eyes the reflective discs on the side of the road and on guideposts.
[SYDNEY REGION, SOUTH COAST AND SOUTHERN TABLELANDS, BRISBANE REGION, TASMANIA]

cattle grate a set of parallel steel bars set in the road (over a shallow pit) where it passes through a fence – cattle will not walk over the steel bars (making a gate unnecessary) but vehicles can drive over. See also **cattle grid**, **cattle-pit**, **cattle ramp**, **grid**[2] and **ramp**.

[TASMANIA]

cattle grid see also **cattle grate**, **cattle-pit**, **cattle ramp**, **grid**[2] and **ramp**. [TASMANIA, ADELAIDE REGION]

cattle-pit see also **cattle grate**, **cattle grid**, **cattle ramp**, **grid**[2] and **ramp**. [PERTH REGION]

cattle ramp see also **cattle grate**, **cattle grid**, **grid**[2] and **ramp**. (In some places a cattle ramp is the timber ramp used for loading cattle onto the back of a truck.) [WIMMERA AND MALLEE, TASMANIA]

cattle tick Catholic (typical school children's word-play insult of the 1950s). From the Irish pronunciation of "Catholic". See also **metholated spirits**, **mickey drip** and **press button**.

[CENTRAL WEST AUSTRALIA, NORTHERN WEST AUSTRALIA, PERTH REGION, WEST CENTRAL QLD, BRISBANE REGION, NORTHERN SOUTH AUSTRALIA, ADELAIDE REGION]

central school a state school in a rural or regional area which provided both primary and lower secondary education (some to year eight, others to year ten). They acted as "feeder schools" for district high schools. See also **area school**, **consolidated school**, **district school**, **high top** and **secondary tops**.

[CENTRAL WEST NSW, FAR WEST NSW, HUNTER VALLEY AND NORTH COAST, NEW ENGLAND DISTRICT, SOUTH COAST AND SOUTHERN TABLELANDS, SYDNEY REGION, THE RIVERINA, MELBOURNE REGION]

chad bad, often used in the adjectival form "chaddy"; as in "Your new car is chad" or "Mr Roberts is a chaddy teacher".

[SYDNEY REGION]

Chaddy Chadstone, a south-eastern suburb of Melbourne. Sometimes restricted to Chadstone Shopping Centre.

[MELBOURNE REGION]

chalet a small self-contained dwelling in the grounds of a house. Now sometimes used of a holiday house. See also **bungalow**[1] and **granny flat**. [TASMANIA, PERTH REGION]

chances expression of doubt that something is likely to happen. As in, "The Magpies will win the semi-final" to which comes the response, "Chances!" (meaning "I don't like their chances").
[BRISBANE REGION]

channel rat a flathead (the fish). [MELBOURNE REGION]

Charlene a female **bevan** or the girlfriend of a **bevan**. (Inspired by the character played by Kylie Minogue on *Neighbours*.) See also **Charmaine** and **Shazza**. [BRISBANE REGION]

Charlie's the Sir Charles Gairdner Hospital. [PERTH REGION]

Charlie's trousers rhyming slang for Charters Towers, north Queensland (used affectionately). [NORTH COAST QLD]

Charmaine see **Charlene** (also **Shazza**).
[CENTRAL COAST QLD, BRISBANE REGION]

charnie bum a lower-class or uneducated person (sometimes just "charnie"). See also **bilby**. [SOUTH COAST AND SOUTHERN TABLELANDS]

chasey a name for various schoolyard chasing games, known by many different names in different regions. See **chasings**, **tag**, **tig**, **tiggy** and **tip**^{2}.
[CENTRAL HIGHLANDS VICTORIA, ADELAIDE REGION, PERTH REGION, NORTHERN VICTORIA, MELBOURNE REGION]

chasings see **chasey** (also **tag**, **tig**, **tiggy** and **tip**^{2}).
[SYDNEY REGION, TASMANIA]

chat lousy, gross, ugly or disgusting (sometimes in the form "chatty"). [SYDNEY REGION]

cheat stick a pool rest. [SYDNEY REGION]

checkside kick regional name for a banana kick in Aussie Rules.
[ADELAIDE REGION, EYRE AND YORKE PENINSULAS, WIMMERA AND MALLEE]

cheerio goodbye. See also **cheery**, **hooray**, **hooroo**, **hurrah**, **oo-roo** and **soup, I'll see you in the**. [SYDNEY REGION]

cheerios small sausages (cocktail frankfurts) eaten cold or hot. See also **Japanese frankfurts** and **little boys**.
[BRISBANE REGION, CENTRAL COAST QLD, NORTH COAST QLD, FAR NORTH QLD, WEST CENTRAL QLD, HUNTER VALLEY AND NORTH COAST, WESTERN DISTRICT]

cheery goodbye – used in place of **cheerio**. See also **hooray**, **hooroo**, **hurrah**, **oo-roo** and **soup, I'll see you in the**.
[EYRE AND YORKE PENINSULAS]

cheese grill an item of school **tuck shop** food consisting of a thin (hot dog) roll cut in half and covered with cheese and grilled.
[PERTH REGION]

cheesy grilled cheese on toast. [PERTH REGION]

cheh (pronounced ch-yeah) only kidding. "This," says a contributor, "is used between friends, so the other person knows the speaker is only joking." [NORTH COAST QLD]

cherrabun freshwater prawns found in Kimberley rivers and pools.
[NORTHERN WEST AUSTRALIA]

cherrynose a type of cicada with a red nose. See also **black prince**, **brown baker**, **brown bomber**[2], **cicada**, **floury baker**, **greengrocer**[2], **pisswhacker**, **tick tock** and **yellow Monday**. [SYDNEY REGION]

cherub a yabby, freshwater prawn. See also **clawchie**, **crawbob**, **crawchie**, **craybob**, **craydab**, **crayfish**, **jilgie**, **lobby**, **lobster**, **marron**, **pink nipper** and **yabby**. [NORTHERN WEST AUSTRALIA]

chevapchichi a small, spicy mince sausage with no skin (now available nationally through supermarket chains).
[ADELAIDE REGION, MELBOURNE REGION]

chewy disagreeable, out of sorts. As in, "You're being a bit chewy this morning, aren't you?" [SYDNEY REGION]

chiak to muck around, create mischief and tomfoolery. (This is a shift from the older – and more widely used – meaning of the word "jeering, taunting, teasing".)
[SOUTH COAST AND SOUTHERN TABLELANDS]

chicken scratch a two-player replacement for a scrum in schoolyard Rugby League. One boy from each team would face the other and bend over. Their heads would touch and they would put their hands behind their backs. The ball would be placed on the ground between them. Someone would count to three and the boys would then "scratch" for the ball with their hands.
[BRISBANE REGION, SOUTH COAST AND SOUTHERN TABLELANDS]

chigger a person who lives in the none-too-salubrious outskirts of Hobart. Also spelled chigga. (From the Hobart suburb of Chigwell.) One contributor writes: "A chigger can often be identified by their clothing: tight black denim jeans, a flannelette checked shirt and work boots." Now obsolete as Chigwell has clambered a little further up the social scale. See also **bennie**, **bethan**, **bevan**, **bog**², **bogan**, **booner**, **boonie**, **chookie**, **cogger**¹, **feral**, **garry**, **scozzer** and **westie**. [TASMANIA]

chilax a combination of "chill out" and "relax". [PERTH REGION]

chilly billy anything that is cold (including the weather). From mass-produced ice marketed under that brand name. [MELBOURNE REGION]

Chinese apple the fruit of the lilly-pilly tree. Also known as "Chinee apple". (The variant "Chinee" dates back to the 19th century and is based on the false assumption that "Chinese" is a plural. That is, if you have "two Chinese", then you have "one Chinee"!) See also **chinky apple** and **chonky apple**. [PERTH REGION, NORTH COAST QLD]

Chinese safety boots thongs or sandals. See also **clackers**, **getters**, **go-backs**, **jandals**, **Japanese flying boots**, **Japanese riding boots**, **Japanese safety boots**, **Jesus boots**, **NT work boots** and **pluggers**. [MELBOURNE REGION]

chinky apple the fruit of the china apple tree. See also **Chinese apple** and **chonky apple**. [BRISBANE REGION, NORTH COAST QLD]

chips kindling, chips of wood used to start a fire. Hence, a "chip heater" was the appliance that was fired up using chips to heat bath water. [HUNTER VALLEY AND NORTH COAST, GIPPSLAND, BRISBANE REGION]

choc foreigner (especially from one of the Mediterranean countries). Rhyming slang: "chocolate frog" (wog). (Derogatory.) See also **Dapto dog** and **Gosford dog**. [WESTERN DISTRICT]

chog heavy metal music. [TASMANIA]

choice excellent. (Sometimes used ironically to suggest the opposite.) See also **duck's nuts** and **nuffest**. [BRISBANE REGION, HUNTER VALLEY AND NORTH COAST, SYDNEY REGION]

chonk a lolly or sweet. [GIPPSLAND]

chonky apple see **Chinese apple** and **chinky apple**. [NORTH COAST QLD]

choodie a good-looking girl, a chick. [ADELAIDE REGION]

chookers okay. As in "Everything's chookers". [SYDNEY REGION]

chookie a person (usually a young male) who drives laps through the main street of town, commonly on Friday and Saturday nights. (Either an abbreviation of "chook chaser" – an off-road bike – or implying that the chookie is driving like a chook with its head chopped off.) Note: a chookie is a type of **bevan**. See also **bennie**, **bethan**, **bog**[2], **bogan**, **booner**, **boonie**, **chigger**, **garry**, **scozzer** and **westie**. [WEST CENTRAL QLD]

chookie laps the laps around town driven by a **chookie**.
[WEST CENTRAL QLD]

chopped drunk. See also **gone to Gowings**, **maggered**, **maggoted**, **maggo**, **off chops** and **off your unit**. [MELBOURNE REGION]

chopper an old cow sold to the abattoir solely for chopping up (for pet food). Also spelled choppa. [WESTERN DISTRICT]

chop picnic what we called a barbecue before the word "barbecue" arrived in Australia. (Now obsolete.) Although reported from many regions, knowledge of this term seems to have been very scattered and irregular. See also **grill**[1].
[SOUTH COAST AND SOUTHERN TABLELANDS, TASMANIA, NORTHERN SOUTH AUSTRALIA, ADELAIDE REGION, SYDNEY REGION, FAR WEST NSW]

chowoon an exclamation of surprise or disbelief (sometimes made more emphatic by the addition of "eh!" as a tag). Also spelled chow woon, chow wun. See also **bulltwang!**; **bunnies to that!**; **eh**; **gammon**; **hells, bells and bootlaces**; **Himmel** and **strike me roan!** [PERTH REGION]

Christmas handshake to grab and crush someone's testicles in a Rugby League scrum. [BRISBANE REGION]

chub change coins suitable for throwing into a poker machine (from the name of a well-known maker of locks and wall safes).
[MELBOURNE REGION]

chuck a beachie to drive around the surrounding streets of a beach. [NORTHERN SOUTH AUSTRALIA]

chuck a bonie to salute an officer (RAAF slang). [NORTH COAST QLD]

chuck a lap to drive around the main streets. See also **chuck a mainy**. [NORTHERN SOUTH AUSTRALIA, BRISBANE REGION, CENTRAL COAST QLD]

chuck a mainy see **chuck a lap**. [EYRE AND YORKE PENINSULAS, NORTHERN SOUTH AUSTRALIA]

chunder daks trousers that have been pulled up too high (above the hips, the waist, and over the stomach) and worn with the shirt tucked in. [SOUTH COAST AND SOUTHERN TABLELANDS, NORTHERN VICTORIA]

chunder suit a formal dinner suit. [MELBOURNE REGION]

chutney a grumpy and irascible older person. [ADELAIDE REGION]

chutty chewing gum. Also spelled chutti. [SYDNEY REGION]

cicada large insects of the family *Cicadidae* (sometimes mistakenly called "locusts"). The regional variation here is found in the pronunciation: in Victoria it is "sick-AY-da" but in New South Wales "sick-AR-da". See also **black prince**, **brown baker**, **brown bomber**[2], **cherrynose**, **floury baker**, **greengrocer**[2], **pisswhacker**, **tick tock** and **yellow Monday**. [MELBOURNE REGION, SYDNEY REGION]

civvies casual clothes, as opposed to school, work or military uniform. [WESTERN DISTRICT, ADELAIDE REGION]

clackers thongs or sandals. See also **Chinese safety boots**, **getters**, **go-backs**, **jandals**, **Japanese flying boots**, **Japanese riding boots**, **Japanese safety boots**, **Jesus boots**, **NT work boots** and **pluggers**. [HUNTER VALLEY AND NORTH COAST]

clag[1] to kiss and cuddle. (Possibly from a familiar brand of glue.) [MELBOURNE REGION]

clag[2] mist or light cloud (bushwalkers' slang). [TASMANIA]

claggies male underwear. ("Of the most embarrassing kind," writes a contributor, "thick, white, undersized boxers with two bands of blue striping around the elastic at the top.") [CENTRAL HIGHLANDS VICTORIA]

Clarence a huntsman spider. See also **triantelope**. [SYDNEY REGION]

clarrie girls' slang for periods (possible abbreviation of "claret").
[CENTRAL WEST NSW]

clawchie an Australian freshwater crayfish, of the genus *Cherax*. See
also **cherub**, **crawchie**, **crawbob**, **craybob**, **craydab**, **crayfish**,
jilgie, **lobby**, **lobster**, **marron**, **pink nipper** and **yabby**. [BRISBANE
REGION]

cleanser an alcoholic beverage (most commonly a beer).
Sometimes extended as "a cleansing ale". [NORTH COAST QLD]

click clack a folding deckchair. [MELBOURNE REGION]

clicker the remote control. ("Who's seen the clicker?" "Have you
looked behind the lounge?" "Yeah, looked there." "You had it last!"
"Don't blame me, I haven't touched the thing!" "Maybe the dog
took it?" "Well, look in its basket then …" and so on, and on, and
on.) [ADELAIDE REGION]

clothes prop man an itinerant seller of clothes props, which were
tall, thin branches cut from saplings with a fork at one end,
used to prop up backyard lines weighed down by wet clothes
(in the days before the rotary hoist). The clothes prop man
(who would cut his own clothes props in the bush and then sell
them door to door) was a well-known figure during the Great
Depression (and for some time afterwards). Also as "clo' prop
man".

[PERTH REGION, SYDNEY REGION, GIPPSLAND, MELBOURNE REGION, ADELAIDE REGION,
NORTHERN VICTORIA]

Cloudland underpants underpants that are too large or too loose
(from the name of a famous Brisbane ballroom). [BRISBANE REGION]

clubbies[1] swimmers (**togs**, **bathers** etc.) acceptable at swimming
clubs that ban board shorts. See also **bathers**, **cossie**, **cozzie**,
costume, **swimmers**, **swimsuit**, **togs** and **trunks**. [BRISBANE REGION]

clubbies[2] members of surf life saving clubs. [BRISBANE REGION]

clumsy as a duck in a ploughed paddock accident-prone. See also
numb nuts and **roo**. [MELBOURNE REGION]

cluster busters see **Speedos**. See also **ballhuggers**, **boasters**, **budgie-huggers**, **budgie-smugglers**, **cockchokers**, **cock jocks**, **codjocks**, **dick bathers**, **dick-pointers**, **dick-pokers**, **dick stickers**, **dick togs**, **dikdaks**, **dipsticks**, **fish frighteners**, **jammers**, **Jimmy clingers**, **knobbies**, **lolly-baggers**, **lolly bags**, **meat-hangers**, **nut huggers**, **nylon disgusters**, **racers**, **racing bathers**, **scungies**[2], **sluggers**, **sluggos**, **slug huggers**, **tights**, **toolies**, **trunks** and **wog togs**. [BRISBANE REGION]

coastal scrag a woman of dubious morals from the north-west coast of Tasmania. [TASMANIA]

coathanger, the Sydney Harbour Bridge (possibly originally coined as a put-down by Melbournians, but embraced by Sydneysiders as an affectionate nickname). See also the **meccano set**.
[SYDNEY REGION]

coats-off day a summer's day at school so hot permission was given for coats to be taken off. [MELBOURNE REGION]

cobber[1] a chocolate-covered lolly.
[MELBOURNE REGION, SYDNEY REGION, CENTRAL WEST AUSTRALIA]

cobber[2] a friend, a mate. Once universally used, now part of the living language only in the island state. See also **cock**, **duck** and **mudcrab**. [TASMANIA]

cobber up make friends (probably now largely obsolete).
[MELBOURNE REGION, GIPPSLAND, WESTERN DISTRICT]

cobbler an Australian eel-tailed catfish. [PERTH REGION]

cobbler's peg a long, thin black seed which sticks to clothing.
[BRISBANE REGION]

cobbler wobbler a stick for hitting the stings out of a **cobbler**.
[PERTH REGION]

cobra a long, white, rockmelon-like fruit (but lacking the sweetness of the rockmelon). A contributor explains: "They are prepared by peeling, slicing up, and then left standing overnight with sugar sprinkled on top. This creates a syrup, which makes the melon sweet, and this is then topped with cream. The locals keep and share the seeds. Everyone aims to have cobras for Christmas Day." [BRISBANE REGION]

cock affectionate form of address (like "mate" and **cobber**[2]). Originating in Britain (and still occasionally in use there and in the US) this is now common in only one Australian state. It is ultimately the same as the word "rooster", and was formerly used to refer to a spirited bloke, in the same way that a rooster is a strutting, feisty bird. See also **cobber**[2], **duck** and **mudcrab**.
[TASMANIA]

cockchokers see **Speedos**. See also **ballhuggers**, **boasters**, **budgie-huggers**, **budgie-smugglers**, **cluster busters**, **cock jocks**, **codjocks**, **dick bathers**, **dick-pointers**, **dick-pokers**, **dick stickers**, **dick togs**, **dikdaks**, **dipsticks**, **fish frighteners**, **jammers**, **Jimmy clingers**, **knobbies**, **lolly-baggers**, **lolly bags**, **meat-hangers**, **nut huggers**, **nylon disgusters**, **racers**, **racing bathers**, **scungies**[2], **sluggers**, **sluggos**, **slug huggers**, **tights**, **toolies**, **trunks** and **wog togs**. [MELBOURNE REGION]

cockeye bob 1. a large whirlwind. 2. a cyclone. Also known as cockeyed bob and as a willy-willy.
[NORTHERN WEST AUSTRALIA, CENTRAL WEST AUSTRALIA, PERTH REGION]

cock jocks see **Speedos**. See also **ballhuggers**, **boasters**, **budgie-huggers**, **budgie-smugglers**, **cluster busters**, **cockchokers**, **codjocks**, **dick bathers**, **dick-pointers**, **dick-pokers**, **dick stickers**, **dick togs**, **dikdaks**, **dipsticks**, **fish frighteners**, **jammers**, **Jimmy clingers**, **knobbies**, **lolly-baggers**, **lolly bags**, **meat-hangers**, **nut huggers**, **nylon disgusters**, **racers**, **racing bathers**, **scungies**[2], **sluggers**, **sluggos**, **slug huggers**, **tights**, **toolies**, **trunks** and **wog togs**. [PERTH REGION, NORTHERN WEST AUSTRALIA, BRISBANE REGION]

cockles small shellfish dug out of the sand, commonly used as bait, sometimes boiled and eaten. See also **eugarie**, **pipi** and **wong**.
[ADELAIDE REGION, MELBOURNE REGION, TASMANIA]

cockroach the Queensland nickname for a resident of New South Wales. See also **Mexican**. [BRISBANE REGION]

cocky[1] a lock of hair sticking up from the head, supposedly resembling a cockatoo's crest. [SYDNEY REGION, MELBOURNE REGION]

cocky[2] a person who keeps lookout while their mates do something dodgy. [PERTH REGION, MELBOURNE REGION, GIPPSLAND]

cockylora a schoolyard catching game, a variant of **British bulldog**. (Also known as "cross over red rover" or "bullrush".) Players ran between safe points on either side of a field attempting to avoid being caught by other players. The catcher had to hold a player long enough to recite "cockylora one, two three". See also **bedlam**, **bullrush** and **red rover**.
[SYDNEY REGION, HUNTER VALLEY AND NORTH COAST, NEW ENGLAND DISTRICT, THE RIVERINA, SOUTH COAST AND SOUTHERN TABLELANDS, CENTRAL WEST NSW, FAR WEST NSW]

code brown the signal given by swimming pool staff when a toddler does number twos in the pool. (That's put you off swimming in public pools for a while, hasn't it?)
[PERTH REGION]

COD gate a "carry or drag" rural gate (either a rough home-made timber gate or a commercial gate that's stopped making any real effort and has sagged despondently across the track). See also **bogan gate**, **Methodist gate** and **wire gate**.
[THE RIVERINA, CENTRAL WEST NSW]

codjocks see **Speedos**. See also **ballhuggers**, **boasters**, **budgie-huggers**, **budgie-smugglers**, **cluster busters**, **cockchokers**, **cock jocks**, **dick bathers**, **dick-pointers**, **dick-pokers**, **dick stickers**, **dick togs**, **dikdaks**, **dipsticks**, **fish frighteners**, **jammers**, **Jimmy clingers**, **knobbies**, **lolly-baggers**, **lolly bags**, **meat-hangers**, **nut huggers**, **nylon disgusters**, **racers**, **racing bathers**, **scungies**[2], **sluggers**, **sluggos**, **slug huggers**, **tights**, **toolies**, **trunks** and **wog togs**. [PERTH REGION]

coffee roll an iced pastry. [CENTRAL COAST QLD, BRISBANE REGION]

coffin a bin to store fish or lobsters. [TASMANIA]

cog[1] people who drive their car around the block late at night. See also **blockie** and **cog-head**. [HUNTER VALLEY AND NORTH COAST]

cog[2] a lout, especially a lout who's a petrol head.
[TASMANIA, HUNTER VALLEY AND NORTH COAST]

cogger[1] see **bennie, bethan, bevan, bog**[2]**, bogan, booner, boonie, chigger, chookie, garry, scozzer** and **westie**.
[HUNTER VALLEY AND NORTH COAST]

cogger[2] cute or precocious, said of a girl or a toddler of either sex (probably now dated). [TASMANIA]

cog-head a petrol head, a person with a fixation on large, loud cars and endless driving around the streets after dark. Abbreviated as **cog**. See also **blockie**. [HUNTER VALLEY AND NORTH COAST]

coinslot buttock cleavage creeping coyly above the top of the pants. See also **builder's smile, councilman's cleavage** and **worker's crack**. [SYDNEY REGION]

college high school years 11 and 12 in the Australian Capital Territory. [SOUTH COAST AND SOUTHERN TABLELANDS]

Collie-ite a person born and living in Collie (Western Australia). Note: a *real* Collie-ite is someone whose parents and grandparents were all born in Collie. [PERTH REGION]

Collins Street cocky an owner of a country property (for tax purposes) who lives and works in Melbourne. Also known as a "Collins Street grazier" or a "Collins Street farmer". Used in some places to refer to all absentee property owners. See also **Pitt Street farmer** and **Queen Street bushie**.
[WIMMERA AND MALLEE, CENTRAL HIGHLANDS VICTORIA, WESTERN DISTRICT, NORTHERN VICTORIA, GIPPSLAND, MELBOURNE REGION]

Coma derogatory nickname for the town of Cooma (in southern New South Wales). [SOUTH COAST AND SOUTHERN TABLELANDS]

come down a flash flood, with dry creeks flooding after a heavy downpour in the Flinders Ranges. [ADELAIDE REGION]

condition weight; fat. "You're putting on a bit of condition" means "you're putting on a bit of weight".
[HUNTER VALLEY AND NORTH COAST]

conky a gum nut. See also **honky nut**. [PERTH REGION]

connie[1] a tram or bus conductor. [MELBOURNE REGION]

connie[2] a stone (usually a small stone suitable for throwing). See also **boondie**[2], **brinnie**, **gibber**, **gonnie**, **goolie**, **ronnie** and **yonnie**.
[THE RIVERINA, GIPPSLAND]

connie[3] the Conservatory in the Fitzroy Gardens, Melbourne.
[MELBOURNE REGION]

connie agate a hard quality playing marble (agate is a variety of quartz). [SYDNEY REGION]

consolidated school a state school in a rural area providing both primary and secondary education. See also **area school**, **central school**, **district school**, **high top** and **secondary tops**.
[CENTRAL HIGHLANDS VICTORIA, GIPPSLAND, MELBOURNE REGION, NORTHERN VICTORIA, WESTERN DISTRICT, WIMMERA AND MALLEE]

continental a large fundraising fete or fair (now possibly obsolete).
[NORTHERN SOUTH AUSTRALIA, THE RIVERINA, CENTRAL WEST NSW, HUNTER VALLEY AND NORTH COAST]

coodies head lice. [PERTH REGION]

coods testicles. See also **ackers**, **goolies**, **nuggets** and **nurries**.
[PERTH REGION, CENTRAL WEST AUSTRALIA]

cooked breads toasted bread. [SYDNEY REGION]

cool cup a plastic cup containing frozen cordial (sometimes "cold cup"). Classic school **tuck shop** tucker.
[BRISBANE REGION, NORTH COAST QLD, HUNTER VALLEY AND NORTH COAST]

cool drink soft drink. See also **cordial**, **fizzy cordial**, **fizzy drink** and **lolly water**.
[ADELAIDE REGION, NORTHERN SOUTH AUSTRALIA, WIMMERA AND MALLEE, EYRE AND YORKE PENINSULAS, PERTH REGION]

Coolie the town of Coolangatta. [HUNTER VALLEY AND NORTH COAST]

coolies a variation on "cool" as a term of approval, but used in a noncommittal way (similar to "fine" or "whatever").
[BRISBANE REGION]

coondie a **boondie** (a rock) so large you can't move it. (However, some contributors remember it as being the other way around: the boondie being the large rock and the coondie the small one.) See also **boondie**[2], **gibber**, **gonnie**, **goolie**, **ronnie** and **yonnie**. [PERTH REGION]

cope to overturn (e.g. a boat). [HUNTER VALLEY AND NORTH COAST]

cop my wallop? Get my drift? Do you understand? [TASMANIA]

copper-top a red-headed person. See also **blood nut** and **ranga**. [PERTH REGION]

Coraki handbag a wine cask. (Note: the town is pronounced CORR-uck-EYE.) See also **bag of death**, **Balga handbag**, **Bellambi handbag**, **boxie**, **box monster**, **Broadmeadows briefcase**, **cardboard handbag**, **death bag**, **Dubbo handbag**, **gin's handbag**, **goon**, **goonbag**, **goonbox**, **goonie**, **goonsack**, **lady in the boat**, **red handbag**, **sack** and **vino collapso**. [HUNTER VALLEY AND NORTH COAST]

corby a grub. A contributor explains: "As schoolboys at Devonport, Tasmania, during the early 1940s it was a common seasonal activity to go 'corbying'. This was the art of fishing corbies from their holes with a length of fine wire." [TASMANIA]

cordial soft drink. Contributors strongly identified cordial as the preferred Tasmanian term. (Adjectives were sometimes used to clarify possible confusion between carbonated soft drinks and syrup to which water was added: "fizzy cordial" versus "water cordial".) See also **cool drink**, **fizzy cordial**, **fizzy drink** and **lolly water**. [TASMANIA, HUNTER VALLEY AND NORTH COAST, CENTRAL WEST NSW]

cordie[1] a drink (usually alcoholic). Abbreviation of **cordial**. [PERTH REGION]

cordie[2] a cadet at Duntroon or one of the Australian Defence Force Academy military colleges. [SOUTH COAST AND SOUTHERN TABLELANDS]

Corinna stubby a longneck of beer. See also **big bot**, **big bud**, **longie**, **long neck** and **tallie**. [TASMANIA]

Corio work boots moccasins. (From the Geelong suburb of Corio.) See also **Broadmeadows wedding shoes**, **moccas**, **Ringwood Reeboks** and **Sunshine stilettos**. [WESTERN DISTRICT]

Coro 1. the Coronation Hotel (popular with university students) 2. Coronation Drive (a scenic road beside the Brisbane River). [BRISBANE REGION]

cossie a swimming costume. Also spelled **cozzie**. What we call our swimming attire seems to be one of the great linguistic divides in Australia. Contributors from New South Wales reported finding **bathers** a rather stuffy and posh word for such a casual piece of clothing. And several reported shopping for cossies when visiting interstate ("You know what I mean – costumes") and being directed to a fancy dress costume shop. Children of "mixed marriages" (parents from different states) report growing up confused as to what to call the gear they swam in. See also **bathers**, **clubbies**[1], **costume**, **swimmers**, **swimsuit**, **togs** and **trunks**. [SYDNEY REGION, HUNTER VALLEY AND NORTH COAST, NEW ENGLAND DISTRICT, THE RIVERINA, SOUTH COAST AND SOUTHERN TABLELANDS, CENTRAL WEST NSW, FAR WEST NSW]

costume a swimming costume. See also **bathers**, **clubbies**[1], **cossie**, **cozzie**, **swimmers**, **swimsuit**, **togs** and **trunks**. [SYDNEY REGION, HUNTER VALLEY AND NORTH COAST, NEW ENGLAND DISTRICT, THE RIVERINA, SOUTH COAST AND SOUTHERN TABLELANDS, CENTRAL WEST NSW, FAR WEST NSW]

could eat a pineapple through a tennis racket has prominent teeth. [PERTH REGION]

councilman's cleavage see **builder's smile**, **worker's crack** and **coinslot**. [SYDNEY REGION]

couple of lamingtons short of a CWA meeting, a not fully informed, a bit slow on the uptake (particularly in relation to getting jokes) or a bit light-on in the intelligence department. This is one of scores of variations on the English slang "not the full quid". See also **dipsticks**, **doughy**, **dubbo**, **gimp**, **Milo**, **moonya**, **munted**, **nuffest** and **veggie**[1]. [CENTRAL WEST AUSTRALIA]

cove chap, fellow. Once heard Australia-wide, this term now seems to thrive only in the Tasmanian climate. [TASMANIA]

cowal a small swampy depression typically found in red-soil country. (From the Kamilaroi Aboriginal language.) [BRISBANE REGION, CENTRAL COAST QLD, NORTH COAST QLD, FAR NORTH QLD, WEST CENTRAL QLD, CENTRAL WEST NSW]

cowboy a country musician with a tin ear, a flat voice, and three wrong chords. Sometimes extended to describe anyone who's not good at their job (especially tradesmen). [SYDNEY REGION, PERTH REGION]

cowboy caviar baked beans. [CENTRAL WEST AUSTRALIA]

cow cordial low fat milk (as opposed to **moo juice** – full cream milk). [MELBOURNE REGION]

cozzie see **bathers**, **clubbies**[1], **cossie**, **costume**, **swimsuit**, **swimmers**, **togs** and **trunks**.
[SYDNEY REGION, HUNTER VALLEY AND NORTH COAST, NEW ENGLAND DISTRICT, THE RIVERINA, SOUTH COAST AND SOUTHERN TABLELANDS, CENTRAL WEST NSW, FAR WEST NSW]

crabhole a depression in a paddock (especially in black soil country). [CENTRAL HIGHLANDS VICTORIA]

crackadog crazy, insane, totally nuts. See also **Baillie**, **Richmond Clinic**, **ward eight**, **ward twenty** and **womba**. [ADELAIDE REGION]

cracked off discarded, disqualified, asked to leave, sent packing. A contributor explains: "This comes from the sport of campdrafting where, if you're disqualified, a whip is cracked to let you know." [CENTRAL COAST QLD]

cracker dust see **crusher dust**. [NORTH COAST QLD]

cranky eccentric. See also **rum 'un**.
[ADELAIDE REGION, CENTRAL HIGHLANDS VICTORIA, EYRE AND YORKE PENINSULAS, GIPPSLAND, MELBOURNE REGION, NORTHERN VICTORIA, PERTH REGION, TASMANIA, WESTERN DISTRICT, WIMMERA AND MALLEE]

crawbob a variant of **craydab**. See also **cherub**, **clawchie**, **crawchie**, **craybob**, **crayfish**, **jilgie**, **lobby**, **lobster**, **marron**, **pink nipper** and **yabby**. [FAR WEST NSW, NEW ENGLAND DISTRICT, CENTRAL WEST NSW]

crawchie Australian freshwater crayfish, of the genus *Cherax*. A small creature with many different names in many different regions. See also **cherub**, **clawchie**, **crawbob**, **craybob**, **craydab**, **crayfish**, **jilgie**, **lobby**, **lobster**, **marron**, **pink nipper** and **yabby**.
[HUNTER VALLEY AND NORTH COAST, NORTH COAST QLD, CENTRAL COAST QLD]

cray[1] crayfish. See also **cherub**, **clawchie**, **crawbob**, **crawchie**, **craybob**, **craydab**, **jilgie**, **lobby**, **lobster**, **marron**, **pink nipper** and **yabby**.

[WIMMERA AND MALLEE, CENTRAL HIGHLANDS VICTORIA, WESTERN DISTRICT, NORTHERN VICTORIA, GIPPSLAND, MELBOURNE REGION, TASMANIA, EYRE AND YORKE PENINSULAS, ADELAIDE REGION, PERTH REGION]

cray[2] a twenty dollar note. See also **crayfish**[2], **lobster**[3], **red back** and **rock lobster**. [PERTH REGION]

craybob 1. craydab. 2. a freshwater crayfish or yabby. See also **cherub**, **clawchie**, **crawchie**, **craydab**, **crayfish**, **jilgie**, **lobby**, **lobster**, **marron**, **pink nipper** and **yabby**.

[FAR WEST NSW, THE RIVERINA, NEW ENGLAND DISTRICT]

craydab Australian freshwater crayfish, of the genus *Cherax*. See also **cherub**, **clawchie**, **crawbob**, **crawchie**, **craybob**, **crayfish**, **jilgie**, **lobby**, **lobster**, **marron**, **pink nipper** and **yabby**.

[FAR WEST NSW, CENTRAL WEST NSW]

crayfish[1] 1. any of various large, edible marine, stalk-eyed decapod crustaceans of the family *Palinuridae*, with large claws and a hard red carapace. 2. Australian freshwater crustacean of the genus *Cherax*. See also **cherub**, **clawchie**, **crawbob**, **crawchie**, **craybob**, **craydab**, **jilgie**, **lobby**, **lobster**, **marron**, **pink nipper** and **yabby**. (Yes, but what did their mothers call them?)

[BRISBANE REGION, CENTRAL COAST QLD, CENTRAL HIGHLANDS VICTORIA, CENTRAL WEST NSW, GIPPSLAND, HUNTER VALLEY AND NORTH COAST, MELBOURNE REGION, NEW ENGLAND DISTRICT, NORTH COAST QLD, NORTHERN VICTORIA, SOUTH COAST AND SOUTHERN TABLELANDS, SYDNEY REGION, THE RIVERINA, WESTERN DISTRICT, WIMMERA AND MALLEE]

crayfish[2] a twenty dollar note. See also **cray**[2], **lobster**[3], **red back** and **rock lobster**. [PERTH REGION, MELBOURNE REGION, GIPPSLAND]

crazy hair day charity fundraising event in which schoolchildren pay a dollar to be allowed to attend school with their hair in different colour(s) or styles. [PERTH REGION]

cream between a slice of ice-cream between two wafers (originally a product name). See also **ice-cream sandwich**.

[WIMMERA AND MALLEE, CENTRAL HIGHLANDS VICTORIA, WESTERN DISTRICT, NORTHERN VICTORIA, GIPPSLAND, MELBOURNE REGION, TASMANIA]

crease leave a batsman's cry in backyard cricket, seeking leave to (a) argue with the umpire or (b) go inside and get a cool drink from Mum. (Sometimes abbreviated to the single word "crease!") [PERTH REGION]

crescent what the English call a shifting spanner and the Americans a monkey wrench. (The full name may have originally been "crescent wrench".) [PERTH REGION]

crew a group of friends. [ADELAIDE REGION]

crib[1] cheating at marbles by pushing the hand forward over the playing line. See also **cribs**, **cribbing**, **duck-shove**, **fernannick**, **fudge** and **phernudge**. [THE RIVERINA]

crib[2] 1. a packed lunch. 2. the bag or container the lunch is packed in. 3. the lunchbreak. The term crib came into Old English in the 11th century from a common West German noun, and originally meant "a receptacle for fodder used in cow sheds". From this humble beginning it came to have many meanings, a number of them naming a container of some sort. According to the *English Dialect Dictionary* (1898) the term crib in the sense of a food container (and, from this, the food it contained) appears as part of the Cornish dialect, and it's from there that it most probably made its way into Australian mining communities (but the term was also in use in Scotland, Northampton and Devon). See also **crib room**.
[CENTRAL WEST AUSTRALIA, NORTHERN WEST AUSTRALIA, PERTH REGION, NORTH COAST QLD, FAR NORTH QLD, HUNTER VALLEY AND NORTH COAST, FAR WEST NSW, CENTRAL COAST QLD, TASMANIA, GIPPSLAND, SOUTH COAST AND SOUTHERN TABLELANDS, EYRE AND YORKE PENINSULAS, NORTHERN SOUTH AUSTRALIA]

cribbing cheating at marbles by moving over the mark. See also **crib**[1], **cribs**, **duck-shove**, **fernannick**, **fudge** and **phernudge**.
[MELBOURNE REGION, TASMANIA]

crib cuddy the place where meals were eaten in the mines of Broken Hill (usually an area cut into the rock face beside a drive). See **crib**[2]. One contributor wrote: "We had to keep our cribs in metal crib tins because the rats in the crib cuddy were as big as bloody cats and could gnaw through anything." See also **crib**[2].
[FAR WEST NSW]

crib room lunch room at heavy industry work sites. See also **crib**[2]. [HUNTER VALLEY AND NORTH COAST, NORTH COAST QLD]

cribs cheating at marbles. See also **crib**[1], **cribbing**, **duck-shove**, **fernannick**, **fudge** and **phernudge**. [MELBOURNE REGION]

crib tin a rectangular-shaped tin with a rounded lid (like a hi-top bread loaf) used by miners to carry their crib in. See also **crib**[2]. [FAR WEST NSW]

cripple surfers' slang for a knee boarder. [HUNTER VALLEY AND NORTH COAST]

crook as Rookwood unwell; often applied to a hangover. (From Rookwood Cemetery, Sydney.) [SYDNEY REGION]

cross-country ballet Australian Rules football. AFL fans respond by calling Rugby League **cross-country wrestling**. See also **football**, **footy**, **hoofa** and **kick and giggle**. [SYDNEY REGION, MELBOURNE REGION]

cross-country wrestling Rugby League. See also **cross-country ballet**.
[CENTRAL HIGHLANDS VICTORIA, GIPPSLAND, MELBOURNE REGION, NORTHERN VICTORIA, WESTERN DISTRICT, WIMMERA AND MALLEE]

crow peck a hard and sharp rap on the skull with the knuckles. See also **camel bite**, **horse bite** and **monkey shine**. [SYDNEY REGION]

CRT a casual relief teacher (formerly, an **emergency teacher**). See also **supply teacher**. [MELBOURNE REGION]

crush, the the time of year when the sugar cane is harvested and crushed (July to September). [NORTH COAST QLD]

crusher dust gravel used on driveways (a waste product of quarries crushing bluestone aggregates).
[NORTHERN SOUTH AUSTRALIA, NORTH COAST QLD]

cubie boarding school slang for a student's cubicle (a portioned-off section of a larger dormitory, containing the boarder's bed, cupboard and desk). [ADELAIDE REGION]

cuda something that's really good (surfing slang). [MELBOURNE REGION]

cungy descriptive term for something that has deteriorated.
[BRISBANE REGION]

Cunnamulla portmanteau sugar bag containing one's belongings and carried over the shoulder. [BRISBANE REGION]

Cunnamulla tune-up randomly swapping the spark-plug leads around on a car (a malicious form of vandalism that can cause major damage). [BRISBANE REGION]

Curly Bells temporary seating at a sports venue made from scaffolding and planking. Also spelled "curlibel", "curly balls" and "curleybelles". (From the name of the original supplier of this seating, Curley Bell of Townsville.)
[NORTH COAST QLD, WEST CENTRAL QLD, FAR NORTH QLD, BRISBANE REGION]

cuss cousin (parallel to the Black American expression "bro").
[SYDNEY REGION]

cut crook to be angry at something or someone. [ADELAIDE REGION]

cut laps yet another term for mindlessly driving a car around the block on a Friday or Saturday night, until asked to move on by the police. [WIMMERA AND MALLEE]

cut lunch and a waterbag, a a long way off; a good distance. In response to the question, "How far away is it, mate?" you could either reply, "A day's travel" or "A cut lunch and a waterbag away". See also **water bottle hike**. [ADELAIDE REGION]

cut out to wind up a job by spending the last of the available cash (possibly on rounds of beer). [NORTH COAST QLD]

cuts corporal punishment with a cane, strap or ruler (usually in twos, fours or sixes).
[SYDNEY REGION, MELBOURNE REGION, ADELAIDE REGION, TASMANIA]

cutter[1] a rough gemstone good enough to be faceted (cut), especially on the sapphire fields. [WEST CENTRAL QLD]

cutter[2] a colourful character, a bit of a lad, a mug lair.
[BRISBANE REGION]

cut the grass there seems to be a regional division in Australia between those who cut the grass and those who **mow the lawn**.
[ADELAIDE REGION, EYRE AND YORKE PENINSULAS, NORTHERN SOUTH AUSTRALIA]

D

D a dozen longnecks of beer. [TASMANIA]

dag bag a school bag made of cotton that could be slung over the shoulder. [SYDNEY REGION]

dagwood dog a deep-fried battered saveloy (the batter being soaked through with cholesterol-rich cooking oil). See also **battered sav**, **death stick**, **dippy dog** and **pluto pup**.
[ADELAIDE REGION, TASMANIA, BRISBANE REGION]

dakabin a local name for the grasstree. [BRISBANE REGION]

Dalkeith diesel a four-wheel-drive vehicle intended only for urban use. Also "Dalkeith tractor". See also **Balmain bulldozer**, **Bronte buggy**, **Burnside bus**, **Kenmore tractor**, **North Shore tank**, **Toorak tractor** and **Turramurra tractor**. [PERTH REGION]

dandy a small container (approximately 100 ml) of ice-cream. (Originally a brand name.) See also **bucket** and **dixie**.
[ADELAIDE REGION, WIMMERA AND MALLEE, EYRE AND YORKE PENINSULAS]

dangle the Dunlops an aircraft lowering the undercarriage as it prepares to land (RAAF slang); also employed by Sydney radio legend Gary O'Callaghan (whether he picked it up from the RAAF or they from him is unclear). [DARWIN AND NORTH COAST NT]

Dapto briefcase cask of wine. See also **bag of death**, **Balga handbag**, **Bellambi handbag**, boxie, box monster, **Broadmeadows briefcase**, cardboard handbag, **Coraki handbag**, death bag, **goon**, **goonbag**, **goonbox**, **goonie**, **goonsack**, **lady in the boat**, red handbag, **sack** and **vino collapso**.
[SOUTH COAST AND SOUTHERN TABLELANDS]

Dapto dog derogatory rhyming slang for "wog". (From the Dapto Dogs – well-known greyhound race meeting.) See also **choc** and **Gosford dog**.
[CENTRAL WEST NSW, FAR WEST NSW, HUNTER VALLEY AND NORTH COAST, NEW ENGLAND DISTRICT, SOUTH COAST AND SOUTHERN TABLELANDS, SYDNEY REGION, THE RIVERINA]

dar cigarette. See also **bulyu**, **bunger**, **busta**, **darb** and **racehorse**[2].
[NORTHERN VICTORIA]

darb cigarette. See also **bulyu**, **bunger**, **busta**, **dar** and **racehorse**[2].
[BRISBANE REGION]

Darlo the inner Sydney suburb of Darlinghurst. [SYDNEY REGION]

Darwin rig acceptable dress for official occasions in the Northern
Territory: according to different contributors this is either long
trousers, shirt and tie, or else short trousers with long socks and a
short-sleeved shirt with a tie. See also **Territory rig**.
[DARWIN AND NORTH COAST NT, THE CENTRE]

Darwin stubby 1. (formerly) an 80 oz bottle of beer. 2. a 2.25 litre
bottle of beer. [DARWIN AND NORTH COAST NT, THE CENTRE, PERTH REGION]

Datto a Datsun car. [NORTH COAST QLD]

Dave generic name for a big bloke who's a bit of a thug.
[SOUTH COAST AND SOUTHERN TABLELANDS]

day bug a day student at a boarding school. See also **day scrag**.
[ADELAIDE REGION, SYDNEY REGION, MELBOURNE REGION, NORTH COAST QLD]

day scrag a day student at a boarding school. See also **day bug**.
[MELBOURNE REGION, ADELAIDE REGION]

DBs desert boots. [PERTH REGION]

dead leg corked thigh. [SYDNEY REGION]

deadly treadly a bicycle (sometimes restricted to a very fast bike,
and sometimes to a fixed-wheel bike with no brakes). Often
abbreviated to **treadly**. See also **grid**[1], **grunter**, **scrap** and **treadly**.
[CENTRAL HIGHLANDS VICTORIA, GIPPSLAND, MELBOURNE REGION, NORTHERN
VICTORIA, WESTERN DISTRICT, WIMMERA AND MALLEE, HUNTER VALLEY AND NORTH
COAST, FAR WEST NSW, PERTH REGION, BRISBANE REGION, DARWIN AND NORTH
COAST NT]

deamon high school slang for a very cool (or popular) person.
[NORTH COAST QLD]

deanie cruising the main street of Albury, New South Wales.
[NORTHERN VICTORIA]

death bag a wine cask. See also **bag of death**, **Balga handbag**,
Bellambi handbag, **boxie**, **box monster**, **Broadmeadows**

briefcase, **cardboard handbag**, **Coraki handbag**, **Dapto briefcase**, **Dubbo handbag**, **gin's handbag**, **goon**, **goonbag**, **goonbox**, **goonie**, **goonsack**, **lady in the boat**, **red handbag**, **sack** and **vino collapso**.
[TASMANIA]

death ray police mobile radar gun. See also **hairdryer**.
[NORTH COAST QLD]

death stick see **battered sav**, **dagwood dog**, **dippy dog** and **pluto pup**. [THE RIVERINA]

deep north far north Queensland. Sometimes spelled "Deep North". From the *Deep South* (of the United States), because of supposedly similar conservative attitudes.
[BRISBANE REGION, CENTRAL COAST QLD, FAR NORTH QLD, NORTH COAST QLD, WEST CENTRAL QLD]

deep sewerage the municipal sewerage system (in contrast to the alternative: a septic tank). [PERTH REGION]

deli what do you call your local, suburban corner shop? It might be a **convenience store**, **milk bar**, or **mixed business**, or it might be called a deli (even though it's not a traditional "delicatessen" selling only smallgoods and fine foods, but sells bread, milk, newspapers and bits of everything).
[ADELAIDE REGION, PERTH REGION, NORTHERN SOUTH AUSTRALIA]

demountable a temporary school building which can be lifted from its foundations and relocated. (Mainly of metal construction, and remembered by contributors as unbearably hot in summer and freezing in winter.) See also **Bristol hut**, **dogbox**, **hot box**, **musset hut**, **portable**, **pre-fab**, **relocatable**, **silver bullet**[1], **terrapin unit** and **transportable**.
[BRISBANE REGION, CENTRAL COAST QLD, CENTRAL WEST NSW, FAR NORTH QLD, FAR WEST NSW, HUNTER VALLEY AND NORTH COAST, NEW ENGLAND DISTRICT, NORTH COAST QLD, SOUTH COAST AND SOUTHERN TABLELANDS, SYDNEY REGION, THE RIVERINA, WEST CENTRAL QLD, PERTH REGION]

dent knocker a panel beater. [ADELAIDE REGION]

depot rubbish dump. See also **dump** and **tip**[1]. [FAR WEST NSW]

depot duck crow (scavenger at local rubbish dumps). [FAR WEST NSW]

depth charger a large bottle of beer. See also **big henry**.
[MELBOURNE REGION]

Dereelians residents of Dereel (a remote, isolated area south of Ballarat). [CENTRAL HIGHLANDS VICTORIA]

derps underpants. See also **reg grundies** and **underdungers**.
[MELBOURNE REGION]

desert chicken corned beef. See also **Burdekin duck**. [BRISBANE REGION]

desert rat someone who lives in the desert/spinifex area north-east of Muttaburra/Aramac. [WEST CENTRAL QLD]

devon[1] mild-flavoured, precooked sausage (usually sold pre-sliced), which seems to travel under many names and speak many languages. See also **baron sausage**, **beef Belgium**, **Belgium sausage**, **bung fritz**, **Byron sausage**, **Empire sausage**, **fritz**, **German sausage**, **luncheon sausage**, **mystery meat**, **polony**, **pork German**, **Strasburg**, **wheel meat** and **Windsor sausage**. (Note: this food item caused a number of contributors to alert us to Broken Hill being linguistically part of South Australia.)
[SYDNEY REGION, HUNTER VALLEY AND NORTH COAST, NEW ENGLAND DISTRICT, THE RIVERINA, SOUTH COAST AND SOUTHERN TABLELANDS, CENTRAL WEST NSW, TASMANIA, MELBOURNE REGION]

devon[2] the bald patch at the back of a man's head.
[SOUTH COAST AND SOUTHERN TABLELANDS]

DGs dark glasses. [SYDNEY REGION, SOUTH COAST AND SOUTHERN TABLELANDS]

dhobi bath or wash (RAN slang). From the Hindi word for laundry. See also **bogey**. [NORTH COAST QLD]

dib dobs worthless (can apply to persons, groups or organisations).
[HUNTER VALLEY AND NORTH COAST]

dibs[1] to lay claim to. See also **bags** and **bar**[3].
[SOUTH COAST AND SOUTHERN TABLELANDS]

dibs[2] marbles. See also **alleys** and **doogs**. [SYDNEY REGION]

dick bathers see **Speedos**. Sometimes abbreviated to DBs. See also **ballhuggers**, **boasters**, **budgie-huggers**, **budgie-smugglers**,

cluster busters, cockchokers, cock jocks, codjocks, dick-pokers, dick stickers, dick togs, dikdaks, dipsticks, fish frighteners, jammers, Jimmy clingers, knobbies, lolly-baggers, lolly bags, meat-hangers, nut huggers, nylon disgusters, racers, racing bathers, scungies[2]**, sluggers, sluggos, slug huggers, tights, toolies, trunks** and **wog togs.**

[ADELAIDE REGION, EYRE AND YORKE PENINSULAS, NORTHERN SOUTH AUSTRALIA, WEST CENTRAL QLD]

dicken an expression of strong agreement (now largely obsolete).

[HUNTER VALLEY AND NORTH COAST, NEW ENGLAND DISTRICT, FAR WEST NSW, ADELAIDE REGION]

dick-pointers see **Speedos**. Sometimes abbreviated to DPs. See also **ballhuggers, boasters, budgie-huggers, budgie-smugglers, cluster busters, cockchokers, cock jocks, codjocks, dick bathers, dick-pokers, dick stickers, dick togs, dikdaks, dipsticks, fish frighteners, jammers, Jimmy clingers, knobbies, lolly-baggers, lolly bags, meat-hangers, nut huggers, nylon disgusters, racers, racing bathers, scungies**[2]**, sluggers, sluggos, slug huggers, tights, toolies, trunks** and **wog togs**.

[GIPPSLAND, SOUTH COAST AND SOUTHERN TABLELANDS, SYDNEY REGION, BRISBANE REGION]

dick-pokers see **Speedos**. Sometimes abbreviated to DPs. See also **ballhuggers, boasters, budgie-huggers, budgie-smugglers, cluster busters, cockchokers, cock jocks, codjocks, dick bathers, dick-pointers, dick stickers, dick togs, dikdaks, dipsticks, fish frighteners, jammers, Jimmy clingers, knobbies, lolly-baggers, lolly bags, meat-hangers, nut huggers, nylon disgusters, racers, racing bathers, scungies**[2]**, sluggers, sluggos, slug huggers, tights, toolies, trunks** and **wog togs**.

[PERTH REGION, MELBOURNE REGION, SYDNEY REGION]

dick stickers see **Speedos**. See also **ballhuggers, boasters, budgie-huggers, budgie-smugglers, cluster busters, cockchokers, cock jocks, codjocks, dick bathers, dick-pointers, dick-pokers, dick togs, dikdaks, dipsticks, fish frighteners, jammers, Jimmy clingers, knobbies, lolly-baggers, lolly bags, meat-hangers, nut huggers, nylon disgusters, racers, racing bathers, scungies**[2]**,

sluggers, sluggos, slug huggers, tights, toolies, trunks and **wog togs**.

[SYDNEY REGION, HUNTER VALLEY AND NORTH COAST, MELBOURNE REGION, THE RIVERINA, NORTHERN VICTORIA, HUNTER VALLEY AND NORTH COAST, SOUTH COAST AND SOUTHERN TABLELANDS]

dick togs see **Speedos**. Sometimes abbreviated to DTs. See also **ballhuggers, boasters, budgie-huggers, budgie-smugglers, cluster busters, cockchokers, cock jocks, codjocks, dick bathers, dick-pointers, dick-pokers, dick stickers, dikdaks, dipsticks, fish frighteners, jammers, Jimmy clingers, knobbies, lolly-baggers, lolly bags, meat-hangers, nut huggers, nylon disgusters, racers, racing bathers, scungies**[2]**, sluggers, sluggos, slug huggers, tights, toolies, trunks** and **wog togs**.

[BRISBANE REGION, NORTH COAST QLD, WEST CENTRAL QLD, CENTRAL COAST QLD, DARWIN AND NORTH COAST NT]

dikdaks see **Speedos**. See also **ballhuggers, boasters, budgie-huggers, budgie-smugglers, cluster busters, cockchokers, cock jocks, codjocks, dick bathers, dick-pointers, dick-pokers, dick stickers, dick togs, dipsticks, fish frighteners, jammers, Jimmy clingers, knobbies, lolly-baggers, lolly bags, meat-hangers, nut huggers, nylon disgusters, racers, racing bathers, scungies**[2]**, sluggers, sluggos, slug huggers, tights, toolies, trunks** and **wog togs**. [THE RIVERINA, BRISBANE REGION]

dimmie abbreviation of "dim sim". [MELBOURNE REGION]

ding[1] a dent in a car panel. See also **dint**.

[SYDNEY REGION, HUNTER VALLEY AND NORTH COAST, MELBOURNE REGION, THE RIVERINA, NORTHERN VICTORIA, HUNTER VALLEY AND NORTH COAST, SOUTH COAST AND SOUTHERN TABLELANDS]

ding[2] (derogatory) Italian or Greek migrant (abbreviation of "dingbat").

[CENTRAL WEST AUSTRALIA, NORTHERN WEST AUSTRALIA, PERTH REGION, MELBOURNE REGION]

dingleberry a dead-set loser in the race of life. Also spelled "dangleberry". [ADELAIDE REGION]

dink 1. to convey as a second person on a horse, bicycle or motorcycle. On a pushbike this might involve conveying the

passenger on the crossbar, on the handlebars, or on the carrier.
2. a ride obtained from being dinked. See also **bar**[2], **dinky**[1], **dinky-double**, **donkey**[1], **double**, **double-dink**, **dub** and **pug**.

[WIMMERA AND MALLEE, CENTRAL HIGHLANDS VICTORIA, WESTERN DISTRICT, NORTHERN VICTORIA, GIPPSLAND, MELBOURNE REGION, THE RIVERINA, TASMANIA, PERTH REGION, CENTRAL WEST AUSTRALIA, SYDNEY REGION, HUNTER VALLEY AND NORTH COAST, SOUTH COAST AND SOUTHERN TABLELANDS, FAR WEST NSW, ADELAIDE REGION, NORTH COAST QLD, CENTRAL COAST QLD, BRISBANE REGION]

dinky[1] see **dink**. See also **bar**[2], **dink**, **dinky-double**, **donkey**[1], **double**, **double-dink**, **dub** and **pug**.

[ADELAIDE REGION, WIMMERA AND MALLEE, EYRE AND YORKE PENINSULAS, PERTH REGION, THE RIVERINA, MELBOURNE REGION]

dinky[2] a small metal tricycle for under-fives. (Dinky Toys was also the brand name of a range of diecast model cars and other vehicles.) [SYDNEY REGION, HUNTER VALLEY AND NORTH COAST]

dinky-double see **dink**. See also **bar**[2], **dinky**[1], **donkey**[1], **double**, **double-dink**, **dub** and **pug**. [BRISBANE REGION]

dint dent in a car panel. See also **ding**[1]. [GIPPSLAND]

dippy dog a **battered sav** dipped in tomato sauce. See also **dagwood dog**, **death stick** and **pluto pup**. [ADELAIDE REGION]

dipsticks 1. see **Speedos**. See also **ballhuggers**, **boasters**, **budgie-huggers**, **budgie-smugglers**, **cluster busters**, **cockchokers**, **cock jocks**, **codjocks**, **dick bathers**, **dick-pointers**, **dick-pokers**, **dick stickers**, **dick togs**, **dikdaks**, **fish frighteners**, **jammers**, **Jimmy clingers**, **knobbies**, **lolly-baggers**, **lolly bags**, **meat-hangers**, **nut huggers**, **nylon disgusters**, **racers**, **racing bathers**, **scungies**[2], **sluggers**, **sluggos**, **slug huggers**, **tights**, **toolies**, **trunks** and **wog togs**. 2. persons who are not too bright and a little slow on the uptake. See also **couple of lamingtons short of a CWA meeting, a**; **doughy**; **dubbo**; **gimp**; **Milo**; **moonya**; **munted**; **nuffest** and **veggie**[1]. [SYDNEY REGION]

dip tin a rectangular galvanised steel bucket with dozens of holes to allow grapes to be dipped into a drying solution (now superseded by plastic tubs). [WIMMERA AND MALLEE]

directly soon. [BRISBANE REGION, CENTRAL COAST QLD, WEST CENTRAL QLD]

dirt bin household garbage bin. (Sometimes called "dirt tin".) See also **garbage bin** and **rubbish bin**. [SYDNEY REGION]

Dirty Acre a block in the middle of the Golden Mile (Kalgoorlie). A contributor writes: "It was sold for 12 bottles of champagne in the 1890s by Tom Brookman and Sam Pearce (the discoverers of the Golden Mile). The small block was quickly covered with five hotels, a brewery and numerous other shops. According to legend, miners would tunnel into the cellars of the hotels to sell stolen gold over the bar." [CENTRAL WEST AUSTRALIA]

dirty duck the Black Swan pub (Wagga Wagga). Also known as the "black duck". [THE RIVERINA]

dishing (up) 1. serving food 2. gossiping.
[HUNTER VALLEY AND NORTH COAST]

dishlicker 1. a greyhound. 2. any dog. See also **panlicker**.
[CENTRAL HIGHLANDS VICTORIA, MELBOURNE REGION]

district school state school in a rural area providing both primary and secondary education. (Sometimes abbreviated to "dis", as in "King Island Dis".) See also **area school**, **central school**, **consolidated school**, **high top** and **secondary tops**. [TASMANIA]

Ditch, the Bass Strait. [TASMANIA]

divvy van a police van. See also **bull wagon**, **bun wagon** and **paddy wagon**. [MELBOURNE REGION]

dixie 1. small container (approximately 100 ml) of ice-cream. See **bucket**, **dandy**. 2. army slang for a small metal mess dish.
[CENTRAL HIGHLANDS VICTORIA, GIPPSLAND, MELBOURNE REGION, NORTHERN VICTORIA, TASMANIA, WESTERN DISTRICT, WIMMERA AND MALLEE, BRISBANE REGION]

doctor, the cooling sea breeze on a hot summer's day. See also **Canberra doctor**, **Esperance doctor** and **Fremantle doctor**.
[PERTH REGION]

dodger bread (now largely obsolete).
[SOUTH COAST AND SOUTHERN TABLELANDS]

do flickey a double roll of pastry with jam and icing.
[SOUTH COAST AND SOUTHERN TABLELANDS]

dog 1. school bag. [THE RIVERINA] 2. trailer on a road train. [CENTRAL WEST AUSTRALIA] 3. to ditch someone (end a friendship). [SYDNEY REGION]

dogbox 1. non-air-conditioned transportable classroom. See also **Bristol hut**, **demountable**, **hot box**, **musset hut**, **portable**, **pre-fab**, **relocatable**, **silver bullet**[1], **terrapin unit** and **transportable**. [ADELAIDE REGION, PERTH REGION] 2. any small inferior house or accommodation. [PERTH REGION] 3. storage extension to a truck crate over the cabin. [WEST CENTRAL QLD] 4. a suburban train with outward swinging doors on both sides providing entry to bench seat compartments without connecting corridors (obsolete). [MELBOURNE REGION]

dogger (derogatory) 1. Anglo-Saxon Australian. 2. person with one Anglo parent and one "wog" parent. [ADELAIDE REGION]

doggie[1] the **dogwatch** (night shift). [HUNTER VALLEY AND NORTH COAST]

doggle[2] supporter of Central District Football Club. [ADELAIDE REGION]

doggy small breed of mackerel. [CENTRAL WEST AUSTRALIA]

dogwatch night shift. [HUNTER VALLEY AND NORTH COAST]

donga[1] 1. arid outback wilderness. 2. open ground surrounding an outback town. [FAR WEST NSW, NORTHERN SOUTH AUSTRALIA]

donga[2] portable accommodation; one man hut (especially as provided in mining camps). [DARWIN AND NORTH COAST NT, THE CENTRE, NORTHERN WEST AUSTRALIA, PERTH REGION, NORTHERN SOUTH AUSTRALIA, CENTRAL WEST AUSTRALIA]

dong-eye catapult. See also **ging**, **gonk**, **shanghai** and **slingshot**. [HUNTER VALLEY AND NORTH COAST]

donk to convey as a second person on a horse, bicycle or motorcycle. See also **bar**[2], **dink**, **dinky**[1], **dinky-double**, **donkey**[1], **double**, **double-dink**, **dub** and **pug**. [SOUTH COAST AND SOUTHERN TABLELANDS]

donkey a variation of **donk**. See also **bar**[2], **dink**, **dinky**[1], **dinky-double**, **double**, **dub** and **pug**. [ADELAIDE REGION, WIMMERA AND MALLEE, EYRE AND YORKE PENINSULAS, NORTHERN SOUTH AUSTRALIA]

donuts nothing, zero, nought. [MELBOURNE REGION]

doogers food. See also **kai**. [ADELAIDE REGION]

dooghan a good bloke. [CENTRAL COAST QLD]

doogs marbles. See also **alleys** and **dibs**[1.]

[NORTHERN WEST AUSTRALIA, PERTH REGION, NORTHERN SOUTH AUSTRALIA, ADELAIDE REGION, SOUTH COAST AND SOUTHERN TABLELANDS]

dooley a drain or gully. [FAR WEST NSW]

Doris someone who is overly interested in the affairs of others; an inquisitive person; a gossip. Sometimes abbreviated to "dorry".

[NORTH COAST QLD]

double 1. to convey as a second person on a horse, bicycle or motorcycle. 2. a ride obtained from being doubled. See also **bar**[2], **dink**, **dinky**[1], **dinky-double**, **donkey**, **dub** and **pug**.

[SYDNEY REGION, HUNTER VALLEY AND NORTH COAST, NEW ENGLAND DISTRICT, THE RIVERINA, SOUTH COAST AND SOUTHERN TABLELANDS, CENTRAL WEST NSW, BRISBANE REGION, CENTRAL COAST QLD, NORTH COAST QLD, FAR WEST NSW]

Double Bay shopping trolley a very expensive, top-of-the-line four-wheel drive intended for urban use only. See also **Balmain bulldozer**, **Bronte buggy**, **Burnside bus**, **Kenmore tractor**, **North Shore tank**, **Toorak tractor** and **Turramurra tractor**.

[SYDNEY REGION]

double-cut roll a bread roll cut through twice and containing two layers of filling (a third cut in the middle making it possible to pull apart and eat as two separate sandwiches).

[EYRE AND YORKE PENINSULAS, ADELAIDE REGION, NORTHERN SOUTH AUSTRALIA]

double-dink see **bar**[2], **dink**, **dinky**[1], **dinky-double**, **donkey**, **double**, **dub** and **pug**.

[WIMMERA AND MALLEE, CENTRAL HIGHLANDS VICTORIA, WESTERN DISTRICT, NORTHERN VICTORIA, GIPPSLAND, MELBOURNE REGION, TASMANIA, PERTH REGION, CENTRAL WEST AUSTRALIA, SOUTH COAST AND SOUTHERN TABLELANDS, SYDNEY REGION, THE RIVERINA]

double-gee 1. a low-growing plant (*Emex australis*) having many hard, sharp, spiny seeds that are painful to step on and will sometimes even penetrate shoe soles. 2. one of these seeds of this plant. From the Afrikaans (Dutch) word *dubbeltjie* (literally, "little double one"); in South African English this became *doublejee*. See also **bullhead**, **California puncture weed**, **caltrop**, **cat head**[1], **cat's eye**[1], **goat's head** and **three-corner jack**. [PERTH REGION]

double grunter double bed. [PERTH REGION]

doubler see **bar**[2], **dink**, **dinky**[1], **dinky-double**, **donkey**, **double**, **double-dink**, **dub** and **pug**. [SYDNEY REGION, BRISBANE REGION]

doughy thick (in the sense of being a bit sleepy or dopey). See also **couple of lamingtons short of a CWA meeting, a**; **dipsticks**; **dubbo**; **gimp**; **Milo**; **moonya**; **munted**; **nuffest** and **veggie**[1]. [BRISBANE REGION, PERTH REGION]

Doveton shuffle (derogatory) wearing flapping moccasins in public (and the manner of walking this entails). [MELBOURNE REGION]

down ball a schoolyard game involving two players, a wall and a tennis ball. (The rules are a combination of handball, squash and tennis – and the cause of a great deal of argument among players!) [MELBOURNE REGION]

down south 1. informal name for a region of Western Australia (Dunsborough to Yallingup). [PERTH REGION] 2. the rest of Australia as seen from the Northern Territory. [DARWIN AND NORTH COAST NT]

downstairs outside the house ("upstairs" being inside the house). Now probably obsolete. [BRISBANE REGION]

drap sack your common everyday drongo, dill, drip or boofhead. See also **rubbernut** and **woppett**. [THE RIVERINA]

drinking fountain the multi-name-bearing piece of plumbing which provides a cool drink on a hot day. See also **bubbler**, **bubble tap**, **drink tap**, **drinking tap**, **fountain** and **water fountain**. [ADELAIDE REGION, BRISBANE REGION, CENTRAL COAST QLD, CENTRAL HIGHLANDS VICTORIA, EYRE AND YORKE PENINSULAS, FAR NORTH QLD, GIPPSLAND, MELBOURNE REGION, NORTH COAST QLD, NORTHERN VICTORIA, PERTH REGION, TASMANIA, WEST CENTRAL QLD, WESTERN DISTRICT, WIMMERA AND MALLEE]

drinking tap see **drinking fountain**. See also **bubbler**, **bubble tap**, **drink tap**, **fountain** and **water fountain**. [WIMMERA AND MALLEE, CENTRAL HIGHLANDS VICTORIA, WESTERN DISTRICT, NORTHERN VICTORIA, GIPPSLAND, MELBOURNE REGION, TASMANIA]

drink tap see **drinking fountain**. See also **bubbler**, **bubble tap**, **drinking tap**, **fountain** and **water fountain**. [PERTH REGION]

drive mining term for a major connecting tunnel. [FAR WEST NSW]

driver's arm the right arm (which, in transport drivers, becomes more tanned than the left). [BRISBANE REGION]

drop drill earthquake/bushfire drill (short for "drop everything and roll to safety"). [PERTH REGION]

drop my strides in Langlands window an expression of scepticism, referring to an event so unlikely that should it happen the speaker undertakes to "drop my strides in Langlands window" (referring to a department store in the main street of Horsham).
[WIMMERA AND MALLEE]

drop of the doings nip of alcohol in a cup of tea. [PERTH REGION]

drop the kids off at the pool evacuate the bowels. [PERTH REGION]

dub short for **double** or **doubler**. [WESTERN DISTRICT]

dubbo slow on the uptake. See also **dipsticks**, **doughy**, **gimp**, **Milo**, **moonya**, **munted**, **nuffest** and **veggie**[1]. [CENTRAL WEST NSW]

Dubbo handbag see also **bag of death**, **Balga handbag**, **Bellambi handbag**, **boxie**, **box monster**, **Broadmeadows briefcase**, **cardboard handbag**, **Coraki handbag**, **death bag**, **goon**, **goonbag**, **goonbox**, **goonie**, **goonsack**, **lady in the boat**, **red handbag**, **sack** and **vino collapso**. [CENTRAL WEST NSW]

dubs[1] the toilet. See also **long drop**. [ADELAIDE REGION]

dubs[2] catching two fish on a double-hooked line. [NORTH COAST QLD]

duchesse dressing table.
[BRISBANE REGION, CENTRAL COAST QLD, NORTH COAST QLD, FAR NORTH QLD, WEST CENTRAL QLD, HUNTER VALLEY AND NORTH COAST, SOUTH COAST AND SOUTHERN TABLELANDS]

duchesse set small mats placed on a dressing table (or **duchesse**).
[BRISBANE REGION]

duck form of address (in the same category as "mate" and "cobber[2]"). See also **cock** and **mudcrab**. [TASMANIA]

duck-shove a form of cheating at marbles (by pushing an opponent's hand as he shoots). See also **cribbing**, **cribs** and **phernudge**. [TASMANIA]

duck's nuts excellent! (A kind of squeal of pleasure.) See also **choice** and **nuffest**. [PERTH REGION]

ducks on the pond a shout of warning, used in shearing sheds to announce the arrival of a lady (the shearers would then watch their language till she left the shed). [NORTHERN SOUTH AUSTRALIA]

duff dessert. [SOUTH COAST AND SOUTHERN TABLELANDS]

dump waste depot/garbage tip. See also **depot** and **tip**[1].
[NEW ENGLAND DISTRICT, ADELAIDE REGION, BRISBANE REGION, PERTH REGION]

dunny budgie large blowfly. See also **bluebottle**, **butcher-shop canary** and **canary**[2]. [NORTHERN VICTORIA, WIMMERA AND MALLEE]

dusty feeling unwell. [SYDNEY REGION]

E

early minute a substitute for "early mark": allowed to go home from school early. In school it often rewarded good behaviour (or to let the teacher get away early). Some have carried the expression into the working world: "The boss's nicked off, so I'm giving myself an early mark/minute."
[TASMANIA, ADELAIDE REGION, NORTHERN SOUTH AUSTRALIA]

East 1. the eastern states of Australia. 2. pertaining to the eastern states. 3. along the coast running north-east from Broome. (Used in such combinations as "over East" or "up East".)
[NORTHERN WEST AUSTRALIA, CENTRAL WEST AUSTRALIA, PERTH REGION]

Eastern Islands, the New Zealand. [SYDNEY REGION]

eastern states 1. those states of Australia which are east of the Nullarbor Plain, especially South Australia, Victoria, New South Wales and (sometimes) Queensland. [PERTH REGION, NORTHERN WEST AUSTRALIA, CENTRAL WEST AUSTRALIA] 2. those states of Australia which are east of South Australia, including Victoria, New South Wales and Queensland. Usage varies, but most South Australians would not consider themselves part of "the eastern states" – and many West Australians would agree. Implied in the expression is often population and power – hence, it's Sydney, Melbourne and (perhaps) Brisbane that are often being pictured by the speaker.
[ADELAIDE REGION, EYRE AND YORKE PENINSULAS, NORTHERN SOUTH AUSTRALIA]

Eastern Suburbs Holden a Mercedes-Benz. A form of snobbery that sees "Mercs" (pronounced with a hard "K") as common family runabouts in Sydney's eastern suburbs. [SYDNEY REGION]

echo a small returnable beer bottle; a stubby.
[EYRE AND YORKE PENINSULAS, ADELAIDE REGION, NORTHERN SOUTH AUSTRALIA]

eh 1. an expression of inquiry or surprise. See also **bulltwang!**; **bunnies to that!**; **chowoon**; **gammon**; **hells, bells and bootlaces**; **Himmel** and **strike me roan!** 2. an expression that invites agreement. 3. a verbal tag with the meaning of "isn't that so?" (similar to the French *n'est-ce pas*). Often no question is implied and the expression is little more than a verbal tic or spoken punctuation mark. "So, you're a north Queenslander, eh? I was born up that way, meself, eh. But ya'd never know from the way I talk, eh?" Sometimes expanded into "waddayareckon, eh?" In some parts of Australia "but" is added to the end of utterances in the same role ("It's a hot day, but") and sometimes the two are combined. See also **eh, but!**

[CENTRAL WEST NSW, BRISBANE REGION, CENTRAL COAST QLD, NORTH COAST QLD, FAR NORTH QLD, WEST CENTRAL QLD, THE CENTRE]

eh, but! meaningless verbal tag, demonstrating how Australians have made Victor Borge's "phonetic punctuation" part of living speech. ("It's a clever thing to do, eh but!") See also **but** and **well.**

[NORTH COAST QLD]

Ekka 1. abbreviation for the Brisbane Exhibition Ground. 2. more commonly the Brisbane Royal Agricultural Show held at that ground. [BRISBANE REGION]

elbum Melbourne pronunciation of "album". One contributor suggests that this vowel turns up in some other words, and makes it impossible for Melbournians to distinguish between the names "Allan" and "Ellen". [MELBOURNE REGION]

elevener the mid-morning break in primary school (also known as **play lunch**, **little lunch** or "morning tea"). This seems to have had a distinct regional restriction as many contributors to the WordMap site insisted that they had never ("never, ever!") heard the word despite (collectively) several thousand years' teaching experience. See also **elevenses**, **levna**, **little lunch**, **little play**, **morning lunch**, **morning play**, **play lunch**, **playtime**, **recess** and **snack.** [WEST CENTRAL QLD]

elevenses 1. the mid-morning break in primary school (also known as **play lunch**, **little lunch** or "morning tea"). See also **elevener**, **levna**, **little lunch**, **little play**, **morning lunch**, **morning play**, **play lunch**, **playtime**, **recess** and **snack.** 2. the start of beer-drinking time. [BRISBANE REGION, WEST CENTRAL QLD]

Elizabethan a person who lives north of Adelaide in the area of Elizabeth. [ADELAIDE REGION]

emergency teacher a relief teacher. Used from the 1960s (and abbreviated to ETs). These staff were later re-named "casual relief teachers" (or **CRT**s). See also **supply teacher**.

[HUNTER VALLEY AND NORTH COAST, WIMMERA AND MALLEE, CENTRAL HIGHLANDS VICTORIA, WESTERN DISTRICT, NORTHERN VICTORIA, GIPPSLAND, MELBOURNE REGION]

Empire pressed meat sausage (served sliced) known by an astonishingly large number of names. According to one contributor, the original name had been **German sausage** (or else a German-sounding name such as **fritz** or **Strasburg**) and it was changed to the patriotic Empire sausage during the First World War. If this is true, it may also be the origin of **Windsor sausage**. See also **baron sausage**, **beef Belgium**, **Belgium sausage**, **bung fritz**, **Byron sausage**, devon, **fritz**, **German sausage**, **luncheon sausage**, **mystery meat**, **polony**, **pork German**, **Strasburg**, **wheel meat** and **Windsor sausage**. [HUNTER VALLEY AND NORTH COAST]

emu bob picking up of litter from an area, usually by an organised group of people, often as a school punishment. Also known as **emu parade**, **emu patrol**, **emu stalk**, **emu walk** and **scab duty**.

[THE RIVERINA, NSW SOUTH COAST AND SOUTHERN TABLELANDS, CENTRAL HIGHLANDS VICTORIA, NORTHERN VICTORIA, MELBOURNE REGION]

emu parade the picking up of litter from an area, usually by an organised group of people. In addition to regional variations, in the army emu parade and **emu patrol** appear to have been the more common expressions. Now sometimes organised by community groups as part of Clean Up Australia Day. See also **emu walk** and **scab duty**.

[SYDNEY REGION, NEW ENGLAND DISTRICT, BRISBANE REGION, NORTH COAST QLD, WESTERN DISTRICT, MELBOURNE REGION, EYRE AND YORKE PENINSULAS, ADELAIDE REGION, NORTHERN SOUTH AUSTRALIA]

emu patrol the picking up of litter from an area, usually by an organised group of people, often as a school punishment. See also **emu bob**, **emu parade**, **emu stalk**, **emu walk** and **scab duty**.

[NORTH COAST QLD, THE RIVERINA, SYDNEY REGION, CENTRAL WEST AUSTRALIA, EYRE AND YORKE PENINSULAS, ADELAIDE REGION, NORTHERN SOUTH AUSTRALIA]

emu stalk another variation on the above. See also **emu bob**, **emu parade**, **emu patrol**, **emu walk** and **scab duty**.

[CENTRAL WEST AUSTRALIA, PERTH REGION]

emu walk once more human behaviour when picking up litter is compared to the *Dromaius novaehollandiae*. See also **emu bob**, **emu parade**, **emu patrol**, **emu stalk** and **scab duty**. [BRISBANE REGION]

English fillet smoked cod. Also known as **South African fillet**. [ADELAIDE REGION, WIMMERA AND MALLEE, EYRE AND YORKE PENINSULAS, PERTH REGION]

Ermo the Sydney suburb of Ermington. [SYDNEY REGION]

escargot the scrolled flat pastries elsewhere known as "snails". (Not that they're being the least bit pretentious, you understand … to do so would be so *à la bourgeoise*.) [MELBOURNE REGION]

Esperance doctor yet another sea breeze with medical qualifications; a strong, cool, southerly wind which blows through Kalgoorlie late in the evening on hot summer nights. See also **Albany doctor**; **Canberra doctor**; **doctor, the** and **Fremantle doctor**. [CENTRAL WEST AUSTRALIA]

Espi the Esplanade Hotel. Contrasts with **'Nade**. [MELBOURNE REGION]

Espy another Esplanade Hotel, this one at St Kilda (once the target of a Save the Espy campaign). [MELBOURNE REGION]

eugarie a mollusc found on surf beaches along the Australian coast. From the Yagara (Brisbane region) Aboriginal language. Known elsewhere as **cockles**, **pipis** or **wongs**. [BRISBANE REGION]

evening the period of the day after midday. (This seems to appear only in parts of the regions listed below. It provoked furious correspondence from contributors, some of whom insisted they'd never encountered this use, while others protested that it was common at their end of town.) [BRISBANE REGION, CENTRAL COAST QLD, FAR NORTH QLD, NORTH COAST QLD, WEST CENTRAL QLD, FAR WEST NSW]

Exaggerator nickname for Launceston's daily newspaper *The Examiner*. [TASMANIA]

ex-govie 1. a house formerly owned by ACT Housing (a government department), but now privately owned. 2. of or relating to such a house. [SOUTH COAST AND SOUTHERN TABLELANDS]

F

face cloth small towelling or flannel cloth for washing with.
[TASMANIA, SOUTH COAST AND SOUTHERN TABLELANDS]. Also "face flannel"
[ADELAIDE REGION, TASMANIA, NORTH COAST QLD, MELBOURNE REGION] or
"facewasher" [BRISBANE REGION, CENTRAL HIGHLANDS VICTORIA, TASMANIA,
ADELAIDE REGION, MELBOURNE REGION, SYDNEY REGION, PERTH REGION, THE
RIVERINA, HUNTER VALLEY AND NORTH COAST] See also **flannel**.

fage a group or cluster of native Australian gum trees.
[CENTRAL WEST AUSTRALIA, NORTHERN WEST AUSTRALIA, PERTH REGION]

fair cop of the saveloy a plaintive cry of protest; a request to be
given a fair go. See also **fair suck of the sav**. [SYDNEY REGION]

fairest and best performance award made to a footballer. See also
best and fairest.
[NORTHERN WEST AUSTRALIA, CENTRAL WEST AUSTRALIA, PERTH REGION]

fair suck of the sav a plaintive cry of protest; a request to be given a
fair go. Now a largely self-conscious anachronism, used for comic
effect. Sometimes taking the form of "fair suck of the sauce
bottle". See also **fair cop of the saveloy**.
[BRISBANE REGION, MELBOURNE REGION, SYDNEY REGION, TASMANIA]

fairy the fluffy, airborne seeds of various plants. See also **Father
Christmas**, **robber**, **Santa Claus** and **wish**.
[CENTRAL HIGHLANDS VICTORIA, GIPPSLAND, MELBOURNE REGION, NORTHERN
VICTORIA, TASMANIA, WESTERN DISTRICT, WIMMERA AND MALLEE]

falcon a hit in the face with a football during a game. From Rugby
League player Mario Fenech who, being of Maltese extraction, was
known as "the Falcon".
[SYDNEY REGION, CENTRAL WEST NSW, NORTH COAST QLD, SOUTH COAST AND
SOUTHERN TABLELANDS, BRISBANE REGION]

fananny-whacking a foul in marbles (pushing the whole hand over
the firing line instead of simply flicking the marble with the
thumb). See also **crib**[1], **cribs**, **cribbing**, **duck-shove**, **fernannick**,
fudge and **phernudge**. [MELBOURNE REGION, CENTRAL HIGHLANDS VICTORIA]

fang 1. to ask for a handout or loan. [NORTH COAST QLD] 2. to drive
fast. See also **bag it**. [GIPPSLAND, SYDNEY REGION]

fanging hungry, *very* hungry! [BRISBANE REGION, NORTH COAST QLD]

farmer's arms (also "farmer's legs") tanned limbs that end in white flesh where sleeves or shorts begin. [TASMANIA]

farms contraction of "fat arms" or "flabby arms". [BRISBANE REGION]

Father Christmas the fluffy, airborne seeds of various plants. See also **fairy**, **robber**, **Santa Claus** and **wish**.

[ADELAIDE REGION, CENTRAL HIGHLANDS VICTORIA, EYRE AND YORKE PENINSULAS, GIPPSLAND, MELBOURNE REGION, NORTHERN VICTORIA, PERTH REGION, TASMANIA, WESTERN DISTRICT, WIMMERA AND MALLEE, BRISBANE REGION, CENTRAL COAST QLD, NORTH COAST QLD, FAR NORTH QLD, WEST CENTRAL QLD, SOUTH COAST AND SOUTHERN TABLELANDS, NORTHERN SOUTH AUSTRALIA]

fenackapants term of endearment (addressed to a child).

[SYDNEY REGION, MELBOURNE REGION]

fence jumper a person involved in an affair or illicit activity.

[TASMANIA]

fernannick to cheat at marbles. See also **crib**[1], **cribs**, **cribbing**, **duck-shove**, **fananny-whacking**, **fudge** and **phernudge**.

[SOUTH COAST AND SOUTHERN TABLELANDS]

ferrets smelly sandshoes or sneakers. [MELBOURNE REGION]

Fibs lycra underpants worn by schoolgirls while playing sport (from a brand name). [SYDNEY REGION, THE RIVERINA]

fiddy a fifty dollar note. See also **golden drinking voucher**, **olive leaf**, **peacemaker**, **pineapple**, **Uncle David** and **yellow belly**[3].

[MELBOURNE REGION]

fifty a glass of beer consisting of equal parts of Toohey's New and Toohey's Old. [SYDNEY REGION]

fighting irons cutlery. Also "eating irons". [NORTH COAST QLD]

fillum pronunciation of "film"; once the common usage of the uneducated, now more commonly employed deliberately for comic effect.

[CENTRAL WEST NSW, FAR WEST NSW, HUNTER VALLEY AND NORTH COAST, NEW ENGLAND DISTRICT, SOUTH COAST AND SOUTHERN TABLELANDS, SYDNEY REGION, THE RIVERINA, BRISBANE REGION, CENTRAL COAST QLD, NORTH COAST QLD, FAR NORTH QLD, WEST CENTRAL QLD, MELBOURNE REGION]

finany finabry, fin slips no second shots allowed (no excuses will be accepted for mistakes made in a game of marbles).
[SOUTH COAST AND SOUTHERN TABLELANDS]

fish frighteners see **Speedos**. See also **ballhuggers**, **boasters**, **budgie-huggers**, **budgie-smugglers**, **cluster busters**, **cockchokers**, **cock jocks**, **codjocks**, **dick bathers**, **dick-pointers**, **dick-pokers**, **dick stickers**, **dick togs**, **dikdaks**, **dipsticks**, **jammers**, **Jimmy clingers**, **knobbies**, **lolly-baggers**, **lolly bags**, **meat-hangers**, **nut huggers**, **nylon disgusters**, **racers**, **racing bathers**, **scungies**[2], **sluggers**, **sluggos**, **slug huggers**, **tights**, **toolies**, **trunks** and **wog togs**. [NEW ENGLAND DISTRICT]

fisho fish and chip shop. [WESTERN DISTRICT]

fish off the land corned beef (or other cold meat) cooked in batter.
[BRISBANE REGION]

fizzin' very happy; excited. [THE RIVERINA]

fizzog a fizzer, a failure, a disappointment. [PERTH REGION]

fizzy cordial soft drink. See also **cool drink**, **cordial**, **fizzy drink** and **lolly water**. [TASMANIA]

fizzy drink soft drink. See also **cool drink**, **cordial**, **fizzy cordial** and **lolly water**.
[SYDNEY REGION, HUNTER VALLEY AND NORTH COAST, NEW ENGLAND DISTRICT, THE RIVERINA, SOUTH COAST AND SOUTHERN TABLELANDS, CENTRAL WEST NSW, FAR WEST NSW, NORTHERN WEST AUSTRALIA, CENTRAL WEST AUSTRALIA, PERTH REGION, WIMMERA AND MALLEE, CENTRAL HIGHLANDS VICTORIA, WESTERN DISTRICT, NORTHERN VICTORIA, GIPPSLAND, MELBOURNE REGION, TASMANIA, ADELAIDE REGION]

flake the name under which shark steaks are sold in seafood shops.
[CENTRAL HIGHLANDS VICTORIA, GIPPSLAND, MELBOURNE REGION, NORTHERN VICTORIA, WESTERN DISTRICT, WIMMERA AND MALLEE, TASMANIA, PERTH REGION, CENTRAL WEST AUSTRALIA, ADELAIDE REGION]

flannel a small towelling or flannel cloth for washing with. See also **face cloth**.
[SYDNEY REGION, PERTH REGION, NORTHERN SOUTH AUSTRALIA, ADELAIDE REGION, EYRE AND YORKE PENINSULAS]

flannelette curtain the imaginary marker between the "right side" and the "wrong side" of the tracks. (From "Iron Curtain".)
[SYDNEY REGION]

flannie a flannelette checked shirt. Sometimes known as "flanno".
[BRISBANE REGION, SYDNEY REGION, SOUTH COAST AND SOUTHERN TABLELANDS,
HUNTER VALLEY AND NORTH COAST, TASMANIA]

flash for cash a police speed camera. [NORTH COAST QLD]

flat bickie as fast as you can; flat out. [GIPPSLAND]

flat dog crocodile. See also **gotcha lizard**, **long flat dog** and **mud
gecko**. [FAR NORTH QLD]

flog to win, to defeat another team or individual in a competitive
sport. [PERTH REGION]

flogged what happened to land that was overfarmed or overstocked.
[WEST CENTRAL QLD]

flogger a woollen jumper or sweater. [PERTH REGION]

flogging a reprimanding, especially by parents (may involve
a verbal reprimand, corporal punishment or both).
[PERTH REGION]

floury baker a type of cicada. See also **black prince**, **brown baker**,
brown bomber[2], **cherrynose**, **cicada**, **greengrocer**[2], **pisswhacker**,
tick tock and **yellow Monday**. [SYDNEY REGION]

fluorescent ducks an invitation to discover the local wildlife –
meaning a bit of smooching in the car by the lake. One
contributor wrote: "When I was younger (and living in
Ballarat) we'd go up to Lake Wendouree to 'see the
fluorescent ducks', or 'the luminous swans' or 'the submarine
races' if we wanted a bit of smooching in the car."
[CENTRAL HIGHLANDS VICTORIA]

fly cemetery a pastry properly called a fruit slice. See also **fly pie**.
[MELBOURNE REGION, BRISBANE REGION]

fly-in fly-out a form of employment: workers are flown in to
work in a mining or pastoral area for a few days or weeks, then
flown back to their city of origin. This enables mining
companies (for instance) to build barracks, rather that whole
towns, to house workers. The most common time now is

reported to be two weeks on and one week off with 12 hour
shifts. Abbreviated to FIFO (especially in job advertisements).
[NORTHERN WEST AUSTRALIA, CENTRAL WEST AUSTRALIA, PERTH REGION, BRISBANE
REGION, CENTRAL COAST QLD, NORTH COAST QLD, FAR NORTH QLD, WEST CENTRAL
QLD, NORTHERN SOUTH AUSTRALIA]

fly pie fruit slice. See also **fly cemetery**.
[PERTH REGION, BRISBANE REGION]

f 'n' v fruit and vegetables (as shopping or meal items).
[DARWIN AND NORTH COAST NT]

football in Queensland formerly Rugby League, but now
ambiguous: either League or AFL. See also **cross-country ballet**,
cross-country wrestling, **footy**, **hoofa** and **kick and giggle**.
[CENTRAL COAST QLD, NORTH COAST QLD]

foot falcon walking, instead of driving, is "taking the foot falcon".
[NORTH COAST QLD]

footpath a grassed strip of land between the front boundary of a
residential block and the edge of the road. Elsewhere (other than
the regions below) this word is restricted to the paved area. See
also **nature strip** and **verge**.
[ADELAIDE REGION, BRISBANE REGION, CENTRAL COAST QLD, CENTRAL WEST NSW,
EYRE AND YORKE PENINSULAS, NEW ENGLAND DISTRICT, NORTH COAST QLD,
WIMMERA AND MALLEE]

Footscray Florsheims ugg boots or slippers. [MELBOURNE REGION]

footy this appears to be a term on the cusp of change. At one time
"footy" always meant AFL, while **football** was used for all other
codes. This, however, appears to be changing, certainly among
some media commentators, with footy now being applied loosely
to all codes. See also **cross-country ballet**, **cross-country
wrestling**, **football**, **hoofa** and **kick and giggle**.
[MELBOURNE REGION, SYDNEY REGION]

footy nicks (or "footy niks") football shorts. [WIMMERA AND MALLEE]

formal blues shorts, blue singlet and thongs. [NEW ENGLAND DISTRICT]

foundation handwriting a style of handwriting taught in some
Australian primary schools in which a few simple movements are

combined and repeated to form letter shapes. See also **Victorian cursive**.

[SYDNEY REGION, HUNTER VALLEY AND NORTH COAST, NEW ENGLAND DISTRICT, THE RIVERINA, SOUTH COAST AND SOUTHERN TABLELANDS, CENTRAL WEST NSW, FAR WEST NSW]

fountain see **bubbler**, **bubble tap**, **drinking fountain**, **drinking tap**, **drink tap** and **water fountain**.

[BRISBANE REGION, CENTRAL COAST QLD, NORTH COAST QLD, FAR NORTH QLD, WEST CENTRAL QLD, WIMMERA AND MALLEE, CENTRAL HIGHLANDS VICTORIA, WESTERN DISTRICT, NORTHERN VICTORIA, GIPPSLAND, MELBOURNE REGION, TASMANIA, EYRE AND YORKE PENINSULAS, ADELAIDE REGION, PERTH REGION]

fourbi four-wheel-drive vehicle. Also spelled "fourby".

[TASMANIA, SYDNEY REGION, BRISBANE REGION]

four-pointer a sandwich consisting of two slices of bread cut diagonally. [TASMANIA]

four-square a schoolyard game; a form of handball in which four squares are chalked on the asphalt playing surface. See also **handball**, **king ping** and **two-square**. [PERTH REGION]

four-wheel drive a tortoise. [ADELAIDE REGION]

fowlhousing dithering, procrastinating. [NEW ENGLAND DISTRICT]

fowl snatchers any rubber-soled shoes.

[TASMANIA, BRISBANE REGION, PERTH REGION]

frang a sausage. [DARWIN AND NORTH COAST NT]

franger a condom.

[NORTHERN SOUTH AUSTRALIA, PERTH REGION, SYDNEY REGION]

free beach a nude beach. [DARWIN AND NORTH COAST NT]

free dress day a school day on which civvies (as opposed to uniforms) are permitted upon making a small payment to a charity collection. See also **casual day**, **mufti day** and **out of uniform day**.

[SYDNEY REGION, NORTH COAST QLD, PERTH REGION, BRISBANE REGION]

freeway, the nickname given (with just a hint of irony) to the dirt road on Cape York Peninsula after it was graded.

[NORTH COAST QLD, FAR NORTH QLD]

Fremantle doctor soothing meteorological medicine consisting of a cooling afternoon sea breeze. Also known as the "Freo Doctor". Now shares its medical qualifications with a number of coastal breezes. See also **Albany doctor**; **Canberra doctor**; **doctor, the** and **Esperance doctor**. [PERTH REGION]

Freo nickname of Fremantle, Western Australia (the use of this nickname in South Australia is associated with AFL).
[PERTH REGION, ADELAIDE REGION]

frilly lizard common water dragon or bearded dragon.
[BRISBANE REGION]

fritz a large, mild-flavoured, precooked sausage, usually sliced thinly and eaten cold. (However, any food which adopts so many aliases should be suspect.) See also **baron sausage**, **beef Belgium**, **Belgium sausage**, **bung fritz**, **Byron sausage**, **devon**, **Empire sausage**, **German sausage**, **luncheon sausage**, **mystery meat**, **polony**, **pork German**, **Strasburg**, **wheel meat** and **Windsor sausage**.
[ADELAIDE REGION, EYRE AND YORKE PENINSULAS, WIMMERA AND MALLEE, FAR WEST NSW]

frog cake a small cake shaped like a frog with an open mouth and covered in icing (usually green, although pink and chocolate are also available). Invented by Balfours bakery of Adelaide in 1922. The frog cake and the **pie floater** are among Adelaide's unique contributions to world gastronomy.
[ADELAIDE REGION, NORTHERN SOUTH AUSTRALIA]

frosty a cold beer. See also **frosty chop**. [WEST CENTRAL QLD]

frosty chop a cold beer. See also **frosty**. [TASMANIA]

frozen a pyramid-shaped flavoured ice block. See also **sonny boy**.
[MELBOURNE REGION]

frozen cup cordial, fruit juice or flavoured milk frozen in plastic cups and served at a party or a school **tuck shop**.
[NORTH COAST QLD]

fruit, the a person who is particularly gorgeous or desirable.
[HUNTER VALLEY AND NORTH COAST]

fruit block a small orchard or vineyard. One contributor says that a variation is a "fruit salad block" – a Riverland property growing a mixture of fruits and/or vines and/or vegetables.
[ADELAIDE REGION, EYRE AND YORKE PENINSULAS, WIMMERA AND MALLEE]

fruit box any juice drink packaged in a small cardboard carton. In some places these beverages are known only by brand names such as **Popper** or **Prima**. See also **Popper** and **Prima**.
[NORTHERN SOUTH AUSTRALIA, ADELAIDE REGION, EYRE AND YORKE PENINSULAS, WIMMERA AND MALLEE, TASMANIA, SOUTH COAST AND SOUTHERN TABLELANDS]

fruit bun a round, sticky glazed bun containing dried fruit. See also **yeast bun**. [BRISBANE REGION]

fruit cup a drink with three coloured layers (green, red and orange) based on lemonade and cordials. [ADELAIDE REGION]

fruiterer known elsewhere as a "greengrocer" or "fruit and veg".
[BRISBANE REGION, MELBOURNE REGION]

fruit fly a female bar patron who accompanies or attaches herself to a gay guy. [BRISBANE REGION]

fruity a fit, hysterics. (Note: "fruities", like wobblies and hissy fits, are normally "chucked".) [NORTHERN SOUTH AUSTRALIA]

fudge to overstep the mark when shooting at a children's game of marbles; to creep up over the agreed mark when playing a shot. See also **cribbing**, **cribs**, **duck-shove** and **phernudge**.
[SYDNEY REGION]

FURTB having partaken of an elegant sufficiency of food (literally: Full Up Ready To Burst). [SYDNEY REGION]

G

Gabba Brisbane Cricket Ground, in the suburb of Woolloongabba. (This is now used nationally, but it is a regionalism in that it was born in Brisbane.) [BRISBANE REGION]

gammon 1. deceitful nonsense; misleading or nonsensical talk; humbug. [CENTRAL WEST AUSTRALIA, DARWIN AND NORTH COAST NT, NORTH COAST QLD] 2. to pretend; to lie jokingly; to kid. [NORTH COAST QLD, DARWIN AND NORTH COAST NT, WEST CENTRAL QLD] 3. false; fake; pretend. [DARWIN AND NORTH COAST NT, NORTHERN VICTORIA, WEST CENTRAL QLD] 4. inadequate, disappointing, lame. [PERTH REGION, THE CENTRE] 5. an exclamation of disbelief, equivalent to "You're joking!" or "As if!" See also **bulltwang!**; **bunnies to that!**; **chowoon**; **eh**; **hells, bells and bootlaces**; **Himmel** and **strike me roan!** [FAR NORTH QLD, DARWIN AND NORTH COAST NT, THE CENTRE] 6. gammon around, to fool around. [DARWIN AND NORTH COAST NT] Sometimes spelled "gammin". Note: contributors say this word group should be pronounced "GAIR-mun".

gang to steal, especially to keep for yourself. See also **tax** and **thump**. [PERTH REGION]

garbage bin a container for household rubbish. See also **dirt bin** and **rubbish bin**.
[SYDNEY REGION, HUNTER VALLEY AND NORTH COAST, NEW ENGLAND DISTRICT, THE RIVERINA, SOUTH COAST AND SOUTHERN TABLELANDS, CENTRAL WEST NSW, FAR WEST NSW, WIMMERA AND MALLEE, CENTRAL HIGHLANDS VICTORIA, WESTERN DISTRICT, NORTHERN VICTORIA, GIPPSLAND, MELBOURNE REGION, TASMANIA, ADELAIDE REGION, EYRE AND YORKE PENINSULAS]

garbo see **bin man** and **rubbish collector**.
[NORTHERN VICTORIA, SYDNEY REGION, PERTH REGION, GIPPSLAND, MELBOURNE REGION, BRISBANE REGION, ADELAIDE REGION]

garry a dag, a socially inadequate male. See also **bennie**, **bethan**, **bog**[2], **bogan**, **booner**, **boonie**, **chigger chookie**, **cogger**[1], **feral**, **mocca**, **scozzer** and **westie**. [MELBOURNE REGION]

gather to muster (sheep, cattle, etc.) [TASMANIA]

gauze flyscreen door; insect screening on windows or verandas.
[FAR WEST NSW]

geebin a nincompoop, an incompetent individual (sometimes the incompetence is in a particular area, such as a "computer geebin"). Pronunciation note: contributors say the "G" is hard.
[BRISBANE REGION]

GEHA acronym for Government Education Housing Authority: accommodation provided for teachers, police officers and other state government employees and their families. (Always used in combination "GEHA house/flat" etc.)
[NORTHERN WEST AUSTRALIA, CENTRAL WEST AUSTRALIA, PERTH REGION]

gent a maggot used as fishing bait.
[EYRE AND YORKE PENINSULAS, ADELAIDE REGION, NORTHERN SOUTH AUSTRALIA]

gentle Annie gently sloping hill. [HUNTER VALLEY AND NORTH COAST]

geo geologist. See also **rock doctor.** [PERTH REGION]

German cake a yeast cake with a crumble topping, sometimes with fruit (apple or apricot) under the crumble. [ADELAIDE REGION]

German sausage a large, mild-flavoured, precooked sausage, usually sliced thinly and eaten cold; a common sandwich filling. See also **beef Belgium**, **Belgium sausage**, **bung fritz**, **Byron sausage**, **devon**, **Empire sausage**, **fritz**, **luncheon sausage**, **mystery meat**, **polony**, **pork German**, **Strasburg**, **wheel meat** and **Windsor sausage.**
[WIMMERA AND MALLEE, CENTRAL HIGHLANDS VICTORIA, WESTERN DISTRICT, NORTHERN VICTORIA, GIPPSLAND, MELBOURNE REGION, TASMANIA]

Gestapo ticket inspector. See also **Met cop**, **Metcard Mafia**, **train dog**, **train fascist**, **train Nazi** and **tram fascist.**
[MELBOURNE REGION]

get off at Redfern coitus interruptus. (On the Sydney rail network Redfern is a station one stop before Central.) See also **go to Melbourne.** [SYDNEY REGION]

get rinsed to have a few alcoholic beverages (sometimes "to get drunk"). Also as "to get on the rinse". [ADELAIDE REGION]

getters informal footwear (thongs, scuffs, plastic shoes etc.) Sometimes known as "getties". See also **Chinese safety boots**, clackers, go-backs, jandals, **Japanese flying boots**, **Japanese riding boots**, **Japanese safety boots**, **Jesus boots**, **NT work boots** and **pluggers**. [DARWIN AND NORTH COAST NT, THE CENTRE]

get your flaps off me! exclamation of complaint, meaning "Leave me alone!" [NORTH COAST QLD]

ghosty children's game in which a bike is pushed along the street or footpath without a rider, and then released to coast by itself. The object of the game is to make the bike go as far as possible before it falls over. [MELBOURNE REGION]

gi- prefix attached to words as an emphasiser, so that "gibig" means "really big" and so on. (From the first part of the word "giant" – as in "ginormous".) [PERTH REGION]

Giant Twin brand of dairy products, available only in country areas north of Adelaide. (The ice-cream, in particular, is commonly asked for by the brand name.) [NORTHERN SOUTH AUSTRALIA]

gibber a stone or pebble. (From Dharruk, the Sydney region Aboriginal language, *giba* meaning "stone".) In some arid areas gibbers dominate the landscape: Sturt's Stony Desert, in the north of South Australia, is a typical gibber desert. The community newspaper at Woomera is called *The Gibber Gabber*. See also **boondie²**, **brinnie**, **connie²**, **gonnie**, **goolie**, **ronnie** and **yonnie**.

[BRISBANE REGION, CENTRAL COAST QLD, CENTRAL WEST AUSTRALIA, CENTRAL WEST NSW, FAR WEST NSW, GIPPSLAND, HUNTER VALLEY AND NORTH COAST, MELBOURNE REGION, NEW ENGLAND DISTRICT, NORTH COAST QLD, NORTHERN SOUTH AUSTRALIA, NORTHERN VICTORIA, SOUTH COAST AND SOUTHERN TABLELANDS, SYDNEY REGION, THE RIVERINA]

gidgie spear-like weapon for catching octopus. (From Nyungar, the south-western WA Aboriginal language.) One contributor writes: "A gidgie was a short spear attached to a rubber loop. You held the end of the loop, pulled the spear back and gripped it (all with one hand) so that you had tension, then released your grip to fire the gidgie."

[CENTRAL WEST AUSTRALIA, NORTHERN WEST AUSTRALIA, PERTH REGION]

gilgai small, often isolated, waterhole.

[NORTH COAST QLD, CENTRAL WEST NSW, NORTHERN SOUTH AUSTRALIA]

gilgie a freshwater crayfish of the genus *Cherax*. They can commonly be found in most streams, rivers and irrigation dams in the south-west of Western Australia. Gilgies can burrow to escape droughts and have a wider distribution than **marron**. See also **clawchie**, **crawchie**, **craydab**, **crayfish**, **lobby**, **lobster**, **marron** and **yabby**. [PERTH REGION]

gilgie's piss low alcohol beer. See also **super** and **unleaded**. [PERTH REGION]

gimp a highly uncoordinated or conspicuously stupid person (derogatory). See also **couple of lamingtons short of a CWA meeting, a**; **dipsticks**; **doughy**; **dubbo**; **Milo**; **moonya**; **munted**; **nuffest** and **veggie**[1]. [BRISBANE REGION, SYDNEY REGION]

ginder haircut (especially a close-cropped haircut). Also as "ginda". According to contributors, in Bunbury in the 1960s a resident of the town named Alf (or possibly Arthur) Ginder lost his hair (possibly from a medical condition) thus giving rise to this expression (or, possibly, just to this myth about the origin of this expression). [PERTH REGION]

ging a shanghai, slingshot or catapult for projecting small stones at great speed; usually a forked stick with a rubber band attached to each fork and a leather pouch joining the rubber bands. (According to some contributors a ging was a rubber band fired from the hand without the aid of a forked stick.) See also **dong-eye**, **gonk**, **shanghai** and **slingshot**.
[GIPPSLAND, CENTRAL WEST AUSTRALIA, BRISBANE REGION, CENTRAL COAST QLD, NORTH COAST QLD, PERTH REGION, ADELAIDE REGION, MELBOURNE REGION]

gingham umbrella. [HUNTER VALLEY AND NORTH COAST]

gin's handbag (racist and derogatory) wine cask. See also **bag of death**, **Balga handbag**, **Bellambi handbag**, **boxie**, **box monster**, **Broadmeadows briefcase**, **cardboard handbag**, **Coraki handbag**, **Dapto briefcase**, **death bag**, **Dubbo handbag**, **goon**, **goonbag**, **goonbox**, **goonie**, **goonsack**, **lady in the boat**, **red handbag**, **sack** and **vino collapso**.
[BRISBANE REGION, WEST CENTRAL QLD, SOUTH COAST AND SOUTHERN TABLELANDS]

Gippi nickname for Gippsland (Victoria). [GIPPSLAND]

girl of ... a female having the name of ... See also **bloke of** ... (As in "That bloke of Evans married the girl of Jones, who lived next-door to the butcher's.")

[HUNTER VALLEY AND NORTH COAST, CENTRAL WEST NSW, FAR WEST NSW]

glass a seven fluid ounce glass of beer (served in a Western Australian or Victorian hotel). See also **butcher**, **handle**, **middy**, **pony**, **pot**, **schooner**[1], **schooner**[2] and **seven**.

[PERTH REGION, MELBOURNE REGION]

globe light globe. See also **bulb**. (Many contributors reported using **bulb** and globe interchangeably, while others reported one predominating over the other.)

[CENTRAL WEST AUSTRALIA, NORTHERN WEST AUSTRALIA, PERTH REGION, SYDNEY REGION]

glom to borrow something and fail to return it, but without the intention of stealing it. [CENTRAL HIGHLANDS VICTORIA, ADELAIDE REGION]

glory vine an ornamental grapevine grown mainly for its vivid red colouring in autumn. See also **ornamental grapevine**.

[WIMMERA AND MALLEE, CENTRAL HIGHLANDS VICTORIA, WESTERN DISTRICT, NORTHERN VICTORIA, GIPPSLAND, MELBOURNE REGION, TASMANIA, EYRE AND YORKE PENINSULAS, ADELAIDE REGION, PERTH REGION]

goat's head burrs; small, sharp seeds. See also **bindi-eye**, **double-gee**, **California puncture weed**, **cat's eye**[1] and **three-corner jack**.

[WEST CENTRAL QLD, NORTH COAST QLD]

gob[1] collective noun for a bunch of worms (especially worms used as bait). [HUNTER VALLEY AND NORTH COAST]

gob[2] to spit. [MELBOURNE REGION, SYDNEY REGION]

go-backs thongs (especially loose or floppy thongs that keep falling off so that you have to "go-back" for them). See also **Chinese safety boots**, **clackers**, **getters**, **jandals**, **Japanese flying boots**, **Japanese riding boots**, **Japanese safety boots**, **Jesus boots**, **NT work boots** and **pluggers**. [CENTRAL HIGHLANDS VICTORIA]

go-cart a small, home-made cart used by children as a downhill racer (propelled by gravity, and stopped, as a rule, by the nearest large object). Elsewhere known as a **billy cart**, **hill trolley**, or

soapbox. Note: the American motorised miniature racing vehicle is spelled differently: Go-Kart. See also **billy cart** and **hill trolley**.
[BRISBANE REGION, ADELAIDE REGION]

goffer can of soft drink (military slang). Royal Navy slang dating back to at least the 1920s (perhaps originally from a soft drink brand name). It now appears to have settled in some Australian regions.
[SOUTH COAST AND SOUTHERN TABLELANDS, BRISBANE REGION, THE RIVERINA]

gogs lollies, sweets. See also **lackers** and **mogs**.
[CENTRAL HIGHLANDS VICTORIA, MELBOURNE REGION]

going the hack displaying hysterical anger. [MELBOURNE REGION]

golden drinking voucher a fifty-dollar note. See also **fiddy**, **olive leaf**, **peacemaker**, **pineapple**, **Uncle David**, **voucher** and **yellow belly**[3]. [SOUTH COAST AND SOUTHERN TABLELANDS]

Goldie the Gold Coast. [BRISBANE REGION]

gold licence a driver's licence for which one becomes eligible after having held a silver licence for five years.
[CENTRAL WEST NSW, FAR WEST NSW, HUNTER VALLEY AND NORTH COAST, NEW ENGLAND DISTRICT, SOUTH COAST AND SOUTHERN TABLELANDS, SYDNEY REGION, THE RIVERINA]

goldsborough morts rhyming slang: shorts (from the famous wool brokerage firm). As with all rhyming slang, often only the first half of the expression was used: "the goldsboroughs", meaning "the shorts". [PERTH REGION]

gone to Gowings formerly an advertising slogan used by Gowing Brothers department store, now employed with a variety of meanings: 1. deteriorating financially. 2. ill, especially with a hangover. 3. failing dismally, as of a racehorse, a football team, etc. 4. having left; departed hastily without a specific destination in mind (or without leaving a forwarding address). 5. drunk. (See also **chopped**, **maggered**, **maggo**, **maggoted**, **off chops** and **off your unit**.) 6. gone nuts, cuckoo, insane. [SYDNEY REGION]

gone to work at Woolies or **Coles** code phrase meaning an unmarried girl who was pregnant has gone to Melbourne to give birth (and possibly have the baby adopted). [THE RIVERINA]

gonk a shanghai, slingshot or catapult. See also **dong-eye**, **ging**, **shanghai** and **slingshot**.

[HUNTER VALLEY AND NORTH COAST, SYDNEY REGION]

gonnie a stone or pebble. See also **boondie**[2], **brinnie**, **connie**[2], **gibber**, **goolie**, **ronnie** and **yonnie**.

[BRISBANE REGION, CENTRAL COAST QLD, NORTH COAST QLD, FAR NORTH QLD, WEST CENTRAL QLD]

good-bye muscle the flabby triceps (upper arms) of an overweight woman (sometimes known as "bye nows"): the under arm skin wobbles as the owner of the arm waves goodbye. See also **aunty arms**, **bingo wings**, **bye nows**, **nannas**, **piano arm**, **reverse biceps**, **ta-ta flaps**, **tuckshop arm** and **widow's curtain**. [SYDNEY REGION]

good, eh! couldn't possibly be better. [TASMANIA]

good night regionally distinctive only when used as an evening greeting rather than as a form of farewell. [BRISBANE REGION]

googery small shelter shed on a farm. [HUNTER VALLEY AND NORTH COAST]

gook the target or hole you aim for in a game of marbles.

[MELBOURNE REGION]

goolie 1. a stone or pebble. See also **boondie**[2], **brinnie**, **connie**[2], **gibber**, **gonnie**, **ronnie** and **yonnie**. 2. an oversized marble.

[SYDNEY REGION, HUNTER VALLEY AND NORTH COAST, NEW ENGLAND DISTRICT, THE RIVERINA, SOUTH COAST AND SOUTHERN TABLELANDS, CENTRAL WEST NSW, BRISBANE REGION, CENTRAL COAST QLD, NORTH COAST QLD]

goolies testicles. See also **ackers**, **coods**, **nuggets** and **nurries**.

[SYDNEY REGION, HUNTER VALLEY AND NORTH COAST, NEW ENGLAND DISTRICT, THE RIVERINA, SOUTH COAST AND SOUTHERN TABLELANDS, CENTRAL WEST NSW, BRISBANE REGION, CENTRAL COAST QLD, NORTH COAST QLD]

goon cheap wine in either cask or flagon. Sometimes known as "gooner" (or **goonbag** for the silver bag containing the wine). See also **bag of death**, **Balga handbag**, **Bellambi handbag**, **boxie**, **box monster**, **Broadmeadows briefcase**, **cardboard handbag**, **Coraki handbag**, **death bag**, **Dubbo handbag**, **gin's handbag**, **goonie**, **goonsack**, **lady in the boat**, **red handbag**, **sack** and **vino collapso**.

[MELBOURNE REGION, PERTH REGION, CENTRAL WEST AUSTRALIA, CENTRAL COAST QLD, ADELAIDE REGION, TASMANIA, HUNTER VALLEY AND NORTH COAST, BRISBANE REGION, THE RIVERINA, DARWIN AND NORTH COAST NT, SOUTH COAST AND SOUTHERN TABLELANDS]

goona manure.

[NORTHERN SOUTH AUSTRALIA, CENTRAL WEST AUSTRALIA, PERTH REGION]

goona to evacuate the bowls. Also spelled "gunna" and "gunnah".

[FAR NORTH QLD]

goonbag cask wine. See also **bag of death**, **Balga handbag**, **Bellambi handbag**, **boxie**, **box monster**, **Broadmeadows briefcase**, **cardboard handbag**, **Coraki handbag**, **death bag**, **Dubbo handbag**, **gin's handbag**, **goon**, **goonie**, **goonsack**, **lady in the boat**, **red handbag**, **sack** and **vino collapso**.

[CENTRAL WEST AUSTRALIA, PERTH REGION, THE RIVERINA, BRISBANE REGION, NORTH COAST QLD, SOUTH COAST AND SOUTHERN TABLELANDS]

goonbox cask wine. See also **bag of death**, **Balga handbag**, **Bellambi handbag**, **boxie**, **box monster**, **Broadmeadows briefcase**, **cardboard handbag**, **Coraki handbag**, **death bag**, **Dubbo handbag**, **gin's handbag**, **goon**, **goonbag**, **goonie**, **goonsack**, **lady in the boat**, **red handbag**, **sack** and **vino collapso**.

[TASMANIA]

goonie cask wine. See also **bag of death**, **Balga handbag**, **Bellambi handbag**, **boxie**, **box monster**, **Broadmeadows briefcase**, **cardboard handbag**, **Coraki handbag**, **death bag**, **Dubbo handbag**, **gin's handbag**, **goon**, **goonbag**, **goonbox**, **goonsack**, **lady in the boat**, **red handbag**, **sack** and **vino collapse**.

[DARWIN AND NORTH COAST NT]

goonie party multiple **goonbags** hung on the Hills hoist, which is spun to pick the next drink at random.

[BRISBANE REGION, CENTRAL WEST NSW]

goon juice a mixture of cask wine and soft drink (supposedly favoured by university students). Also known as "goonie juice".

[CENTRAL HIGHLANDS VICTORIA]

goon monkey habitual drinker of cheap cask wine.

[SOUTH COAST AND SOUTHERN TABLELANDS]

goonsack bladder from a wine cask.. See also **bag of death**, **Balga handbag**, **Bellambi handbag**, **boxie**, **box monster**, **Broadmeadows briefcase**, **cardboard handbag**, **Coraki handbag**,

death bag, **Dubbo handbag**, **gin's handbag**, **goon**, **goonbag**, **goonbox**, **goonie**, **lady in the boat**, **red handbag**, **sack** and **vino collapso**.

[SOUTH COAST AND SOUTHERN TABLELANDS]

goonya Aboriginal word for a white person. See also **wadjella**.

[ADELAIDE REGION, EYRE AND YORKE PENINSULAS, NORTHERN SOUTH AUSTRALIA]

goose club a fundraising raffle for modest, donated prizes. (Elsewhere often known as a "chook raffle".)

[PERTH REGION, NORTH COAST QLD, BRISBANE REGION]

goose juice alcohol. [MELBOURNE REGION]

goozy spit. See also **grot**.

[EYRE AND YORKE PENINSULAS, NORTHERN SOUTH AUSTRALIA, ADELAIDE REGION, PERTH REGION, CENTRAL WEST AUSTRALIA]

Gosford dog[1] toilet, rhyming slang for "bog". See also **choc**, **Dapto dog**, **dubs** and **long drop**. [SYDNEY REGION]

Gosford dog[2] derogatory rhyming slang for "wog". [SYDNEY REGION]

gotcha lizard crocodile. See also **flat dog**, **long flat dog** and **mud gecko**. [FAR NORTH QLD]

gotchas barbecue tongs. See also **nickernackers** and **snicker-snacks**.

[PERTH REGION]

go to Melbourne adolescent term for having sex and "going all the way". Contrast with **get off at Redfern**. [SYDNEY REGION]

got their licence off the Weeties packet expression of complaint about a bad driver. [MELBOURNE REGION]

government house a house owned by ACT Housing, a government department. Often shortened to "govie". See also **guvvie**.

[SOUTH COAST AND SOUTHERN TABLELANDS]

government school state school.

[SOUTH COAST AND SOUTHERN TABLELANDS, DARWIN AND NORTH COAST NT, THE CENTRE, NORTHERN WEST AUSTRALIA, CENTRAL WEST AUSTRALIA, PERTH REGION]

govvie wagon any government vehicle. [CENTRAL WEST AUSTRALIA]

Goyder's line line of demarcation between the drier north of
South Australia and the south. Drawn in 1865 by G. W. Goyder
(1826–98), surveyor-general of South Australia marking the
northern limit for safe agricultural development. Also known as
"Goyder's line of rainfall" or simply, "the Goyder line".
[EYRE AND YORKE PENINSULAS, ADELAIDE REGION, NORTHERN SOUTH AUSTRALIA]

grade prefix before school year. Elsewhere "form", "class" or "year".
[BRISBANE REGION, CENTRAL COAST QLD, FAR NORTH QLD, NORTH COAST QLD, WEST
CENTRAL QLD]

gramma a type of pumpkin (*Cucurbita moschate*) with an
elongated shape and orange flesh and skin. (Some contributors
report spelling this vegetable "grammer", while others report
making exceptionally fine pies out of it!)
[SYDNEY REGION, HUNTER VALLEY AND NORTH COAST, NEW ENGLAND DISTRICT, THE
RIVERINA, SOUTH COAST AND SOUTHERN TABLELANDS, CENTRAL WEST NSW, FAR
WEST NSW]

granny flat a partially or fully self-contained dwelling at the rear of
a house. See also **bungalow**[1] and **chalet**.
[SYDNEY REGION, NORTHERN SOUTH AUSTRALIA, TASMANIA, MELBOURNE REGION]

grass castle a large, ostentatiously lavish house (assumed to be
built by profits from drug dealing).
[SOUTH COAST AND SOUTHERN TABLELANDS, NORTHERN VICTORIA]

grasshopper kangaroo or wallaby. [CENTRAL COAST QLD]

greaser a menacing or "dirty" look. [BRISBANE REGION, SYDNEY REGION]

green can a can of beer: specifically Victoria Bitter ("VB" for short).
See also **blue can**, **red can**, **white can** and **yellow can**.
[THE CENTRE, DARWIN AND NORTH COAST NT, MELBOURNE REGION, FAR NORTH
QLD, WESTERN DISTRICT, SYDNEY REGION, NORTHERN WEST AUSTRALIA]

greengrocer[1] a retailer of fruit and vegetables. Elsewhere a **fruiterer**.
[ADELAIDE REGION, TASMANIA, PERTH REGION, SYDNEY REGION]

greengrocer[2] a type of cicada. See also **black prince**, **brown baker**,
brown bomber[2], **cherry nose**, **cicada**, **floury baker**, **pisswhacker**,
tick tock and **yellow Monday**. [SYDNEY REGION]

green slip certificate of compulsory third party car insurance.
[CENTRAL WEST NSW, FAR WEST NSW, HUNTER VALLEY AND NORTH COAST, NEW ENGLAND DISTRICT, SOUTH COAST AND SOUTHERN TABLELANDS, SYDNEY REGION, THE RIVERINA]

green title freehold title to land as distinct from strata (or purple) title. From the colour of the shading used to denote freehold title by the Titles Office of Western Australia. [PERTH REGION]

Gregory's familiar street directory and road atlas. See also **Melways** and **Referdex**. [SYDNEY REGION]

grenade a small-sized stubby of beer. Also known as "hand grenade". [BRISBANE REGION, SYDNEY REGION]

grey ghost[1] a parking inspector (from the colour of their uniform). See also **blue bomber**, **brown bomber**, **grey meanie** and **sticker licker**.
[WIMMERA AND MALLEE, CENTRAL HIGHLANDS VICTORIA, WESTERN DISTRICT, NORTHERN VICTORIA, GIPPSLAND, MELBOURNE REGION, PERTH REGION]

grey ghost[2] a one hundred dollar note. See also **grey nurse**.
[SYDNEY REGION]

greylead lead pencil.
[CENTRAL HIGHLANDS VICTORIA, GIPPSLAND, MELBOURNE REGION, NORTHERN VICTORIA, WESTERN DISTRICT, WIMMERA AND MALLEE, THE RIVERINA]

grey meanie a parking officer. See also **blue bomber**, **brown bomber**, **grey ghost** and **sticker licker**. [MELBOURNE REGION]

grey nomads retirees who holiday in the northern regions of Australia during the winter. [NORTH COAST QLD, MELBOURNE REGION]

grey nurse a one hundred dollar note. See also **grey ghost**[2].
[SYDNEY REGION]

grid[1] bicycle. (According to one contributor this was occasionally expanded to "grid iron".) See also **deadly treadly**, **grunter**, **scrap** and **treadly**.
[EYRE AND YORKE PENINSULAS, BRISBANE REGION, HUNTER VALLEY AND NORTH COAST, SYDNEY REGION, MELBOURNE REGION, CENTRAL WEST AUSTRALIA, WIMMERA AND MALLEE, DARWIN AND NORTH COAST NT, PERTH REGION, THE RIVERINA]

grid[2] a set of parallel steel bars set in the road (over a shallow pit) where it passes through a fence – cattle will not walk over the steel bars making a gate unnecessary. See also **cattle grate**, **cattle grid**, **cattle ramp** and **ramp**. [WEST CENTRAL QLD]

grill[1] barbecue. See also **chop picnic**. [PERTH REGION]

grill[2] a person of southern European ancestry. Possibly originally a play on the word "Greek". [FAR WEST NSW]

grinder an individual of doubtful integrity or trustworthiness. [FAR WEST NSW]

gromnick means "results of extensive IQ testing have shown this person to be a dill". See also **gronk**. [TASMANIA]

gronk see **gromnick**. [SYDNEY REGION]

grot spit. See also **goozy**. [WESTERN DISTRICT]

ground lice sheep. See also **land lice**, **maggot-taxi** and **mountain maggots**. [GIPPSLAND]

grouper member of a **group settlement**. [NORTHERN WEST AUSTRALIA, CENTRAL WEST AUSTRALIA, PERTH REGION]

group settlement a 1920s settlement scheme whereby the underdeveloped south-west of Western Australia was to be settled by British immigrants, many of them ex-soldiers. The scheme was run in cooperation with the British and Australian national governments. However, the properties were small and the infrastructure primitive, limiting the success of the scheme. [NORTHERN WEST AUSTRALIA, CENTRAL WEST AUSTRALIA, PERTH REGION]

group settler member of a **group settlement**. [NORTHERN WEST AUSTRALIA, CENTRAL WEST AUSTRALIA, PERTH REGION]

grub a non-union member who benefits from pay and conditions negotiated by the union (and paid for by their workmates' union fees). [MELBOURNE REGION]

grunter pushbike. See also **deadly treadly**, **grid**[1], **scrap** and **treadly**. [CENTRAL HIGHLANDS VICTORIA]

gubba Aboriginal name for a white person. See also **goonya**, **guddiyah** and **wadjella**. [HUNTER VALLEY AND NORTH COAST]

guddiyah Aboriginal name for a white person. See also **gubba**, **goonya** and **wadjella**. [NORTHERN WEST AUSTRALIA]

gudgeon a person with the air of the unwashed about them. [MELBOURNE REGION]

guernsey 1. the top part of a footy player's uniform. (Contributors suggest that Australian Rules football players wear guernseys, while Rugby and soccer players wear **jerseys**.) See also **jersey** and **jumper**. 2. **get a guernsey** to be selected to play in a team. [FAR WEST NSW, BRISBANE REGION, NEW ENGLAND DISTRICT, DARWIN AND NORTH COAST NT, MELBOURNE REGION]

gullie a person who is unsophisticated, unemployed and uninspiring. [THE RIVERINA]

Gullie, **The** the village of Collingullie, 20 km west of Wagga Wagga. [THE RIVERINA]

gully raker a thunderstorm that brings heavy rain. [NEW ENGLAND DISTRICT]

gully wind evening wind, often strong, that blows off the Mt Lofty Ranges over Adelaide in summer when the wind turns south-easterly. [ADELAIDE REGION]

gumby[1] a pimple. See also **acker** and **zots**. [HUNTER VALLEY AND NORTH COAST]

gumby[2] a tram conductor (or any public transport employee). From their green uniforms (and the green cartoon character of this name). [MELBOURNE REGION]

gumi a raft made predominantly of inner tubes from cars or trucks. "If you're lucky," writes one contributor, "you can get hold of large tractor tyres for a super gumi." The same contributor reports informal gumi races on the Murrumbidgee. [THE RIVERINA]

gum suckers Victorians. (The term dates back to the early 19th century when it was common for people to chew on balls of gum

taken from acacia trees. Somehow the label stuck to the colony of Victoria more than any other.)
[CENTRAL WEST AUSTRALIA, NORTHERN WEST AUSTRALIA, PERTH REGION]

guncher heavy gust of wind (a sailing term). [TASMANIA]

Gundy the town Goondiwindi (which is correctly pronounced GUNDA-windi). [BRISBANE REGION]

gunna a procrastinator; a person who promises but fails to deliver (they're always "gunna" do this and "gunna" do that – but, somehow, it never happens). [SYDNEY REGION, MELBOURNE REGION]

guvvie a government-funded residence, usually offering low-cost accommodation.
[SOUTH COAST AND SOUTHERN TABLELANDS, WEST CENTRAL QLD]

gympie hammer a heavy hammer, square in section but with a very short handle about 20 cm in length. Sometimes abbreviated to "gympie". [PERTH REGION, ADELAIDE REGION]

H

had the bean broken, faulty, defective. See also **had the chad**.

[SYDNEY REGION]

had the chad broken, faulty, defective. See also **had the bean**.

[ADELAIDE REGION]

hair clip two slender prongs, made from sprung metal, to hold hair in place. Also known as "hairpin". More widely known as a "bobby pin". See also **hair slide**.

[ADELAIDE REGION, CENTRAL HIGHLANDS VICTORIA, EYRE AND YORKE PENINSULAS, GIPPSLAND, MELBOURNE REGION, NORTHERN VICTORIA, PERTH REGION, TASMANIA, WESTERN DISTRICT, WIMMERA AND MALLEE]

hairdryer hand-held police radar gun. See also **death ray**.

[BRISBANE REGION]

hair slide two slender prongs, made from sprung metal, to hold hair in place. See also **hair clip**.

[CENTRAL HIGHLANDS VICTORIA, GIPPSLAND, MELBOURNE REGION, NORTHERN VICTORIA, TASMANIA, WESTERN DISTRICT, WIMMERA AND MALLEE]

hairy mary kiwi fruit. [SYDNEY REGION]

half-job a person who has an easy job (such as a stop-go man at a school street crossing or with a road gang).

[SOUTH COAST AND SOUTHERN TABLELANDS, NEW ENGLAND DISTRICT]

half up, **half down** a girl's hairstyle (the front half of the hair tied up in a hair band, and the back loose). See also **Pollyanna** and **waterfall**. [ADELAIDE REGION]

ham and beef shop a delicatessen. (Now largely obsolete.)

[MELBOURNE REGION, TASMANIA, SYDNEY REGION]

handball a schoolyard game played with a tennis ball on a court drawn in chalk on the asphalt. Also known as "two-square". See also **four-square** and **king ping**.

[SYDNEY REGION, BRISBANE REGION, HUNTER VALLEY AND NORTH COAST]

handle a beer glass with a handle. See also **butcher**, **glass**, **middy**, **pony**, **pot**, **schooner**[1], **schooner**[2] and **seven**.
[BRISBANE REGION, CENTRAL COAST QLD, CENTRAL HIGHLANDS VICTORIA, DARWIN AND NORTH COAST NT, FAR NORTH QLD, GIPPSLAND, MELBOURNE REGION, NORTH COAST QLD, NORTHERN VICTORIA, THE CENTRE, WEST CENTRAL QLD, WESTERN DISTRICT, PERTH REGION, WIMMERA AND MALLEE]

hanger[1] a young person hanging around a place (such as a shopping mall) for no particular purpose (usually in a group).
[MELBOURNE REGION]

hanger[2] a high mark in Aussie Rules.
[MELBOURNE REGION, WIMMERA AND MALLEE, CENTRAL HIGHLANDS VICTORIA]

hard-play the asphalt/bitumen-covered part of the school playground. See also **quadrangle**. [ADELAIDE REGION]

hard rubbish collection periodic, often annual, collection of large items of rubbish (broken appliances, furniture etc.) by local councils. [MELBOURNE REGION]

hard rubbish shopping the raiding of heaps of large items of rubbish on footpaths awaiting collection. [MELBOURNE REGION]

he the central figure in children's games; the player who is **in**, **it** or **up**.
[ADELAIDE REGION, CENTRAL HIGHLANDS VICTORIA, EYRE AND YORKE PENINSULAS, GIPPSLAND, MELBOURNE REGION, NORTHERN VICTORIA, PERTH REGION, TASMANIA, WESTERN DISTRICT, WIMMERA AND MALLEE, NORTHERN WEST AUSTRALIA, CENTRAL WEST AUSTRALIA, PERTH REGION]

head like a busted sofa wild or unruly hair. See also **revolving mallee root**. [TASMANIA]

head like a half-sucked mango and a body like a burst sausage unattractive. (Derogatory – but you'd worked that out, hadn't you?) [BRISBANE REGION]

Hector notorious thunderstorm that occurs in the Tiwi Islands about mid-afternoon most days in the **build-up**.
[DARWIN AND NORTH COAST NT]

helicopter a dragonfly (*Odonata anisoptera*). [ADELAIDE REGION]

hells, bells and bootlaces an exclamation of surprise. See also **bulltwang!**, **bunnies to that!**, **chowoon**, **eh**, **gammon**, **Himmel** and **strike me roan!** [BRISBANE REGION]

Herman a drunk; someone sleeping rough. (A contributor writes: "From Herman the German a homeless bloke who used to roam Ballarat streets until his death in the 1990s.")

[CENTRAL HIGHLANDS VICTORIA]

hey a tag word used as a sentence terminator. See also **eh**.

[BRISBANE REGION, CENTRAL COAST QLD, NORTH COAST QLD, FAR NORTH QLD, WEST CENTRAL QLD, PERTH REGION]

hide-and-go-seek children's game in which one player seeks all the others, who are in hiding. The seeker is **he**, **it** or **up**. The rules often required the seeker to run back to a home base before the person whose hiding place has just been found. (Sometimes said as "hidey-go-see".) See also **hide-and-seek** and **hidey**.

[BRISBANE REGION, SYDNEY REGION, TASMANIA, NEW ENGLAND DISTRICT]

hide-and-seek the same game as **hide-and-go-seek** and **hidey**.

[SYDNEY REGION, PERTH REGION]

hidey (sometimes known as "hideys" or "hidings") the same game as **hide-and-go-seek** and **hide-and-seek**.

[WIMMERA AND MALLEE, CENTRAL HIGHLANDS VICTORIA, WESTERN DISTRICT, NORTHERN VICTORIA, GIPPSLAND, MELBOURNE REGION, TASMANIA, SYDNEY REGION, ADELAIDE REGION]

high-blocked (of a building) built up on stumps of at least one and a half metres in height. See also **low-blocked**.

[BRISBANE REGION, CENTRAL COAST QLD, FAR NORTH QLD, NORTH COAST QLD, WEST CENTRAL QLD]

high set house elevated on blocks or poles (the bottom level may be subsequently built in); a house that has the garage underneath. See also **low set**. [NORTH COAST QLD, FAR NORTH QLD]

high top a combined primary and high school. See also **area school**, **central school**, **consolidated school**, **district school** and **secondary tops**. [NORTH COAST QLD]

Hill, the Parliament House, Canberra. See also **House, the**.

[SOUTH COAST AND SOUTHERN TABLELANDS]

hills people residents of the Dandenong Hills (in the Melbourne area); often intended to identify those with alternative lifestyles.

[MELBOURNE REGION]

hill trolley a home-built downhill racer. See also **billy cart**, **go-cart** and **soapbox.** [PERTH REGION]

Himmel an exclamation of surprise employed by the descendants of German settlers in the Barossa Valley when speaking English. (From the German word for "Heaven".) See also **bulltwang!; bunnies to that!; chowoon; eh; gammon; hells, bells and bootlaces** and **strike me roan!** [ADELAIDE REGION]

hipstick children's game closely resembling **British bulldog** and **red rover**. See also **bedlam**, **bullrush** and **cockylora**. [PERTH REGION]

hit-and-run a form of cricket in which the batter must run if they hit the ball. Also called "tip-and-run" or "nick-and-run". See also **tippety-run**, **tippy-go-run** and **tipsy-run**.
[BRISBANE REGION, CENTRAL COAST QLD, CENTRAL HIGHLANDS VICTORIA, CENTRAL WEST NSW, GIPPSLAND, HUNTER VALLEY AND NORTH COAST, MELBOURNE REGION, NEW ENGLAND DISTRICT, NORTH COAST QLD, NORTHERN VICTORIA, SOUTH COAST AND SOUTHERN TABLELANDS, SYDNEY REGION, TASMANIA, THE RIVERINA, WESTERN DISTRICT, WIMMERA AND MALLEE]

hobby haars a mythical monster used to frighten children into good behaviour. [MELBOURNE REGION]

holda to carry out a task with gusto and fervour. A contributor writes: "I think it originated as a shortening of the phrase 'hold your foot on the accelerator of your car'." [TASMANIA]

home place of safety in a children's game. See also **bar**[1].
[PERTH REGION, ADELAIDE REGION]

honkie person from Hong Kong. [SYDNEY REGION]

honky nut a large gum nut. ("Good for throwing!" wrote one belligerent contributor.) See also **conky**.
[NORTHERN WEST AUSTRALIA, CENTRAL WEST AUSTRALIA, PERTH REGION]

hoody a hooded jumper or pullover.
[SOUTH COAST AND SOUTHERN TABLELANDS]

hoofa Australian Rules football. See also **cross-country ballet**, **football**, **footy** and **kick and giggle.** [PERTH REGION]

hooking wood collecting firewood. [TASMANIA]

hoon a noisy or aggressive adolescent showing off in a car.
[PERTH REGION, SYDNEY REGION, MELBOURNE REGION, CENTRAL WEST NSW, CENTRAL
COAST QLD, NORTH COAST QLD, TASMANIA]

hoops, **doing** driving a car in tight circles at full throttle, causing the
rear wheels to skid. Also known as "circlework", "doughnut" and
"doughies". See also **two-bob**. [CENTRAL WEST NSW]

hooray goodbye. This (possibly now dated) expression was
seen by some contributors as a class indicator (only speakers
of "Broad Australian" employing it). Other contributors
pointed out that when pronounced with the stress on the
second syllable it indicates joy or celebration, and only with
the stress on the first syllable does it mean "goodbye". See
also **cheerio**, **cheery**, **hooroo**, **hurrah**, **oo-roo** and **soup**, **I'll
see you in the**.
[BRISBANE REGION, MELBOURNE REGION, HUNTER VALLEY AND NORTH COAST, PERTH
REGION, SYDNEY REGION, NORTH COAST QLD]

hooroo goodbye. See also **cheerio**, **cheery**, **hooray**, **hurrah**, **oo-roo**
and **soup**, **I'll see you in the**.
[DARWIN AND NORTH COAST NT, BRISBANE REGION, SYDNEY REGION, HUNTER VALLEY
AND NORTH COAST, CENTRAL HIGHLANDS VICTORIA, ADELAIDE REGION]

hoppo bumpo a children's game involving hopping on one leg
while attempting to knock over the other players, the last one
standing being the winner.
[CENTRAL HIGHLANDS VICTORIA, MELBOURNE REGION, TASMANIA, ADELAIDE REGION,
SYDNEY REGION]

hornets aged feral female cattle (they look calm, but they've got
plenty of sting). [WEST CENTRAL QLD]

horse bite a sharp blow to the skin with a cupped hand. See also
camel bite, **crow peck** and **monkey shine**. [SYDNEY REGION]

horsey a type of "bomb" dive designed to make the maximum
splash in the swimming pool. Also spelled "horsie". See also
banana, **can-opener** and **peg leg**.
[PERTH REGION, FAR WEST NSW, MELBOURNE REGION]

hospital kick (in AFL) a kick that might result in an injury. One
contributor writes: "When a ball is kicked high and straight up in

the air footballers will sit under the ball waiting to mark it, and can risk a clash of bodies which can result in injury."
[ADELAIDE REGION]

hospital pass (in Rugby League/Union) a pass that might result in an injury. A contributor writes: "A hospital pass is a floating pass in Rugby League, Rugby Union or even touch football that gets the receiver tackled hard without time to defend."
[NORTH COAST QLD, SYDNEY REGION]

hot box a transportable classroom. See also **Bristol hut**, **demountable**, **dogbox**, **musset hut**, **portable**, **pre-fab**, **relocatable**, **silver bullet**[1], **terrapin unit** and **transportable**.
[PERTH REGION]

hot enough for cotton frocks and plastic handbags very hot weather. [ADELAIDE REGION]

House, the Parliament House, Canberra. See also **Hill, the**.
[SOUTH COAST AND SOUTHERN TABLELANDS]

houso occupant of a Housing Commission home. [SYDNEY REGION]

how's your mother's chooks? once a form of affectionate greeting, this has been dated by the disappearance of chook runs from suburban backyards. [SYDNEY REGION]

hoy to throw out; to dispose of. [SYDNEY REGION]

hum to smell bad. [PERTH REGION]

humbug 1. to irritate or annoy. 2. to bludge or beg cigarettes or drinks. One contributor writes: "Signs in hotels in Tennant Creek and Katherine state no humbugging allowed."
[DARWIN AND NORTH COAST NT, THE CENTRE, NORTHERN WEST AUSTRALIA]

humpy a modest shack or house; a makeshift dwelling. From the Yagara Aboriginal language (Brisbane region). See also **badger box**.
[NORTH COAST QLD, FAR NORTH QLD, TASMANIA, NORTHERN SOUTH AUSTRALIA]

hungus an enthusiastic foodie: always hungry, always eating.
[CENTRAL COAST QLD]

hurrah goodbye. See also **cheerio**, **cheery**, **hooray**, **hooroo**, **oo-roo** and **soup, I'll see you in the**.
[BRISBANE REGION, CENTRAL COAST QLD, NORTH COAST QLD, FAR NORTH QLD, WEST CENTRAL QLD]

hut holiday house; beach cottage (perhaps built from second-hand materials). [NORTH COAST QLD]

hydro the name given in Tasmania to electricity. (From the Tasmanian Hydro-Electric Commission.) [TASMANIA]

hydro bill an electricity bill. [TASMANIA]

hydro pole power pole. See also a **SEC pole**, **Stobie pole**, **telegraph pole** and **telepole**. [TASMANIA]

hyena Tasmanian tiger or thylacine (*Thylacinus cynocephalus*). [TASMANIA]

I

iceblock[1] a frozen, flavoured confection on a stick. See also **by jingo**, **icy pole**, **juicy** and **Paddle-pop**.

[ADELAIDE REGION, BRISBANE REGION, CENTRAL COAST QLD, CENTRAL WEST NSW, EYRE AND YORKE PENINSULAS, HUNTER VALLEY AND NORTH COAST, NEW ENGLAND DISTRICT, NORTH COAST QLD, SOUTH COAST AND SOUTHERN TABLELANDS, SYDNEY REGION, THE RIVERINA, WIMMERA AND MALLEE, PERTH REGION]

iceblock[2] a block of frozen flavoured confection served in a wafer cube (or, in the past, in a cube of waxed cardboard).

[MELBOURNE REGION]

ice-cream sandwich an ice-cream between two wafer biscuits. See also **cream between**. [PERTH REGION]

ice cup frozen cordial in a plastic cup (sometimes frozen orange juice or flavoured milk). See also **cool cup**.

[DARWIN AND NORTH COAST NT, HUNTER VALLEY AND NORTH COAST, CENTRAL HIGHLANDS VICTORIA]

icy pole a frozen flavoured confection on a stick. See also **by jingo**, **iceblock** and **Paddle-pop**. (Originally icy pole was a brand name.)

[SYDNEY REGION, HUNTER VALLEY AND NORTH COAST, NEW ENGLAND DISTRICT, THE RIVERINA, SOUTH COAST AND SOUTHERN TABLELANDS, CENTRAL WEST NSW, FAR WEST NSW, WIMMERA AND MALLEE, CENTRAL HIGHLANDS VICTORIA, WESTERN DISTRICT, NORTHERN VICTORIA, GIPPSLAND, MELBOURNE REGION, TASMANIA, EYRE AND YORKE PENINSULAS, ADELAIDE REGION, PERTH REGION]

igloo a plastic tunnel for growing herbs and vegetables (functioning as a hothouse or greenhouse). [MELBOURNE REGION]

Illahorror grim nickname given to the Illawarra region following two gruesome murders that filled the headlines in the 1990s.

[SOUTH COAST AND SOUTHERN TABLELANDS]

I'm not made of wood and water "I can't be expected to do everything at once!" (now largely obsolete). [SYDNEY REGION]

in the player who is the centre of the action in a children's game (for example, the one who must find, or catch, or tag the others). See also **it**, **he** and **up**.

[BRISBANE REGION, CENTRAL COAST QLD, CENTRAL WEST NSW, HUNTER VALLEY AND NORTH COAST, NEW ENGLAND DISTRICT, NORTH COAST QLD, SOUTH COAST AND SOUTHERN TABLELANDS, SYDNEY REGION, THE RIVERINA]

Inceston (derogatory) nickname for Launceston. [TASMANIA]

incursion the visit to a school by a performer or speaker (play on the word "excursion"). [MELBOURNE REGION, PERTH REGION]

Indroo abbreviation of Indooroopilly (Brisbane suburb). Sometimes also as "Indrops". [BRISBANE REGION]

in-ground pool domestic swimming pool set into the ground (in a suburban backyard). See also **below-ground pool**. (The contrast is with "above-ground pool" – that being a cheaper and more temporary installation.)
[SYDNEY REGION, HUNTER VALLEY AND NORTH COAST, NEW ENGLAND DISTRICT, THE RIVERINA, SOUTH COAST AND SOUTHERN TABLELANDS, CENTRAL WEST NSW, FAR WEST NSW, BRISBANE REGION, CENTRAL COAST QLD, NORTH COAST QLD, FAR NORTH QLD, WEST CENTRAL QLD, TASMANIA, WIMMERA AND MALLEE, CENTRAL HIGHLANDS VICTORIA, WESTERN DISTRICT, NORTHERN VICTORIA, GIPPSLAND, MELBOURNE REGION]

injection a cry to allow a player to pause their involvement in a children's game. ("Accompanied," explained one contributor, "by a hand sign miming injecting something intramuscularly. Generally used when one wanted to stop playing for a while to do something else, such as talk to someone outside the game. To rejoin the game one merely said 'Uninjection.'") [SYDNEY REGION]

inside the eastern half of New South Wales, as seen by the residents of the Far West. [FAR WEST NSW]

in-to label given to interference in a children's game (such as marbles). (Sometimes known as "innos".) May have begun as an abbreviation of "interruption" or "interference" but is now pronounced "in toe". [MELBOURNE REGION, BRISBANE REGION]

Ipswichian resident of Ipswich (Brisbane suburb). [BRISBANE REGION]

iron pony motorbike (most common on properties where motorbikes have replaced horses for working cattle).
[WEST CENTRAL QLD]

iron ringer the local name for "true locals" in the western New South Wales town Cobar (i.e. born and bred in the town).
[FAR WEST NSW]

the Isa Mount Isa. [WEST CENTRAL QLD]

it the player who is the centre of the action in a children's game (for example, the one who must find, or catch, or tag the others). See also **he**, **in** and **up**.

[MELBOURNE REGION, GIPPSLAND, BRISBANE REGION, ADELAIDE REGION, PERTH REGION, CENTRAL HIGHLANDS VICTORIA]

Italian lawn concrete paving (possibly painted green). See also **Lebanese lawn** and **Leichhardt grass**. [PERTH REGION]

It must be rough on the bay! verbal response to seeing a flock of seagulls in the city (e.g. at the Melbourne Cricket Ground) well away from the waters of Port Phillip Bay. [MELBOURNE REGION]

I've been to Manly joking response to the question "Have you been overseas?" [SYDNEY REGION]

J

jacks[1] police. [SYDNEY REGION]

jacks[2] a children's game, originally played with the knucklebones from a leg of lamb, later with plastic replicas of these. [SYDNEY REGION]

jack sharp 1. a low-growing plant (*Emex australis*) having many hard, sharp, spiny seeds that are extremely painful to step on and which will sometimes even puncture the soles of shoes. 2. one of the seeds of this plant. See also **bullhead**, **California puncture weed**, **caltrop**, **cat head**[1], **cat's eye**[1], **double-gee**, **goat's head** and **three-corner jack**. [ADELAIDE REGION]

jacky jacky common name for a small brown lizard. See also **Jimmy lizard**. [WEST CENTRAL QLD]

jaggy leg when a hair on your leg gets caught in your clothing that is jaggy leg (and can be surprisingly painful). [MELBOURNE REGION]

jammers see **Speedos**. See also **ballhuggers**, **boasters**, **budgie-huggers**, **budgie-smugglers**, **cluster busters**, **cockchokers**, **cock jocks**, **codjocks**, **dick bathers**, **dick-pointers**, **dick-pokers**, **dick stickers**, **dick togs**, **dikdaks**, **dipsticks**, **fish frighteners**, **Jimmy clingers**, **knobbies**, **lolly-baggers**, **lolly bags**, **meat-hangers**, **nut huggers**, **nylon disgusters**, **racers**, **racing bathers**, **scungies**[2], **sluggers**, **sluggos**, **slug huggers**, **tights**, **toolies**, **trunks** and **wog togs**. [MELBOURNE REGION]

jandals rubber footwear, thongs. Possibly a contraction of "Japanese sandals". Several contributors suggest this term is of New Zealand origin (and was brought to parts of Australia by Kiwis looking for a better life). See also **Chinese safety boots**, **clackers**, **getters**, **go-backs**, **Japanese flying boots**, **Japanese riding boots**, **Japanese safety boots**, **Jesus boots**, **NT work boots** and **pluggers**. [PERTH REGION, SYDNEY REGION, BRISBANE REGION]

Japanese flying boots rubber footwear, thongs. See also **Chinese safety boots**, **clackers**, **getters**, **go-backs**, **jandals**, **Japanese riding boots**, **Japanese safety boots**, **Jesus boots**, **NT work boots** and **pluggers**. [TASMANIA]

Japanese frankfurts cocktail frankfurts. See also **cheerios** and **little boys.** [BRISBANE REGION]

Japanese riding boots rubber footwear, thongs. See also **Chinese safety boots**, **jandals**, **Japanese flying boots**, **Japanese safety boots**, **Jesus boots** and **NT work boots**.

[DARWIN AND NORTH COAST NT, ADELAIDE REGION, BRISBANE REGION, WEST CENTRAL QLD]

Japanese safety boots rubber footwear, thongs. According to one contributor, this is sometimes varied to "Japanese (or Chinese) parachute boots". See also **Chinese safety boots**, **clackers**, **getters**, **go-backs**, **jandals**, **Japanese flying boots**, **Japanese riding boots**, **Jesus boots**, **NT work boots** and **pluggers**.

[CENTRAL WEST AUSTRALIA, DARWIN AND NORTH COAST NT, NORTHERN WEST AUSTRALIA]

jard 1. to believe a lie. 2. to deceive, to fool someone by making a false claim. 3. to refute, to show a statement to be false. 4. to rebuke or snub someone.

[BRISBANE REGION, PERTH REGION, THE RIVERINA, SOUTH COAST AND SOUTHERN TABLELANDS]

jarrah jerker timber-getter, bush worker.

[NORTHERN WEST AUSTRALIA, CENTRAL WEST AUSTRALIA, PERTH REGION]

JCs leather sandals with brown crisscross straps. (Sometimes called "Jesus sandals" or **Roman sandals**.) See also **Jesus boots**.

[SOUTH COAST AND SOUTHERN TABLELANDS, SYDNEY REGION]

Jeff's shed the Melbourne Exhibition Centre. (From Jeff Kennett, Premier of Victoria 1992–99.) [MELBOURNE REGION]

jelly cake a lamington-style cake. Its making is described by one contributor thus: "A plain cake (sometimes cut into cubes), dipped in pink almost-set jelly and covered with desiccated coconut (sometimes with the addition of cream in the middle)." See also **pink lamington**.

[SYDNEY REGION, GIPPSLAND, MELBOURNE REGION, WESTERN DISTRICT, CENTRAL WEST AUSTRALIA, ADELAIDE REGION]

jersey the top part of a footy player's uniform. See also **guernsey** and **jumper.** [SYDNEY REGION, WEST CENTRAL QLD]

Jesus boots 1. thongs. See also **Chinese safety boots**, **clackers**, **getters**, **go-backs**, **jandals**, **Japanese flying boots**, **Japanese riding boots**, **Japanese safety boots**, **NT work boots** and **pluggers**. 2. brown leather sandals. See **JCs** and **Roman sandals**.
[NORTH COAST QLD, MELBOURNE REGION]

jig to truant from school. [SYDNEY REGION]

jilgie Australian freshwater crayfish, of the genus Cherax. From the Nyungar Aboriginal language (south-western Western Australia). See also **cherub**, **clawchie**, **crawbob**, **crawchie**, **craybob**, **craydab**, **crayfish**, **lobby**, **lobster**, **marron**, **pink nipper** and **yabby**.
[PERTH REGION]

jimbo a gate-crasher, a person who joins an activity uninvited.
[BRISBANE REGION]

Jimmy clingers see **Speedos**. See also **ballhuggers**, **boasters**, **budgie-huggers**, **budgie-smugglers**, **cluster busters**, **cockchokers**, **cock jocks**, **codjocks**, **dick bathers**, **dick-pointers**, **dick-pokers**, **dick stickers**, **dick togs**, **dikdaks**, **dipsticks**, **fish frighteners**, **jammers**, **knobbies**, **lolly-baggers**, **lolly bags**, **meat-hangers**, **nut huggers**, **nylon disgusters**, **racers**, **racing bathers**, **scungies**^{2}, **sluggers**, **sluggos**, **slug huggers**, **tights**, **toolies**, **trunks** and **wog togs**. [WEST CENTRAL QLD]

Jimmy lizard a small brown lizard. See also **jacky jacky**.
[BRISBANE REGION]

jingie a powerful evil spirit in Aboriginal mythology. Also spelled "jingy" or "jinga". From the Nyungar Aboriginal language (south-western Western Australia).
[NORTHERN WEST AUSTRALIA, CENTRAL WEST AUSTRALIA, PERTH REGION]

jinker shopping trolley. [ADELAIDE REGION]

job and knock an agreement between a boss and a worker whereby the worker can leave early if he finishes the job quickly. The equivalent of "job and finish". A contributor explains: "It's used, for example, on an extremely hot day when everyone is tired and the job is going slowly to speed the job up. This is achieved by working through all lunchbreaks and smoko breaks." [PERTH REGION]

joey another name for **bindi-eye**. From the idea that when you stand on one you hop around like a young kangaroo – a joey. See also **bindi-eye, bindy, jo-jo** and **prickle**.
[HUNTER VALLEY AND NORTH COAST]

jo-jo 1. a low-growing plant (*Soliva pterosperma*) often found in lawns with small spiky burrs which painfully impale bare feet. 2. one of these burrs. (An acronym for "jump on, jump off".) See also **bindi-eye, bindy, joey** and **prickle**.
[HUNTER VALLEY AND NORTH COAST, PERTH REGION, SOUTH COAST AND SOUTHERN TABLELANDS]

jolly joker a brand name that became a generic name for an **iceblock**[1] or **icy pole**. [BRISBANE REGION]

joogie a small, freshwater marron usually residing in rivers and streams. [PERTH REGION]

joombie (derogatory) a member of the burgeoning peasant underclass. [BRISBANE REGION]

jubbard an odd-job man on a cattle station. Possibly from an Aboriginal source word. [DARWIN AND NORTH COAST NT, THE CENTRE]

jubbly frozen cordial or fruit juice. Also spelled "jublee".
[MELBOURNE REGION]

jubee a drink of cordial. [BRISBANE REGION]

jubilee cake a plain cake containing sultanas or other dried fruit (created for the 100th anniversary of the founding of South Australia in 1936).
[EYRE AND YORKE PENINSULAS, ADELAIDE REGION, NORTHERN SOUTH AUSTRALIA, FAR WEST NSW]

jubilee twist a type of sweet, plaited bun. [PERTH REGION]

juicy an **iceblock**[1]. See also **by jingo, icy pole** and **Paddle-pop**.
[BRISBANE REGION]

jumper the top part of a footy player's uniform. See also **guernsey** and **jersey**. [ADELAIDE REGION]

jump-up the point where a road or track rises abruptly from one level to another. One contributor writes: "I've found jump-up used where a road or track has been cut by a watercourse of some kind causing a gully with steep sides." Another contributor says: "Jump-up is a commonly used term for a slight but abrupt rise, often in otherwise flat country."

[THE CENTRE, WEST CENTRAL QLD, FAR NORTH QLD, NORTHERN SOUTH AUSTRALIA, FAR WEST NSW]

K

kai food, tucker. (From Neomelanesian pidgin.) See also **doogers**.
[FAR NORTH QLD]

kanga money. [MELBOURNE REGION]

kangaroo tail a type of Australian palm.
[SYDNEY REGION, HUNTER VALLEY AND NORTH COAST, NEW ENGLAND DISTRICT, THE
RIVERINA, SOUTH COAST AND SOUTHERN TABLELANDS, CENTRAL WEST NSW, FAR
WEST NSW, WIMMERA AND MALLEE, CENTRAL HIGHLANDS VICTORIA, WESTERN
DISTRICT, NORTHERN VICTORIA, GIPPSLAND, MELBOURNE REGION, TASMANIA, ADELAIDE
REGION, EYRE AND YORKE PENINSULAS]

kangawallafox collective name for Australian animals such as
kangaroos, wallabies and foxes. [FAR WEST NSW]

kazza mazza calamari. [SYDNEY REGION]

keepings off a schoolyard game in which a circle of players toss a
ball while trying to keep it out of the hands of a player in the
middle of the circle. [MELBOURNE REGION, TASMANIA, GIPPSLAND]

kelvinator originally a brand-name refrigerator that, in places, has
become the generic word for a refrigerator.
[EYRE AND YORKE PENINSULAS, FAR WEST NSW]

Kenmore tractor one of the many names for a city-only four-wheel
drive. See also **Balmain bulldozer**, **Bronte buggy**, **Burnside bus**,
North Shore tank, **Toorak tractor** and **Turramurra tractor**.
[BRISBANE REGION]

kick and giggle AFL football. See also **cross-country ballet**,
football, **footy** and **hoofa**. [BRISBANE REGION]

Kickastickalong an imaginary remote country town. To be found
on the same map as **Bundiwallop**, **Oodnagalahbi** and
Wheelyabarraback. [SYDNEY REGION, TASMANIA]

kick-to-kick a game in which two groups kick a football across a
playground and attempt to "mark" (catch) the ball before
returning it. In some places called "end to end".
[CENTRAL HIGHLANDS VICTORIA, GIPPSLAND, MELBOURNE REGION, NORTHERN
VICTORIA, WESTERN DISTRICT, WIMMERA AND MALLEE, PERTH REGION]

kill kiln (as in hop kiln or oast house). [TASMANIA]

Killiecrankie diamond a type of gemstone (possibly clear topaz) found near Killiecrankie, Flinders Island, Bass Strait. [TASMANIA]

killing the pig working very hard. [HUNTER VALLEY AND NORTH COAST]

kinder abbreviation of **kindergarten**. See also **kindie**.
[CENTRAL HIGHLANDS VICTORIA, TASMANIA, THE RIVERINA, MELBOURNE REGION, PERTH REGION, SYDNEY REGION]

kindergarten first year in primary school. (From the German word coined by Friedrich Froebel, literally "children's garden".). In some places kindergarten is part of the school, in other places it is a separate preschool institution (and sometimes children attend for less than a full week). See also **preparatory class**, **reception class** and **transition**.
[CENTRAL WEST NSW, FAR WEST NSW, HUNTER VALLEY AND NORTH COAST, NEW ENGLAND DISTRICT, SOUTH COAST AND SOUTHERN TABLELANDS, SYDNEY REGION, THE RIVERINA]

kindie abbreviation of **kindergarten**. Sometimes as "kindy". See also **kinder** and **kindergarten**.
[SYDNEY REGION, ADELAIDE REGION, BRISBANE REGION, PERTH REGION, DARWIN AND NORTH COAST NT, THE CENTRE, EYRE AND YORKE PENINSULAS, NORTHERN SOUTH AUSTRALIA, MELBOURNE REGION, SOUTH COAST AND SOUTHERN TABLELANDS]

kindy nap an afternoon sleep. See also **nana nap**. [NORTH COAST QLD]

king a schoolyard game (a variant of **brandy**). [MELBOURNE REGION]

king brown a large bottle of beer. See also **big bud**. [PERTH REGION]

king cobra to go to bed in your work clothes *and* with your work boots on! (One step worse than to **black snake**.) [PERTH REGION]

king ping schoolyard game more commonly called **handball**, and also known as **four-square**, **two-square**. King ping is sometimes called "king pin" or "KP". [SYDNEY REGION, PERTH REGION]

King River prawn untreated faecal matter released into waterways. See also **blind mullet**, **blind trout**, **Bondi cigar**, **brown trout**, **pollywaffle** and **Werribee trout**. [TASMANIA]

Kirup syrup homemade grappa sold by the flagon. (Kirup is a small country town in the south-west of Western Australia.)
[PERTH REGION]

kiss and cuddle game soccer. See also **catch and kiss**. [PERTH REGION]

kit bag Gladstone bag (a light travelling bag or small portmanteau opening into two compartments).
[GIPPSLAND, NORTHERN SOUTH AUSTRALIA, ADELAIDE REGION]

kitchener bun a doughnut-like cake filled with cream or mock cream, and often jam as well. (According to some contributors this was originally known as a "berliner" and was given the more patriotic name of kitchener bun during the First World War.)
[EYRE AND YORKE PENINSULAS, ADELAIDE REGION, NORTHERN SOUTH AUSTRALIA]

kite a cheque or bank cheque, especially when paid as wages to rural workers. [SOUTH COAST AND SOUTHERN TABLELANDS]

kittle the mess of empty stubbies, cans and used beer glasses which accumulate on a table during a drinking party. [PERTH REGION]

knackers affectionate form of greeting among males (similar to "mate") . See also **cobber**, **cock**, **duck** and **mudcrab**. [TASMANIA]

knobbies see **Speedos**. See also **ballhuggers**, **boasters**, **budgie-huggers**, **budgie-smugglers**, **cluster busters**, **cockchokers**, **cock jocks**, **codjocks**, **dick bathers**, **dick-pointers**, **dick-pokers**, **dick stickers**, **dick togs**, **dikdaks**, **dipsticks**, **fish frighteners**, **jammers**, **Jimmy clingers**, **lolly-baggers**, **lolly bags**, **meat-hangers**, **nut huggers**, **nylon disgusters**, **racers**, **racing bathers**, **scungies**[2], **sluggers**, **sluggos**, **slug huggers**, **tights**, **toolies**, **trunks** and **wog togs**. [PERTH REGION]

knock 'em down a violent thunderstorm with strong winds, lashing rain and plenty of lightning and thunder. (These, a contributor explains, tend to occur only at the end of the wet season, and take their name from the fact that they knock down the two-metre-tall cattle grass.) [DARWIN AND NORTH COAST NT, THE CENTRE]

knockers a brothel. [CENTRAL WEST AUSTRALIA]

koitch an axe. [PERTH REGION]

koonac freshwater crayfish found in Western Australia (of the genus *Cherax*). Koonacs are relatively large crayfish, growing up to 200 mm long. Their distribution is more inland than for **marron**, and they are often found in seasonal rivers and swamps which dry up during summer. [CENTRAL WEST AUSTRALIA, PERTH REGION]

koori an Aboriginal person from southern New South Wales or Victoria.

[SYDNEY REGION, SOUTH COAST AND SOUTHERN TABLELANDS, THE RIVERINA, MELBOURNE REGION, NORTHERN VICTORIA, GIPPSLAND]

kumanji word used as a substitute for the identifying name of a deceased person. One contributor explains: "This word is an Arrernte (Aranda) Aboriginal word, spelled 'kwementyaye' using the most recent Arrernte orthography. This is a term applied by Arrernte people to those who have died, and sometimes to people who share the same kin or a close family relationship." Another contributor adds, "This word is spelled 'kummanjayi' in Warlpiri, used in place of a dead person's name or words that sound similar. Words that become kummanjayi are decided on by the dead person's family." [DARWIN AND NORTH COAST NT, THE CENTRE]

kylie[1] a boomerang or a similarly shaped object cut from thin gauge metal and used to throw at fish in shallow waters as an alternative to spearing. Also spelled "kylee". From the Nyungar Aboriginal language (south-western Western Australia). [PERTH REGION]

kylie[2] a blue-coloured incontinence cloth placed under the lower sheet on hospital beds. [PERTH REGION]

kyogle this word was used as a label for any passenger train between Brisbane and Sydney between the completion of the standard gauge link to Brisbane (in 1930) and the introduction of diesels (in the mid-1950s). From the northern NSW town of that name.

[BRISBANE REGION]

L

Lachlan lilac a biennial herb, *Echium plantagineum*, native to the Mediterranean area, but widely naturalised in settled parts of Australia, having blue-purple flowers. Widely regarded as a noxious weed. See also **blue weed**, **Murrumbidgee sweet pea**, **Paterson's curse**, **Riverina bluebell** and **Salvation Jane**.

[SYDNEY REGION, HUNTER VALLEY AND NORTH COAST, NEW ENGLAND DISTRICT, THE RIVERINA, SOUTH COAST AND SOUTHERN TABLELANDS, CENTRAL WEST NSW, FAR WEST NSW]

lacka band abbreviation for elastic band. See also **lacker band** and **lacky band**. [THE RIVERINA, GIPPSLAND]

lackers lollies. See also **gogs** and **mogs**.

[CENTRAL HIGHLANDS VICTORIA, WIMMERA AND MALLEE]

lacker band a rubber band. See also **lacka band** and **lacky band**.

[WIMMERA AND MALLEE, CENTRAL HIGHLANDS VICTORIA, WESTERN DISTRICT, NORTHERN VICTORIA, GIPPSLAND, MELBOURNE REGION, TASMANIA, SOUTH COAST AND SOUTHERN TABLELANDS, THE RIVERINA, ADELAIDE REGION]

lackies elastic bands for your hair. [PERTH REGION]

lacky band a rubber band. Also spelled "lackey band" and "lackie band". See also **lacka band** and **lacker band**.

[PERTH REGION, BRISBANE REGION, SOUTH COAST AND SOUTHERN TABLELANDS, SYDNEY REGION, NORTHERN WEST AUSTRALIA, CENTRAL WEST AUSTRALIA, MELBOURNE REGION]

lady in the boat cheap cask wine; Coolibah moselle. (From the illustration on the box of a popular brand.) Sometimes as "lady 'n' boat". See also **bag of death**, **Balga handbag**, **Bellambi handbag**, **boxie**, **box monster**, **Broadmeadows briefcase**, **cardboard handbag**, **Coraki handbag**, **death bag**, **Dubbo handbag**, **gin's handbag**, **goon**, **goonbag**, **goonbox**, **goonie**, **goonsack**, **red handbag**, **sack** and **vino collapso**.

[NORTHERN WEST AUSTRALIA, DARWIN AND NORTH COAST NT]

Lake Cat-eye nickname for Lake Cathie (both the town and the lagoon). [HUNTER VALLEY AND NORTH COAST]

land lice sheep. See also **ground lice**, **maggot-taxi** and **mountain maggots**.

[NORTHERN SOUTH AUSTRALIA, EYRE AND YORKE PENINSULAS, ADELAIDE REGION]

lapper an adolescent driver who does laps around suburban streets, usually late at night with a loud stereo and a noisy exhaust. [WEST CENTRAL QLD]

lappo the car in which the **lapper** does his laps. [PERTH REGION]

lappy the **lapper** and his **lappo** return, but this time they are driving up and down the same stretch of road repeatedly after doing U-turns at the end of the laps. (Well, it keeps the neighbours amused.) [NORTHERN VICTORIA]

larridoodlin a reprimanding (perhaps involving corporal punishment). [BRISBANE REGION]

last tango in Nanango going bush for a final fling. [BRISBANE REGION]

latte set trendy inner-city dwellers. [SYDNEY REGION]

laughing gear the mouth (when employed in an eating, rather than speaking or breathing, capacity); as in, "Wrap your laughing gear around this" (accompanied by an offer of food). [SOUTH COAST AND SOUTHERN TABLELANDS, SYDNEY REGION]

Launceston the issue here is pronunciation. The Tasmanian (and therefore correct) pronunciation is LON-sess-ton. Mainlanders tend to say LORN-sess-ton, while the older British pronunciation has only two syllables: LORN-ston. [TASMANIA]

laundry trough a large sink installed in a laundry. See also **laundry tub**, **trough**, **trove**, **wash trough** and **wash tub**. (According to some contributors, in Tasmania this was once pronounced to rhyme with "cow".) [WIMMERA AND MALLEE, CENTRAL HIGHLANDS VICTORIA, WESTERN DISTRICT, NORTHERN VICTORIA, GIPPSLAND, MELBOURNE REGION, TASMANIA, EYRE AND YORKE PENINSULAS, ADELAIDE REGION, PERTH REGION]

laundry tub a large sink installed in a laundry (as I just said – aren't you paying attention?). See also **laundry trough**, **trough**, **trove**, **wash trough** and **wash tub**. [SYDNEY REGION, HUNTER VALLEY AND NORTH COAST, NEW ENGLAND DISTRICT, THE RIVERINA, SOUTH COAST AND SOUTHERN TABLELANDS, CENTRAL WEST NSW, BRISBANE REGION, CENTRAL COAST QLD, NORTH COAST QLD]

lawn sale the sale of unwanted domestic items from the front lawn of the house; garage sale. [DARWIN AND NORTH COAST NT]

lazy wind a cold, biting wind; it's too lazy to go around you, it blows straight through you!

[MELBOURNE REGION, SOUTH COAST AND SOUTHERN TABLELANDS, CENTRAL COAST QLD, BRISBANE REGION]

learner's permit a learner driving licence.

[SYDNEY REGION, HUNTER VALLEY AND NORTH COAST, NEW ENGLAND DISTRICT, THE RIVERINA, SOUTH COAST AND SOUTHERN TABLELANDS, CENTRAL WEST NSW, FAR WEST NSW, BRISBANE REGION, CENTRAL COAST QLD, NORTH COAST QLD, FAR NORTH QLD, WEST CENTRAL QLD, NORTHERN WEST AUSTRALIA, CENTRAL WEST AUSTRALIA, PERTH REGION, MELBOURNE REGION]

leavers 1. Year 12 students who take a rest and recreation holiday at the completion of their exams 2. the holiday itself. [PERTH REGION]

Lebanese lawn a cement covered front or back yard. See also **Italian lawn** and **Leichhardt grass**. [SYDNEY REGION]

left foot stab pass removed; got rid off; given the flick; taken out of the equation. [NORTHERN SOUTH AUSTRALIA]

left without a sandshoe or galosh lost everything (usually in either a gamble or a swindle). [SYDNEY REGION]

Lego child's building bricks. The issue here is pronunciation: while the rest of Australia says LEGG-o Adelaidians say LAY-go.

[ADELAIDE REGION]

Leichhardt grass concreted front or back yard (especially when painted green). From the Sydney suburb of Leichhardt and its maintenance-minded residents. See also **Italian lawn** and **Lebanese lawn**.

[SYDNEY REGION, HUNTER VALLEY AND NORTH COAST, NEW ENGLAND DISTRICT, THE RIVERINA, SOUTH COAST AND SOUTHERN TABLELANDS, CENTRAL WEST NSW, FAR WEST NSW]

lemon spread sweet spread made from lemons, sugar and egg yolks, sometimes called "lemon butter", "lemon cheese" or "lemon curd".

[BRISBANE REGION, SYDNEY REGION, SOUTH COAST AND SOUTHERN TABLELANDS]

leper-line the 20th parallel of South latitude above which it was intended to keep all cases of leprosy (now obsolete).

[NORTHERN WEST AUSTRALIA, CENTRAL WEST AUSTRALIA, PERTH REGION]

levna name given to the morning break at state schools (at eleven o'clock). See also **elevener**, **elevenses**, **little lunch**, **little play**, **morning lunch**, **morning play**, **play lunch**, **playtime**, **recess** and **snack**. [BRISBANE REGION]

Lewisham conversational response to a particularly daffy remark, taking the form of: "It won't be long, and it won't be Lewisham." Being translated from Ancient Aussie this (now obsolete) expression means: "It won't be long before they're coming to take you away, and it won't be to the general hospital (at Lewisham) but to the psychiatric unit." [SYDNEY REGION]

lids boogy board surfers. (From "Esky lids", which their boards allegedly resemble.) [SYDNEY REGION]

like the bird on the biscuit tin on the outside looking in (from the old Arnott's trademark). [SYDNEY REGION]

Lincoln weed a common roadside weed; mustard weed.
[ADELAIDE REGION, WIMMERA AND MALLEE, EYRE AND YORKE PENINSULAS]

linen press a linen cupboard; a storage cupboard for linen, towels, etc. See also **manchester cupboard**. [BRISBANE REGION, SYDNEY REGION]

linger-and-die a long, steep hill. [HUNTER VALLEY AND NORTH COAST]

Lismoron a resident of Lismore, northern New South Wales. (Apparently a mocking self-reference coined by the Lismorons themselves.) [HUNTER VALLEY AND NORTH COAST]

little aths little athletics. [MELBOURNE REGION, TASMANIA]

little boys cocktail frankfurts (rhyming slang from "saveloys"). See also **cheerios** and **Japanese frankfurts**.
[WIMMERA AND MALLEE, CENTRAL HIGHLANDS VICTORIA, WESTERN DISTRICT, NORTHERN VICTORIA, GIPPSLAND, MELBOURNE REGION, TASMANIA, ADELAIDE REGION, EYRE AND YORKE PENINSULAS, SYDNEY REGION, HUNTER VALLEY AND NORTH COAST, NEW ENGLAND DISTRICT, THE RIVERINA, SOUTH COAST AND SOUTHERN TABLELANDS, CENTRAL WEST NSW, FAR WEST NSW, NORTHERN SOUTH AUSTRALIA]

little green cart the mythical vehicle that would take you away to the home for the terminally confused. From the verbal warning that the little green cart is on its way. See also **Lewisham**.
[SYDNEY REGION]

little lunch 1. the mid-morning break in primary school. See also **elevener, elevenses, levna, little play, morning lunch, morning play, play lunch, playtime, recess** and **snack**. 2. a snack eaten then.

[SYDNEY REGION, HUNTER VALLEY AND NORTH COAST, NEW ENGLAND DISTRICT, THE RIVERINA, SOUTH COAST AND SOUTHERN TABLELANDS, CENTRAL WEST NSW, BRISBANE REGION, CENTRAL COAST QLD, NORTH COAST QLD, TASMANIA, FAR NORTH QLD]

little play morning break in primary school. See also **elevener, elevenses, levna, little lunch, little play, morning lunch, morning play, play lunch, playtime, recess** and **snack**. [MELBOURNE REGION]

little tacker a child. See also **bluetongue**[1] and **passion killers**.

[NORTHERN SOUTH AUSTRALIA, ADELAIDE REGION]

lobby an Australian freshwater crayfish, of the genus *Cherax*. (Typically Australian diminutive formed from "lobster".) See also **cherub, clawchie, crawbob, crawchie, craybob, craydab, crayfish, jilgie, lobster, marron, pink nipper** and **yabby**.

[BRISBANE REGION, CENTRAL COAST QLD, FAR NORTH QLD, NORTH COAST QLD, WEST CENTRAL QLD]

lobster[1] an Australian freshwater crayfish, of the genus *Cherax*. See also **cherub, clawchie, crawbob, crawchie, craybob, craydab, crayfish, jilgie, lobby, marron, pink nipper** and **yabby**. [TASMANIA]

lobster[2] any of various large, edible, marine stalk-eyed decapod crustaceans of the family *Palinuridae*, with large claws and a hard red carapace. See also **crayfish**.

[ADELAIDE REGION, BRISBANE REGION, CENTRAL COAST QLD, CENTRAL HIGHLANDS VICTORIA, CENTRAL WEST NSW, EYRE AND YORKE PENINSULAS, GIPPSLAND, HUNTER VALLEY AND NORTH COAST, MELBOURNE REGION, NEW ENGLAND DISTRICT, NORTH COAST QLD, NORTHERN VICTORIA, SOUTH COAST AND SOUTHERN TABLELANDS, SYDNEY REGION, TASMANIA, THE RIVERINA, WESTERN DISTRICT, WIMMERA AND MALLEE]

lobster[3] a twenty dollar note. See also **cray**[2], **crayfish**[2], **red back** and **rock lobster**. [PERTH REGION, SYDNEY REGION, MELBOURNE REGION]

logodile a floating log which cunningly disguises itself as a crocodile, and thus frightens the life out of the humans with which it shares the waterways.

[DARWIN AND NORTH COAST NT, NORTHERN VICTORIA]

lolly-baggers see **Speedos**. See also **ballhuggers**, **boasters**, **budgie-huggers**, **budgie-smugglers**, **cluster busters**, **cockchokers**, **cock jocks**, **codjocks**, **dick bathers**, **dick-pointers**, **dick-pokers**, **dick stickers**, **dick togs**, **dikdaks**, **dipsticks**, **fish frighteners**, **jammers**, **Jimmy clingers**, **knobbies**, **lolly bags**, **meat-hangers**, **nut huggers**, **nylon disgusters**, **racers**, **racing bathers**, **scungies**[2], **sluggers**, **sluggos**, **slug huggers**, **tights**, **toolies**, **trunks** and **wog togs**.
[CENTRAL WEST AUSTRALIA, MELBOURNE REGION]

lolly bags see **Speedos**. See also **ballhuggers**, **boasters**, **budgie-huggers**, **budgie-smugglers**, **cluster busters**, **cockchokers**, **cock jocks**, **codjocks**, **dick bathers**, **dick-pointers**, **dick-pokers**, **dick stickers**, **dick togs**, **dikdaks**, **dipsticks**, **fish frighteners**, **jammers**, **Jimmy clingers**, **knobbies**, **lolly-baggers**, **meat-hangers**, **nut huggers**, **nylon disgusters**, **racers**, **racing bathers**, **scungies**[2], **sluggers**, **sluggos**, **slug huggers**, **tights**, **toolies**, **trunks** and **wog togs**. [SYDNEY REGION]

lollypop lady the person who holds up the stop sign at school crossings. Also "lollypop man". (Sometimes applied to the council worker who directs traffic around road works.)
[MELBOURNE REGION, HUNTER VALLEY AND NORTH COAST, SYDNEY REGION, BRISBANE REGION]

lolly water soft drink. See also **cool drink**, **cordial**, **fizzy cordial** and **fizzy drink**. [ADELAIDE REGION, SYDNEY REGION, MELBOURNE REGION]

London bun a rolled sweet bun containing diced apple. Elsewhere known as an **apple scroll** or a "Chelsea bun". [ADELAIDE REGION]

long doughnut a long bun of doughnut dough split along its length with jam and cream in the middle. See also **kitchener bun**.
[BRISBANE REGION]

long drop earth closet toilet. See also **dubs**.
[ADELAIDE REGION, EYRE AND YORKE PENINSULAS, NORTHERN SOUTH AUSTRALIA, WEST CENTRAL QLD, NORTH COAST QLD, TASMANIA, NEW ENGLAND DISTRICT]

long flat dog crocodile (Experts say: "Crikey! They bite!"). See also **flat dog**, **gotcha lizard** and **mud gecko**.
[NORTH COAST QLD, DARWIN AND NORTH COAST NT]

long-grass where the homeless people camp on the outskirts of urban centres. [DARWIN AND NORTH COAST NT]

long-grasser a homeless (possibly itinerant) person.
[DARWIN AND NORTH COAST NT]

longie abbreviation of **long neck**. See also **big bot**, **big bud**, **Corinna stubby** and **tallie**. [PERTH REGION]

long neck 750 ml bottle of beer as opposed to a (shorter) stubbie. See also **big bot**, **big bud**, **Corinna stubby**, **longie** and **tallie**.
[WEST CENTRAL QLD, PERTH REGION, ADELAIDE REGION, SYDNEY REGION, TASMANIA, MELBOURNE REGION, BRISBANE REGION]

long paddock grass growing along the edge of the road; when cattle or sheep are being moved to feed on this grass (especially during times of drought) they are "on the long paddock".
[WEST CENTRAL QUEENSLAND, FAR WEST NSW, WIMMERA AND MALLEE, WESTERN DISTRICT]

Lonnie Launceston. [TASMANIA]

loosely wrapped slightly mentally unhinged; highly idiosyncratic; does not have a firm grip on reality. [ADELAIDE REGION]

low-blocked a building on stumps of less than about 1.5 m in height. See also **high-blocked**.
[BRISBANE REGION, CENTRAL COAST QLD, FAR NORTH QLD, NORTH COAST QLD, WEST CENTRAL QLD]

low set a single storey house. By contrast a **high set** house would either be two storeys or would have a garage underneath.
[NORTH COAST QLD, FAR NORTH QLD]

luncheon sausage a large, mild-flavoured, precooked sausage, usually sliced thinly and eaten cold. See also **baron sausage**, **beef Belgium**, **Belgium sausage**, **bung fritz**, **Byron sausage**, **devon**, **Empire sausage**, **fritz**, **German sausage**, **mystery meat**, **polony**, **pork German**, **Strasburg**, **wheel meat** and **Windsor sausage**.
[BRISBANE REGION, CENTRAL COAST QLD, NORTH COAST QLD, FAR NORTH QLD, WEST CENTRAL QLD, CENTRAL HIGHLANDS VICTORIA]

lunch shed a shed on school grounds (separate from the classrooms) in which children eat or shelter on rainy days. See also **play shed, shelter shed** and **weather shed.**

[NORTHERN VICTORIA, MELBOURNE REGION]

lux to vacuum clean. (From the brand name Electrolux.)

[HUNTER VALLEY AND NORTH COAST, TASMANIA]

M

macca macadamia nut. See also **bopple**.
[HUNTER VALLEY AND NORTH COAST]

Mackay cedar a type of wood. [NORTH COAST QLD]

Mad Mary untidy or unkempt (particularly refers to hair).
[THE RIVERINA]

maggered as drunk as a skunk. Possibly from **maggoted** as
pronounced by someone who is as drunk as a skunk. See also
chopped, gone to Gowings, maggo, off chops and **off your unit.**
[NORTHERN VICTORIA, GIPPSLAND, SYDNEY REGION]

maggo dead drunk. Abbreviation of **maggoted**. See also **chopped,
gone to Gowings, maggered, maggo, off chops** and **off your unit.**
[PERTH REGION]

maggoted extremely drunk. See also **chopped, gone to Gowings,
maggered, maggo, off chops** and **off your unit.**
[HUNTER VALLEY AND NORTH COAST, SYDNEY REGION, PERTH REGION]

maggot bag a meat pie. A "maggot bag and blood" is a meat pie
with tomato sauce.
[HUNTER VALLEY AND NORTH COAST, CENTRAL COAST QLD, WEST CENTRAL QLD,
EYRE AND YORKE PENINSULAS, ADELAIDE REGION, NORTHERN SOUTH AUSTRALIA,
BRISBANE REGION]

maggot-taxi 1. a sheep. See also ground lice, land lice and
mountain maggots. [BRISBANE REGION] 2. a dead body. [CENTRAL
HIGHLANDS VICTORIA, NORTHERN VICTORIA, GIPPSLAND]

magpie-lark a common black-and-white bird, *Grallina cyanoleuca*,
with a loud piping voice, pairs often sing in antiphonic duet;
ranges across the entire mainland, absent from Tasmania. See also
mudlark, Murray magpie and **peewee.** [SYDNEY REGION]

mainland, the 1. continental Australia. [TASMANIA] See also **Australia,
big island, north island** and **the other side.** 2. **Tasmania.** [KING AND
FLINDERS ISLANDS]

mainlander 1. a resident of continental Australia. [TASMANIA] 2. a
resident of Tasmania. [KING AND FLINDERS ISLANDS]

maisonette a semi-detached house; a duplex townhouse.
[ADELAIDE REGION, EYRE AND YORKE PENINSULAS, NORTHERN SOUTH AUSTRALIA, HUNTER VALLEY AND NORTH COAST, MELBOURNE REGION]

malt sandwich a bottle of beer. See also **brown sandwich**.
[THE RIVERINA]

manchester cupboard a cupboard for storing linen, towels, etc. See also **linen cupboard**. [SYDNEY REGION]

man fern any tree fern. [TASMANIA]

mango madness feelings of oppression and agitation brought on by the **build-up**. [DARWIN AND NORTH COAST NT]

maralinga breadbox microwave oven. [NORTHERN SOUTH AUSTRALIA]

mare's eggs equine faecal matter (good for the roses). [TASMANIA]

Marrickville Mercedes Chrysler Valiant; derogatory reference to the automotive tastes of young Greek males in the 1970s and 1980s.
[SYDNEY REGION]

marron are the largest freshwater crayfish in the south-west of Western Australia and one of the largest freshwater crayfish species on earth. Note: the scientific names for the two species of marron are currently under review. The popular name comes from the Nyungar Aboriginal language (south-western WA). See also **cherub**, **clawchie**, **crawbob**, **crawchie**, **craybob**, **craydab**, **crayfish**, **jilgie**, **lobby**, **lobster**, **pink nipper** and **yabby**.
[PERTH REGION]

matriculation college a secondary college providing schooling for years 11 and 12. [SOUTH COAST AND SOUTHERN TABLELANDS, TASMANIA]

meat-hangers see **Speedos**. See also **ballhuggers**, **boasters**, **budgie-huggers**, **budgie-smugglers**, **cluster busters**, **cockchokers**, **cock jocks**, **codjocks**, **dick bathers**, **dick-pointers**, **dick-pokers**, **dick stickers**, **dick togs**, **dikdaks**, **dipsticks**, **fish frighteners**, **jammers**, **Jimmy clingers**, **knobbies**, **lolly-baggers**, **lolly bags**, **nut huggers**, **nylon disgusters**, **racers**, **racing bathers**, **scungies**[2], **sluggers**, **sluggos**, **slug huggers**, **tights**, **toolies**, **trunks** and **wog togs**.
[HUNTER VALLEY AND NORTH COAST, NORTHERN SOUTH AUSTRALIA, BRISBANE REGION, SYDNEY REGION]

meat store a butcher's shop.
[EYRE AND YORKE PENINSULAS, NORTHERN SOUTH AUSTRALIA, ADELAIDE REGION]

meccano set 1. an enormous set of traffic lights at the intersection of the Hume Highway and Henry Lawson Drive in Sydney. 2. the Sydney Harbour Bridge. (From the name of a once popular construction kit.) [SYDNEY REGION]

melon hole a lumpy hole found in black soil country caused by expansion and contraction of the soil with changing water content, and capable of breaking an axle if crossed at speed.
[CENTRAL COAST QLD]

Melways familiar suburban road map in Melbourne. See **Gregory's** and **Referdex**. [MELBOURNE REGION]

mermaid a Queensland Transport Department officer with a portable weighbridge for checking the load weights of semis (so called because "they have scales"). [BRISBANE REGION]

messages small shopping errands (now largely obsolete); to "do the messages" was to do the shopping.
[MELBOURNE REGION, SYDNEY REGION, CENTRAL COAST QLD]

Metcard Mafia a ticket inspector on Melbourne's public transport system. A contributor explains that the mafia tag comes from their black suits and black overcoats. See also **Gestapo**, **Met cop**, **train fascist**, **train Nazi** and **tram fascist**.
[MELBOURNE REGION]

Met cop a ticket inspector on Melbourne's public transport system. They can hand out fines and make things difficult for those attempting to travel without having their "Metcard" handy. See also **Gestapo**, **Metcard Mafia**, **train dog**, **train fascist**, **train Nazi** and **tram fascist**. [MELBOURNE REGION]

Methodist gate a farm gate so heavy, stiff or awkward only a Methodist can open or close it without swearing. See also **bogan gate**, **COD gate** and **wire gate**. [BRISBANE REGION]

metholated spirits Methodists. See also **cattle tick**, **mickey drip** and **press button**. [BRISBANE REGION]

metwurst spicy German sausage that is reported to be a staple of SA lunches. Also "mettie". Sometimes jokingly referred to as "metwist". "Slashed metwurst" is a sliced 250 g block of **metwurst** from the butcher. [ADELAIDE REGION]

Mexican 1. someone from Victoria. [THE RIVERINA, SOUTH COAST AND SOUTHERN TABLELANDS] 2. someone from New South Wales (or further south). [BRISBANE REGION, CENTRAL COAST QLD, NORTH COAST QLD, FAR NORTH QLD, WEST CENTRAL QLD]

Mexico more formally "the southern states": New South Wales and Victoria. [BRISBANE REGION]

mickey drip Catholic (derogatory schoolboy slang from the 1950s). See also **cattle tick**, **metholated spirits** and **press button**. [CENTRAL WEST AUSTRALIA, NORTHERN WEST AUSTRALIA, PERTH REGION]

Mickey Weston (or "Wesson") a beer gut. A contributor who claimed to know the original, from whom the label came, said that whenever ribbed about his large paunch the original Mickey Weston would reply: "They don't put bay windows on dunnies". [BRISBANE REGION]

middy a medium-sized glass of beer (standard NSW size approximately 285 ml; standard WA size approximately 200 ml). From the notion that it is midway between a glass and a schooner. See also **butcher**, **glass**, **handle**, **pony**, **pot**, **schooner**[1], **schooner**[2] and **seven**. [CENTRAL WEST NSW, FAR WEST NSW, HUNTER VALLEY AND NORTH COAST, NEW ENGLAND DISTRICT, SOUTH COAST AND SOUTHERN TABLELANDS, SYDNEY REGION, THE RIVERINA]

milkbar[1] a corner store (what is now called a "convenience store"); a small shop selling a range of soft drinks, snack foods, smallgoods, bread and other grocery items. Also **convenience store**, **deli** and **mixed business**. [BRISBANE REGION, MELBOURNE REGION, TASMANIA]

milkbar[2] a small shop selling milk shakes, soft drinks, **spiders** (ice-cream sodas), confectionery, snack foods and hamburgers (but no smallgoods, bread or grocery items). Now largely obsolete. [SYDNEY REGION]

milkshake a milky-coloured playing marble. [BRISBANE REGION]

milky/milko the person who delivered milk to your door (back in the days when milk was delivered to your door). [ADELAIDE REGION, EYRE AND YORKE PENINSULAS]

Milo someone who is a little bit slow on the uptake. (Note: both Milo and Quik are brands of milk flavouring, and anyone who wasn't quick must be a ...) See also **couple of lamingtons short of a CWA meeting, a; dipsticks; doughy; dubbo; gimp; moonya; munted; nuffest** and **veggie**[1]. [NORTH COAST QLD]

minda 1. (derogatory) a bit of an idiot (from Minda Incorporated, service provider for the intellectually disabled – originally the Mentally Intellectually and Neurologically Disabled Association). See also **banger, nuff nuff, oxygen thief, random** and **roo**. 2. a type of unfashionable sandal; girls' school sandals common in Adelaide in the 1980s. [ADELAIDE REGION, NORTHERN SOUTH AUSTRALIA]

Ming Wing the Sir Robert Menzies School of Humanities Building at Monash University, housing the faculties of Arts and Economics. [MELBOURNE REGION]

mint cool. See **mintox**. [PERTH REGION]

Mintabie time later than expected; taking more time than promised; the pace at which life runs in Mintabie (as contrasted with the restless pace at which the hands of the clock whiz around elsewhere). From the opal mining town in the north of South Australia. [NORTHERN SOUTH AUSTRALIA]

mintox very good; cool. Also, **mint**. It's unclear which came first: mint later expanded into mintox, or mintox later contracted into mint. [PERTH REGION]

mixed business a corner shop; a **milk bar**; a **deli**. [SYDNEY REGION]

mixed lollies (obsolete) when lollies were sold from big jars (and not in packets) it was possible to buy a bag of mixed lollies to the value of ... (whatever small change you found in your pocket). [MELBOURNE REGION, SOUTH COAST AND SOUTHERN TABLELANDS]

mixup cordial mixed with water and ready to drink. [HUNTER VALLEY AND NORTH COAST]

mizzle a combination of mist and drizzle. [TASMANIA]

mocca one who favours moccasins as everyday footwear; a member of the burgeoning peasant underclass; a **bogan**, a **bevan**, a **bevchick**, a **westie**. See also **bennie**, **bethan**, **bog**², **bogan**, **booner**, **boonie**, **chigger**, **chookie**, **cogger**¹, **feral**, **garry**, **scozzer** and **westie**. [CENTRAL HIGHLANDS VICTORIA]

moccas moccasins. Sometimes "moccies". See also **Broadmeadows wedding shoes**, **Ringwood Reeboks** and **Sunshine stilettos**. [MELBOURNE REGION]

Mockery, The nickname given to any newspaper officially called *The Mercury* (for instance *The Hobart Mercury* and *The Illawarra Mercury* – both being known locally as **The Mockery**). [TASMANIA, SOUTH COAST AND SOUTHERN TABLELANDS]

mogs lollies or sweets. See also **gogs** and **lackers**. [MELBOURNE REGION]

monger stupid person; slow-witted person (especially a dope smoker). Abbreviated as "mong". See also **couple of lamingtons short of a CWA meeting, a**; **dipsticks**; **dubbo** and **Milo**. [NEW ENGLAND DISTRICT, ADELAIDE REGION, PERTH REGION]

mongo 1. a Rugby League player. 2. a Rugby Union player who changes codes to play League. [CENTRAL WEST NSW, FAR WEST NSW, HUNTER VALLEY AND NORTH COAST, NEW ENGLAND DISTRICT, SOUTH COAST AND SOUTHERN TABLELANDS, SYDNEY REGION, THE RIVERINA]

monkey shine a headlock accompanied by a ferocious rubbing of the scalp with the palm. See also **camel bite**, **crow peck** and **horse bite**. [SOUTH COAST AND SOUTHERN TABLELANDS]

mono to lift one wheel of a bike so as to be riding on one wheel only; usually expressed as "pop a mono". [CENTRAL WEST AUSTRALIA]

moo juice full cream milk (low fat milk is **cow cordial**). [MELBOURNE REGION]

moompie a mouse; sometimes in full as a "moompie mouse". See also **noofy**. [EYRE AND YORKE PENINSULAS]

moonya stupid (offensive, derived from the Moonya Spastic Centre in Wonthaggi). See **minda**, **crowl**. See also **couple of lamingtons short of a CWA meeting, a**; **dipsticks**; **doughy**; **dubbo**; **gimp**; **Milo**; **munted**; **nuffest** and **veggie**[1]. [GIPPSLAND]

more complaints than Sydney Hospital a whinger. [SYDNEY REGION]

more front than Myers brash or outrageously self-confident. [MELBOURNE REGION]

morning lunch morning tea; in schools (in some regions) this would be known as **little lunch** or **play lunch**. See also **elevener**, **elevenses**, **levna**, **little play**, **morning play**, **recess** and **snack**. [ADELAIDE REGION, EYRE AND YORKE PENINSULAS, NORTHERN SOUTH AUSTRALIA, TASMANIA]

morning play the mid-morning break in primary school. See also **elevener**, **elevenses**, **levna**, **little lunch**, **little play**, **morning lunch**, **play lunch**, **recess** and **snack**. [PERTH REGION, MELBOURNE REGION]

morning sticks kindling wood for lighting the fire at the start of the day. See also **mornings wood**. [TASMANIA]

mornings wood kindling for starting the fire at the beginning of the day. See also **morning sticks**. [NORTH COAST QLD, CENTRAL HIGHLANDS VICTORIA, TASMANIA]

morphia (or "morph") nickname commonly given to a person perceived as being "a slow working dope". [THE RIVERINA]

Mosman shopping trolley a city-based four-wheel drive. See also **Balmain bulldozer**, **Bronte buggy**, **Burnside bus**, **Kenmore tractor**, **North Shore tank**, **Toorak tractor** and **Turramurra tractor**. [SYDNEY REGION]

mothers' milk Victoria Bitter (VB) beer. See also **green can**, **veeb**, **Victor Bravo**, **vitamin B** and **vomit bomb**. [WIMMERA AND MALLEE]

mountain maggots sheep. See also **ground lice**, **land lice** and **maggot-taxi**. [GIPPSLAND]

mountain oyster the discarded testicle of a castrated bull calf. These were invariably fed to the dogs, but visitors were often threatened with "mountain oysters in garlic butter for tea tonight". See also **prairie oyster**. [GIPPSLAND, NORTH COAST QLD]

mountain people residents of the Blue Mountains, west of Sydney. See also **plains people**. [SYDNEY REGION]

Mount Isa by the sea a derogatory nickname for Townsville (a contributor explains this is a reference to the comparative lack of green surroundings and predominance of industrial plants and refineries). [NORTH COAST QLD]

mow the lawn in some parts of Australia householders **cut the grass** while in the following regions they mow the lawn:

[CENTRAL HIGHLANDS VICTORIA, GIPPSLAND, MELBOURNE REGION, NORTHERN VICTORIA, WESTERN DISTRICT, WIMMERA AND MALLEE, SYDNEY REGION, BRISBANE REGION]

mozz to condemn a person to failure by confidently predicting they will succeed spectacularly: "to put the mozz on someone". [SOUTH COAST AND SOUTHERN TABLELANDS, MELBOURNE REGION]

Mrs Kerfoops 1. an affectionate form of address for a girl or woman. 2. used to refer to an unknown or unspecified woman. 3. a fictional character against whom you may be compared unfavourably. 4. a sneering put-down for any girl or woman who was thought to "have tickets on herself". [SYDNEY REGION, MELBOURNE REGION, HUNTER VALLEY AND NORTH COAST, THE RIVERINA, GIPPSLAND]

muckadilla a disorganised person; a messer. [CENTRAL COAST QLD]

mudcrab term of greeting; usually in a similar way to "mate", **cobber**[2] or "sport". See also **cock** and **duck**. [DARWIN AND NORTH COAST NT]

muddy a mud crab. [NORTH COAST QLD]

mud gecko a crocodile. See also **flat dog**, **gotcha lizard** and **long flat dog**. [FAR NORTH QLD]

mudlark a common black-and-white bird, *Grallina cyanoleuca*, with a loud piping voice, pairs often sing in antiphonic duet; ranges across the entire mainland, absent from Tasmania. See also **magpie lark**, **Murray magpie** and **peewee**. [ADELAIDE REGION, PERTH REGION]

mud stump an ant bed. [WEST CENTRAL QLD]

mufti day casual clothes day. See also **casual day**, **free dress day** and **out of uniform day**.
[NORTHERN VICTORIA, SOUTH COAST AND SOUTHERN TABLELANDS, SYDNEY REGION]

muley a small fish; a pilchard or sardine.
[NORTHERN WEST AUSTRALIA, CENTRAL WEST AUSTRALIA, PERTH REGION, BRISBANE REGION, CENTRAL COAST QLD, NORTH COAST QLD, FAR NORTH QLD, SYDNEY REGION, HUNTER VALLEY AND NORTH COAST, SOUTH COAST AND SOUTHERN TABLELANDS]

munchie a shark (surfers' slang). [BRISBANE REGION]

mundoee the foot. Also spelled "mundowie" and "mundooey".
[CENTRAL COAST QLD, NORTH COAST QLD, FAR NORTH QLD]

mung bean a totally useless person. According to one contributor this is used to refer to itinerant tourists (but not in their presence!), while another suggests it's used of "feral greenies living an alternative lifestyle".
[SOUTH COAST AND SOUTHERN TABLELANDS, PERTH REGION, CENTRAL HIGHLANDS VICTORIA]

munger an abbreviation of **mung bean**. One contributor writes that "it is used in the Kununurra–Ord River region for seasonal workers picking melons, pumpkins or doing any manual day labour in that area". [NORTHERN WEST AUSTRALIA]

mungery ill; out of sorts; angry; bad-tempered; in a foul mood. Pronunciation note: the "G" is soft, so the word is pronounced "munj-ery". [NORTH COAST QLD]

munji my lover, my boyfriend, my man (from Port Lincoln Aboriginal slang). [EYRE AND YORKE PENINSULAS]

munted stupid; uncool; tired; out of energy; broken but not quite destroyed. Possibly originally from a racially offensive South African word brought to Australia by migrants from that country, and here softened and given a range of different applications. See also **couple of lamingtons short of a CWA meeting, a**; **dipsticks**; **doughy**; **dubbo**; **gimp**; **Milo**; **moonya**; **nuffest** and **veggie**[1].
[PERTH REGION, SOUTH COAST AND SOUTHERN TABLELANDS, TASMANIA]

munya going crazy; over-excited. [FAR NORTH QLD, NORTH COAST QLD]

Mur'bah abbreviation of Murwillumbah (in northern New South Wales). [HUNTER VALLEY AND NORTH COAST]

Murray magpie common black-and-white bird, *Grallina cyanoleuca*, with a loud piping voice, pairs often sing in antiphonic duet; ranges across the entire mainland, absent from Tasmania. See also **magpie lark**, **mudlark** and **peewee**.
[ADELAIDE REGION, WIMMERA AND MALLEE, EYRE AND YORKE PENINSULAS]

Murray mud a drink made by pouring cola soft drink over ice-cream. [WIMMERA AND MALLEE]

Murray weed a kind of weed that began to grow in Adelaide gardens after water was piped to the area from the Murray River.
[ADELAIDE REGION]

murri Queensland Aboriginal person. [BRISBANE REGION]

Murrumbidgee sweet pea a biennial herb, *Echium plantagineum*, native to the Mediterranean area, but widely naturalised in settled parts of Australia, having blue-purple flowers. Regarded as a noxious weed. See also **blue weed**, **Lachlan lilac**, **Paterson's curse**, **Riverina bluebell** and **Salvation Jane**.
[SYDNEY REGION, HUNTER VALLEY AND NORTH COAST, NEW ENGLAND DISTRICT, THE RIVERINA, SOUTH COAST AND SOUTHERN TABLELANDS, CENTRAL WEST NSW, FAR WEST NSW]

musset hut an early type of portable classroom (possibly from the name of the designer). Sometimes referred to as "mustard huts" both from their yellow colour and as a play on "musset". See also **Bristol hut**, **demountable**, **dogbox**, **hot box**, **portable**, **pre-fab**, **relocatable**, **silver bullet**[1], **terrapin unit** and **transportable**.
[TASMANIA]

muttai sweet corn, usually still on the cob, boiled and eaten as a vegetable. (From a Tamil word from South India. Just how it ended up in Taree and the Macleay River district is unknown.)
[HUNTER VALLEY AND NORTH COAST, NEW ENGLAND DISTRICT]

mutton fish abalone. [TASMANIA]

mystery meat devon, fritz or any form of processed meat product;
or the contents of a sausage or meat pie. See also **baron sausage**,
beef Belgium, **Belgium sausage**, **bung fritz**, **Byron sausage**,
devon, **Empire sausage**, **fritz**, **German sausage**, **luncheon
sausage**, **polony**, **pork German**, **Strasburg**, **wheel meat** and
Windsor sausage. [SYDNEY REGION, HUNTER VALLEY AND NORTH COAST]

N

'Nade (pronounced nard) WA abbreviation for any hotel called "The Esplanade". Victorian hotels of this name are abbreviated to **Espi.** [PERTH REGION]

nags small containers of nitrogen dioxide (used as propellent for whipped cream) inhaled recreationally by teenagers. Also known as "nangs" and **nitros.** [PERTH REGION]

nana nap afternoon sleep. See also **kindy nap.** [NORTH COAST QLD]

nangas, the the middle of nowhere. [NEW ENGLAND DISTRICT]

nannas flabby skin under the upper arm. See also **aunty arms, bingo wings, bye-nows, good-bye muscle, piano arm, reverse biceps, ta-ta flaps, tuckshop arm** and **widow's curtain.**
[SOUTH COAST AND SOUTHERN TABLELANDS]

narki fast-running flightless bird (*Gallinula mortierii*) with dark greenish-brown plumage and conspicuous white marks on the flanks. Also known as the "Tasmanian native hen" or just "native hen". [TASMANIA]

nature strip[1] a grassed strip of land between the front yard of a home and the edge of the road. See also **berm, footpath** and **verge.**
[CENTRAL HIGHLANDS VICTORIA, GIPPSLAND, MELBOURNE REGION, NORTHERN VICTORIA, TASMANIA, WESTERN DISTRICT, WIMMERA AND MALLEE, SOUTH COAST AND SOUTHERN TABLELANDS, SYDNEY REGION, PERTH REGION]

nature strip[2] a grassed median strip between two lanes of a major road. [TASMANIA, SOUTH COAST AND SOUTHERN TABLELANDS, SYDNEY REGION]

Nedlands mother a young woman whose only ambition in life is to marry a wealthy professional man and settle down in a huge house in the Perth suburb of Nedlands. [PERTH REGION]

negs bad, horrible (short for negative). Also as "negsy".
[SYDNEY REGION]

nellie bin (or "nelly bin") a rectangular plastic bin with a lid originally intended to store ice and fish, now creatively adapted to many uses. (Perhaps originally "Nally bin" from the name of the manufacturer.) [NORTH COAST QLD]

Nerangotang a resident of the town of Nerang (south-east Queensland). [BRISBANE REGION]

neville good at school, dresses like a geek, universally disliked – short for "neville no-friends"; sometimes the longer version takes the form of "scott neville", meaning "'s got no mates, never will". See also **nigel**, **nof** and **scott**.

[SYDNEY REGION, NORTH COAST QLD, SOUTH COAST AND SOUTHERN TABLELANDS, MELBOURNE REGION]

Newey nickname for the city of Newcastle. [SYDNEY REGION]

nibble pie small meat pie (also known as a party pie).

[WESTERN DISTRICT, MELBOURNE REGION]

nickernackers kitchen tongs. Also spelled "knickernackers" and "knicker-knackers". See also **gotchas** and **snicker-snacks**.

[GIPPSLAND, MELBOURNE REGION]

Nicknock nickname for the NSW town of Cessnock. Also spelled "Nik Nok". [HUNTER VALLEY AND NORTH COAST]

nigel school slang for someone who is often seen to be alone. Also as "nigel no-friends" and "nigel no-mates". In some places "barry" has been adopted and used in place of nigel. See also **neville** and **nof**.

[SYDNEY REGION, HUNTER VALLEY AND NORTH COAST, ADELAIDE REGION, BRISBANE REGION, DARWIN AND NORTH COAST NT, SOUTH COAST AND SOUTHERN TABLELANDS, MELBOURNE REGION]

nigelate to isolate someone; to ignore them; to send them to Coventry; to treat them as a **nigel**.

[SYDNEY REGION, HUNTER VALLEY AND NORTH COAST, ADELAIDE REGION, BRISBANE REGION, DARWIN AND NORTH COAST NT, SOUTH COAST AND SOUTHERN TABLELANDS, MELBOURNE REGION]

night a period of the day deemed to begin not at sunset, but from the moment school/work ends for the day (from that moment on the rest of that day is called night.) Used in this way it makes sense to speak of having cricket practice "tomorrow night after school".

[BRISBANE REGION, WIMMERA AND MALLEE, CENTRAL HIGHLANDS VICTORIA, MELBOURNE REGION]

nikky swim swimming naked. [PERTH REGION]

nipper[1] a rouseabout in an underground mine.
[CENTRAL WEST AUSTRALIA]

nipper[2] small fishing bait. [SOUTH COAST AND SOUTHERN TABLELANDS]

nitros small containers of nitrogen dioxide (used as propellent for whipped cream) inhaled recreationally by teenagers. Also known as **nags**. [HUNTER VALLEY AND NORTH COAST]

no David Murrays no worries (rhyming slang from a well-known furniture store in Adelaide).
[ADELAIDE REGION, EYRE AND YORKE PENINSULAS, NORTHERN SOUTH AUSTRALIA]

nof acronym: "not one friend"; belonging to the same class of social misfits as a "nigel no-friends". See also **neville**, **nigel** and **scott**.
[NORTHERN VICTORIA]

nointer 1. a spoiled or difficult child. 2. a "guts"; an over-eater. (From a British dialect word for a mischievous person, one who needed a good thrashing, which in turn comes from the obsolete verb *to anoint* in the sense of "to chastise or thrash".) Sometimes pronounced as "nineter". [TASMANIA]

nonpareil small dots of coloured confectionery, otherwise known as hundreds and thousands. (From the French *nonpareil* "without equal".) [TASMANIA, ADELAIDE REGION]

noodle ("or noodling") to go through the dumps of opal mines at Coober Pedy to find missed "potch" (opal that has no play of colour and is of no value); fossicking through opal waste dumps for opals (often a tourist activity). [NORTHERN SOUTH AUSTRALIA]

noofy a mouse. See also **moompie**. [EYRE AND YORKE PENINSULAS]

Noongar an Aboriginal person of the south-west of Western Australia. Also as **Nyungah**. [PERTH REGION]

Normie a resident of the city of Newcastle.
[HUNTER VALLEY AND NORTH COAST]

Normo the Sydney suburb of Normanhurst. [SYDNEY REGION]

northern phonecard a straw or piece of cardboard inserted into the coin refund of a public telephone so as to obtain free phone calls.

(The northern component refers to Wollongong's northern suburbs, and is a product of the constant rivalry between the area north of Lake Illawarra and that south of the lake and Dapto.) [SOUTH COAST AND SOUTHERN TABLELANDS]

north island mainland Australia. See also **Australia**; **big island**; **mainland, the** and **other side, the.** [TASMANIA]

North Shore tank yet another term for a city only four-wheel drive. To be compared with (deep breath): **Balmain bulldozer**, **Bronte buggy**, **Burnside bus**, **Kenmore tractor**, **Rose Bay shopping trolley**, **Toorak tractor** and **Turramurra tractor**. [SYDNEY REGION]

nosebleed a bleeding from the nose. See also **blood nose** and **bloody nose**. (One contributor suggests that a nosebleed was a medical event while blood nose meant the result of a fight.) [SYDNEY REGION, HUNTER VALLEY AND NORTH COAST, NEW ENGLAND DISTRICT, THE RIVERINA, SOUTH COAST AND SOUTHERN TABLELANDS, CENTRAL WEST NSW, BRISBANE REGION, CENTRAL COAST QLD, NORTH COAST QLD, TASMANIA]

not EVEN! An ironic remark, used to mean that you *are* in fact doing something (or the person addressed is doing what they have just denied). A contributor explains: "The phrase is commonly used on its own as a reply to someone (to dispute what they have just said)". [NORTH COAST QLD, FAR NORTH QLD]

NT work boots a pair of thongs. See also **Chinese safety boots**, **clackers**, **getters**, **go-backs**, **jandals**, **Japanese flying boots**, **Japanese riding boots**, **Japanese safety boots**, **Jesus boots** and **pluggers.** [THE CENTRE]

nuffest 1. silly or stupid. (See also **couple of lamingtons short of a CWA meeting, a**; **dipsticks**; **doughy**; **dubbo**; **gimp**; **Milo**; **moonya**; **munted** and **veggie**[1].) 2. cool. A contributor explains the apparent contradiction thus: "its attraction is that you can say someone is 'nuff' without having to disclose what you mean. This allows you tentatively to suggest that you think a potential love match is cool but with the option of claiming that you actually meant the opposite should your companions not agree!" See also **choice** and **duck's nuts.** [DARWIN AND NORTH COAST NT]

nuff nuff an insult, although exactly what the insult means our contributors were unable to agree upon. Their suggestions included: 1. an idiot who does something stupid, but thinks they're cool. 2. an intellectually disabled person. (See also **window licker**.) 3. someone with a harelip. 4. someone on social security who has had a very tough life, possibly a drug addict. 5. a person who was poorly educated or not terribly bright. 6. a straightforward dill or idiot. (See also **banger**, **minda**, **oxygen thief**, **random** and **roo**.) So there you are – take your pick. (Do I need to add that it's an fairly offensive expression?)
[MELBOURNE REGION, WESTERN DISTRICT, SYDNEY REGION]

nuggets testicles. See also **ackers**, **coods**, **goolies** and **nurries**.
[BRISBANE REGION]

numb nuts 1. a person acting the fool. 2. someone who is clumsy or accident-prone. (See also **clumsy as a duck in a ploughed paddock** and **roo**.) 3. a term of endearment.
[PERTH REGION, SOUTH COAST AND SOUTHERN TABLELANDS, CENTRAL COAST QLD]

numpty a nonentity (a politically correct form of abuse); RAN slang. [SOUTH COAST AND SOUTHERN TABLELANDS]

Nunga an Aboriginal person of southern South Australia. The term comes from the coastal Wirangu language.
[ADELAIDE REGION, EYRE AND YORKE PENINSULAS, NORTHERN SOUTH AUSTRALIA]

nurrabunga embarrassing, dorky (especially as a verbal response to someone who has just said something embarrassing).
[THE RIVERINA]

nurries testicles. See also **ackers**, **coods**, **goolies** and **nuggets**.
[PERTH REGION]

nutbag a funny person; the clown in the group; (affectionately) a bit of an idiot. See also **nutbar**. [MELBOURNE REGION]

nutbar a funny person; the clown in the group; (affectionately) a bit of an idiot. See also **nutbag**. [MELBOURNE REGION]

nut huggers see **Speedos**. See also **ballhuggers**, **boasters**, **budgie-huggers**, **budgie-smugglers**, **cluster busters**, **cockchokers**, **cock jocks**, **codjocks**, **dick bathers**, **dick-pointers**, **dick-pokers**, **dick**

stickers, **dick togs**, **dikdaks**, **dipsticks**, **fish frighteners**, **jammers**, **Jimmy clingers**, **knobbies**, **lolly-baggers**, **lolly bags**, **meat-hangers**, **nylon disgusters**, **racers**, **racing bathers**, **scungies**[2], **sluggers**, **sluggos**, **slug huggers**, **tights**, **toolies**, **trunks** and **wog togs**.

[SOUTH COAST AND SOUTHERN TABLELANDS]

nutmeg football slang: to intentionally pass the ball through a player's legs. [ADELAIDE REGION, BRISBANE REGION, MELBOURNE REGION]

nylon disgusters see **Speedos**. See also **ballhuggers**, **boasters**, **budgie-huggers**, **budgie-smugglers**, **cluster busters**, **cockchokers**, **cock jocks**, **codjocks**, **dick bathers**, **dick-pointers**, **dick-pokers**, **dick stickers**, **dick togs**, **dikdaks**, **dipsticks**, **fish frighteners**, **jammers**, **Jimmy clingers**, **knobbies**, **lolly-baggers**, **lolly bags**, **meat-hangers**, **nut huggers**, **racers**, **racing bathers**, **scungies**[2], **sluggers**, **sluggos**, **slug huggers**, **tights**, **toolies**, **trunks** and **wog togs**. [SYDNEY REGION]

Nyungah an Aboriginal person of south-west Western Australia. Also as **Noongar**. [PERTH REGION]

O

OAF acronym: Old Adelaide Family (that is, a descendent of an early settler and, quite possibly, a snob). [ADELAIDE REGION]

Obie nickname for the Ocean Beach Hotel, Cottesloe Beach, Perth. It appears to have begun as the abbreviations OB and OBH, which were then pronounced Obie. (Said by one contributor to be very popular with visitors to Perth from rural Western Australia, whose utes often feature OB stickers on their back windows.)
[CENTRAL WEST AUSTRALIA, NORTHERN WEST AUSTRALIA, PERTH REGION]

offa off your face (on either drugs or alcohol). [TASMANIA, PERTH REGION]

off chops as drunk as a skunk. See also **chopped**, **gone to Gowings**, **maggered**, **maggoted**, **maggo** and **off your unit**. [SYDNEY REGION]

off-peak heater a type of electric room-heater containing cast-iron or terracotta bricks, permanently plugged in, which comes on at off-peak power usage times and heats the bricks which then store and release the heat until the next off-peak period. ("From the outside," writes one contributor, "it looks like an ugly filing cabinet.") Note: elsewhere "off peak" refers to a hot water supply that is heated by off-peak power.
[TASMANIA]

off your unit having consumed an injudicious quantity of either alcohol or drugs (i.e. as drunk as a skunk). See also **chopped**, **gone to Gowings**, **maggered**, **maggoted**, **maggo** and **off chops**.
[PERTH REGION]

old fella one's father. ("Not, however," warns one contributor, "to be spoken within earshot of the old fella!")
[NORTH COAST QLD, SYDNEY REGION]

old mate 1. substituted for a friend's name when referring to him in conversation. 2. form of address to a stranger.
[HUNTER VALLEY AND NORTH COAST, FAR NORTH QLD, NORTH COAST QLD]

olive leaf a fifty dollar note. See also **fiddy**, **golden drinking voucher**, **peacemaker**, **pineapple**, **Uncle David** and **yellow belly**[3].
[SYDNEY REGION]

omo someone who gets very drunk very quickly (from Omo laundry liquid: "only a third of a cup needed".) See also **cadbury** and **one pot screamer**. [SOUTH COAST AND SOUTHERN TABLELANDS]

one hand salute using one hand to wave away flies while trying to eat at a picnic or barbecue. Also known as the "Great Australian Salute". [PERTH REGION]

one pot screamer someone who gets very drunk very quickly. Note: the more common colloquialism is "two-pot screamer". See also **cadbury** and **omo**. [SYDNEY REGION]

on the barbed (or **barb**) **wire** 1. on a drinking spree (with a serious commitment to the consumption of XXXX beer). 2. drunk on XXXX beer. [BRISBANE REGION]

on the gas a night of drinking and partying. [SYDNEY REGION]

Oodnagalahby mythical remote outback town. (Belongs on the same map as **Bundiwallop**, **Kickastickalong** and **Wheelyabarraback**.) [ADELAIDE REGION]

oo-roo goodbye; farewell. See also **cheerio**, **cheery**, **hooray**, **hooroo**, **hurrah** and **soup, I'll see you in the.**

[ADELAIDE REGION, SYDNEY REGION, MELBOURNE REGION, WESTERN DISTRICT, TASMANIA, DON BURKE]

oosh acronym: Out of Hours School Care (a sort-of acronym … where the "H" comes from is not entirely clear). See also **afters** and **BASC**. [SYDNEY REGION]

orange roughie the deepwater, slow-maturing marine fish *Hoplostethus atlaticus* (orange-red in colour with pale orange fins). An important commercial fish found in the waters of Tasmania, Victoria and southern New South Wales. (The "roughie" part of the name seems to come from the fact that this fish is notoriously ugly.)

[TASMANIA, SOUTH COAST AND SOUTHERN TABLELANDS, MELBOURNE REGION]

ornamental grapevine a type of grapevine with leaves turning vivid red in autumn. See also **glory vine**.

[SYDNEY REGION, HUNTER VALLEY AND NORTH COAST, NEW ENGLAND DISTRICT, THE RIVERINA, SOUTH COAST AND SOUTHERN TABLELANDS, CENTRAL WEST NSW, BRISBANE REGION, CENTRAL COAST QLD, NORTH COAST QLD]

other side, the mainland Australia. See also **Australia**, **big island**, **the mainland** and **north island**. [TASMANIA]

othersider a person living east of the Nullarbor Plain. Sometimes as "t'othersider".

[CENTRAL WEST AUSTRALIA, NORTHERN WEST AUSTRALIA, PERTH REGION]

otto bin a large rubbish bin on wheels. See also **sulo bin** and **wheely bin**. [SYDNEY REGION, HUNTER VALLEY AND NORTH COAST, BRISBANE REGION]

out of uniform day a day on which casual clothing may be worn instead of uniforms or suits upon the payment of a small sum to a designated charity. See also **casual day**, **free dress day** and **mufti day**. [MELBOURNE REGION]

over the shoulder boulder holder jokey schoolboy label for a bra.

[MELBOURNE REGION, SYDNEY REGION]

oxford a dollar (rhyming slang: Oxford scholar). [SYDNEY REGION]

oxygen thief an idiot; a useless person; a waste of space. See also **banger**, **minda**, **nuff nuff**, **random** and **roo**.

[WEST CENTRAL QLD, PERTH REGION, SYDNEY REGION]

P

pad school writing pad or school notebook.

[BRISBANE REGION, CENTRAL COAST QLD, FAR NORTH QLD, NORTH COAST QLD, WEST CENTRAL QLD]

Paddle-pop® a frozen, flavoured confection on a stick. (A trademarked name, occasionally used as if it were a generic name.) See also **by jingo**, **iceblock** and **icy pole**.

[SYDNEY REGION, HUNTER VALLEY AND NORTH COAST, NEW ENGLAND DISTRICT, THE RIVERINA, SOUTH COAST AND SOUTHERN TABLELANDS, CENTRAL WEST NSW, BRISBANE REGION, CENTRAL COAST QLD, NORTH COAST QLD]

Paddo[1] the Sydney suburb of Paddington. [SYDNEY REGION]

Paddo[2] 1. the Brisbane suburb of Paddington. 2. the Paddington Tavern, Brisbane. [BRISBANE REGION]

paddock chicken wild rabbit.

[HUNTER VALLEY AND NORTH COAST, NEW ENGLAND DISTRICT, THE RIVERINA, SOUTH COAST AND SOUTHERN TABLELANDS, CENTRAL WEST NSW, FAR WEST NSW, CENTRAL COAST QLD, NORTH COAST QLD, FAR NORTH QLD, WEST CENTRAL QLD]

paddocks an informal type of cricket played by primary school children with bowlers at both ends taking turns to bowl. "From memory," writes one contributor, "batters were individuals from the field, not teams." [THE RIVERINA]

pale abbreviation of Coopers Pale Ale. [ADELAIDE REGION]

Palmie the Sydney suburb of Palm Beach. [SYDNEY REGION]

pang yang an improvised meal of leftovers ("Usually Sunday tea," explains a contributor, "after midday roast dinner.") [TASMANIA]

pan licker dog. See also **dishlicker**. [SYDNEY REGION]

panno a panel van. [SYDNEY REGION]

parade an assembly of everyone in the school; in some schools weekly, in others daily. Commonly held outdoors. See also **assembly**. [BRISBANE REGION]

pares parents. [MELBOURNE REGION]

parkland a public garden or park. (With capitals – the Park Lands – it refers to the area of park surrounding Adelaide as part of William Light's (the city's founder) original plan.)
[ADELAIDE REGION, EYRE AND YORKE PENINSULAS, NORTHERN SOUTH AUSTRALIA]

parra[1] a non-resident invading a beach suburb. (From the western Sydney suburb of Parramatta.) [SYDNEY REGION]

Parra[2] the Sydney suburb of Parramatta. [SYDNEY REGION]

passion killers 1. small children. See also **bluetongue**[1] and **little tacker**. 2. high-waisted (unglamorous) women's underpants.
[PERTH REGION]

Paterson's curse a biennial herb, *Echium plantagineum*, native to the Mediterranean area, but widely naturalised in settled parts of Australia, having blue-purple flowers. See also **Lachlan lilac**, **Murrumbidgee sweet pea**, **Riverina bluebell** and **Salvation Jane**.
[SYDNEY REGION, HUNTER VALLEY AND NORTH COAST, NEW ENGLAND DISTRICT, THE RIVERINA, SOUTH COAST AND SOUTHERN TABLELANDS, CENTRAL WEST NSW, FAR WEST NSW, WIMMERA AND MALLEE, CENTRAL HIGHLANDS VICTORIA, WESTERN DISTRICT, NORTHERN VICTORIA, GIPPSLAND, MELBOURNE REGION, TASMANIA, PERTH REGION]

pay doughnuts, it will a poor financial return; a fruitless endeavour; a bad investment; a dividend of $0:0. [PERTH REGION]

peacemaker a fifty dollar note. See also **fiddy**, **golden drinking voucher**, **olive leaf**, **pineapple**, **Uncle David** and **yellow belly**[3].
[SYDNEY REGION]

peachy 1. the quandong (or wild peach). 2. a boys' game (played with quandong seeds threaded on string – the object being to smash the opponent's quandong or "bullie"); also known as **bullies**. [FAR WEST NSW, THE RIVERINA, NORTHERN SOUTH AUSTRALIA]

peanut butter a paste made from finely ground roasted peanuts, used as a spread etc. See also **peanut paste**.
[BRISBANE REGION, SYDNEY REGION, HUNTER VALLEY AND NORTH COAST, NEW ENGLAND DISTRICT, THE RIVERINA, SOUTH COAST AND SOUTHERN TABLELANDS, CENTRAL WEST NSW, FAR WEST NSW, WIMMERA AND MALLEE, CENTRAL HIGHLANDS VICTORIA, WESTERN DISTRICT, NORTHERN VICTORIA, GIPPSLAND, MELBOURNE REGION, TASMANIA, ADELAIDE REGION, EYRE AND YORKE PENINSULAS]

peanut country the red earth around Kingaroy, Queensland (a peanut-producing area). [BRISBANE REGION]

peanut paste a smooth paste made from finely ground roasted peanuts, used as a spread etc. Some contributors suggested that at one time there may have been (in some states) a ban on the use of "butter" as a label for non-dairy products, while others suggested peanut paste is the Australian name and peanut butter the American one. See also **peanut butter**.

[BRISBANE REGION, CENTRAL COAST QLD, NORTH COAST QLD, FAR NORTH QLD, WEST CENTRAL QLD, ADELAIDE REGION, WIMMERA AND MALLEE, EYRE AND YORKE PENINSULAS, PERTH REGION, CENTRAL WEST AUSTRALIA]

peewee a common black-and-white bird, *Grallina cyanoleuca*, with a loud piping voice; pairs often sing in antiphonic duet; ranges across the entire mainland; absent from Tasmania. See also **magpie lark**, **mudlark** and **Murray magpie**.

[SYDNEY REGION, BRISBANE REGION, CENTRAL WEST NSW]

peg to throw (a ball, stone etc.)

[HUNTER VALLEY AND NORTH COAST, SYDNEY REGION, BRISBANE REGION]

peg leg a type of "bomb" dive into a swimming pool. (You want to try it? Here are the operating instructions: jump into the water with one leg tucked under your arms, up towards your chest, the other extended straight out. You will now be banned from the municipal pool for the rest of the season.) See also **banana**, **can-opener** and **horsey**. [HUNTER VALLEY AND NORTH COAST]

pelican pick a digging implement with one pointed end and one round end used for difficult areas that are too hard for machinery to reach. (Mining slang.) [CENTRAL WEST AUSTRALIA]

Pendo the Sydney suburb of Pendle Hill. [SYDNEY REGION]

Penno the Sydney suburb of Pennant Hills. [SYDNEY REGION]

people's palace a tight pair of pants. (From the name of the Salvation Army's hostels.) [BRISBANE REGION]

phernudge to overstep the mark when shooting at a children's game of marbles; to creep over the agreed mark when playing a shot. Sometimes as "fnudge" or **fudge**. See also **cribbing**, **cribs** and **duck-shove**. [MELBOURNE REGION, TASMANIA]

phlegm cake vanilla slice. See also **pus pie**, **snot-block** and **wet Nellie**. [HUNTER VALLEY AND NORTH COAST, PERTH REGION]

physsie abbreviation of "physical culture" (a regimented exercise program). [SOUTH COAST AND SOUTHERN TABLELANDS, SYDNEY REGION]

piano arms the flabby triceps area of an overweight woman's upper arms. See also **aunty arms**, **bingo wings**, **bye-nows**, **good-bye muscle**, **nannas**, **reverse biceps**, **ta-ta flaps**, **tuckshop arm** and **widow's curtain**. [SYDNEY REGION]

pie cart where you buy a **pie floater**. [ADELAIDE REGION]

piece a sandwich. (Some contributors remark on how puzzling this usage is in those regions where it is uncommon or unknown, while others suggest it may be of Scottish origin.) See also **sambo**, **sanga** and **schnitter**.
[WESTERN DISTRICT, FAR WEST NSW, ADELAIDE REGION, PERTH REGION, MELBOURNE REGION]

piecey a piece of bread, normally half a sandwich; a expression used (most commonly) when addressing small children.
[MELBOURNE REGION]

pie floater a hot meat pie served upside down on pea soup, with a generous dollop of tomato sauce. (If you're looking for a pie floater you could try the **pie cart** outside the railway station, North Terrace, Adelaide.) [ADELAIDE REGION]

piff to throw (a ball, stone etc.).
[MELBOURNE REGION, NORTHERN SOUTH AUSTRALIA, NORTHERN VICTORIA, GIPPSLAND]

pigeon a derogatory term used to indicate a weak or useless person (Australian army slang). [NORTHERN VICTORIA]

piggin', **goin'** going out to catch a wild pig with a dog and a knife.
[FAR WEST NSW]

piggy (or "piggy spider") a harmless insect; the segmented wood lice with many small legs that curls up into an armoured sphere; a slater. [TASMANIA, SYDNEY REGION]

Pilliga yowie a wild, hairy creature surviving (in small numbers) in the most remote parts of Australia. According to some scientists it

shares DNA with such legendary creatures as the "drop bear" and the "hoop snake". Others, however, claim it is more closely related to the bunyip. The debate continues. See also **Binjour bear**.
[CENTRAL WEST NSW]

pilling under the influence of drugs consumed as pills. [PERTH REGION]

pimply squash a member of the gourd family with thick skin covered in small bumps. [HUNTER VALLEY AND NORTH COAST]

pinch a hill; a steep rise.
[SYDNEY REGION, NORTHERN VICTORIA, WESTERN DISTRICT, NEW ENGLAND DISTRICT]

pineapple a fifty dollar note. See also **fiddy**, **golden drinking voucher**, **olive leaf**, **peacemaker**, **Uncle David** and **yellow belly**[3].
[WESTERN DISTRICT, ADELAIDE REGION, SYDNEY REGION]

piner a timber-getter employed in the Huon pine trade. [TASMANIA]

piner's punt a type of boat used by **piners** when transporting logs down a river (the logs are floated, they are not carried in the boat). [TASMANIA]

pink-eyed salmon alternative name for Barramundi, especially used when the barramundi season is closed. [NORTH COAST QLD]

pinkie[1] the lesser bilby. (From the Kaurna Aboriginal language.)
[ADELAIDE REGION, EYRE AND YORKE PENINSULAS, NORTHERN SOUTH AUSTRALIA]

pinkie[2] a parking ticket.
[CENTRAL HIGHLANDS VICTORIA, GIPPSLAND, MELBOURNE REGION, NORTHERN VICTORIA, WESTERN DISTRICT, WIMMERA AND MALLEE]

Pink Lady voluntary helper in a hospital (from the colour of their uniforms). [SYDNEY REGION]

pink lamington lamington-style cake which is pink, rather than chocolate, in colour. Here's the recipe: take a plain sponge cake, cut it into cubes, dip these in pink almost-set jelly, split them in half, re-join them with fresh cream and cover them with desiccated coconut. Also called **jelly cakes**. Originally lamingtons (both the pink and the chocolate varieties) were made from stale cake, as a way of finding a use for old cake. However, this tends to make very dry lamingtons and is not recommended. It's perfectly alright to make your lamingtons with fresh cake. (I'm glad we cleared that up.) [SYDNEY REGION]

pink nipper a yabby-like estuarine crustacean. See also **cherub**, **clawchie**, **crawbob**, **crawchie**, **craybob**, **craydab**, **crayfish**, **jilgie**, **lobby**, **lobster**, **marron** and **yabby**.

[BRISBANE REGION, CENTRAL COAST QLD, NORTH COAST QLD, FAR NORTH QLD, WEST CENTRAL QLD]

pipe loaf a loaf of bread baked in a round corrugated tin so that the finished loaf has the shape of a piece of corrugated pipe. See also **tank loaf**.

[MELBOURNE REGION, ADELAIDE REGION, NORTHERN SOUTH AUSTRALIA, SYDNEY REGION]

pipi a mollusc found on surf beaches along the Australian coast. Dug up by fishermen for bait. Pipi is from a Maori source word. See also **cockle**, **eugarie** and **wong**.

[BRISBANE REGION, MELBOURNE REGION, SOUTH COAST AND SOUTHERN TABLELANDS, SYDNEY REGION, HUNTER VALLEY AND NORTH COAST]

piping shrike the Australian magpie.

[EYRE AND YORKE PENINSULAS, ADELAIDE REGION, NORTHERN SOUTH AUSTRALIA]

pisling a sound defeat; well and truly beaten. See also **pizzling**.

[WEST CENTRAL QLD]

pisswhacker a type of cicada that urinates on your hand when held. See also **black prince**, **brown baker**, **brown bomber**[2], **cicada**, **cherrynose**, **floury baker**, **greengrocer**[2], **tick tock** and **yellow Monday**. [SYDNEY REGION]

Pitt Street, as busy as run off your feet; no time to catch your breath; flat out like a lizard drinking. [SYDNEY REGION]

Pitt Street farmer an owner of a country property (often held for tax loss purposes) who lives and works in Sydney. See also **Collins Street cocky** and **Queen Street bushie**.

[SYDNEY REGION, HUNTER VALLEY AND NORTH COAST, NEW ENGLAND DISTRICT, THE RIVERINA, SOUTH COAST AND SOUTHERN TABLELANDS, CENTRAL WEST NSW, FAR WEST NSW]

Pitt Street skier a wealthy business type who travels to the snowfields regularly with the best, the latest and the most

expensive clothing and equipment – and who then spends the weekend drinking *gluhwein* near the fireplace.
[SOUTH COAST AND SOUTHERN TABLELANDS]

pivot head a tourist (surveying the scenery as if their head rotated on a pivot). [CENTRAL HIGHLANDS VICTORIA]

Pizza Hut Abel Smith Lecture Theatre at the University of Queensland. [BRISBANE REGION, SYDNEY REGION]

pizzling a sound defeat; well and truly beaten. See also **pisling**.
[NORTHERN SOUTH AUSTRALIA]

Plains, The nickname given to the Sydney metropolitan area by residents of the Blue Mountains. [SYDNEY REGION]

plains people nickname given by residents of the Blue Mountains to Sydneysiders who live between the foothills and the coast. Contrasts with **mountain people.** [SYDNEY REGION]

playground duty the rostered time a teacher spends supervising students in a school playground. See also **yard duty**.
[TASMANIA, SYDNEY REGION, HUNTER VALLEY AND NORTH COAST, NEW ENGLAND DISTRICT, THE RIVERINA, SOUTH COAST AND SOUTHERN TABLELANDS, CENTRAL WEST NSW, BRISBANE REGION, CENTRAL COAST QLD, NORTH COAST QLD, PERTH REGION]

play lunch 1. the mid-morning break in primary school. 2. a snack eaten then. See also **elevener, elevenses, levna, little lunch, little play**, **morning lunch**, **morning play**, **playtime**, **recess** and **snack**.
[SYDNEY REGION, HUNTER VALLEY AND NORTH COAST, NEW ENGLAND DISTRICT, THE RIVERINA, SOUTH COAST AND SOUTHERN TABLELANDS, CENTRAL WEST NSW, FAR WEST NSW, WIMMERA AND MALLEE, CENTRAL HIGHLANDS VICTORIA, WESTERN DISTRICT, NORTHERN VICTORIA, GIPPSLAND, MELBOURNE REGION, TASMANIA, PERTH REGION]

play shed a shed on school grounds, usually open on one side (and separate from the classrooms), in which children could play in wet weather. See also **lunch shed**, **shelter shed** and **weather shed**.
[BRISBANE REGION, CENTRAL COAST QLD, NORTH COAST QLD, FAR NORTH QLD, WEST CENTRAL QLD]

playtime mid-morning recess in primary schools. See also **elevener, elevenses, levna, little lunch, little play, morning lunch**, **morning play**, **play lunch**, **recess** and **snack**.
[BRISBANE REGION, MELBOURNE REGION, SYDNEY REGION, FAR WEST NSW, PERTH REGION, NORTHERN VICTORIA, GIPPSLAND]

plod a work sheet. Sometimes known as "plod card". (From a Cornish dialect word, originally meaning "a short, dull story". Does that sum up work for you?)

[NORTHERN SOUTH AUSTRALIA, CENTRAL WEST AUSTRALIA, NORTHERN WEST AUSTRALIA, PERTH REGION]

pluggers a pair of thongs with only one plug under the foot to hold the footwear together (by contrast with double pluggers). See also **Chinese safety boots**, **clackers**, **getters**, **go-backs**, **jandals**, **Japanese flying boots**, **Japanese riding boots**, **Japanese safety boots**, **Jesus boots** and **NT work boots**. [BRISBANE REGION, NORTH COAST QLD]

plunge ("or plunge bath") a bath.

[ADELAIDE REGION, BRISBANE REGION, CENTRAL COAST QLD, EYRE AND YORKE PENINSULAS, FAR NORTH QLD, NORTH COAST QLD, NORTHERN SOUTH AUSTRALIA, WEST CENTRAL QLD]

pluto pup a frankfurt dipped in thick batter then deep-fried in nice, saturated fat, cholesterol-rich oil and finally dipped in tomato sauce before being served on a stick. A culinary treat. (This classic Australian dish is officially classified by the great gourmands of the world as *vieux cuisine*.) See also **battered sav**, **dagwood dog**, **death stick** and **dippy dog**.

[PERTH REGION, SOUTH COAST AND SOUTHERN TABLELANDS]

poddy cow or ("poddy calf") a young cow; a calf that's hand-fed.

[HUNTER VALLEY AND NORTH COAST, CENTRAL WEST NSW]

poddy mullet a small mullet (suitable for use as bait).

[HUNTER VALLEY AND NORTH COAST]

podge to hurry someone; to urge them along. [THE RIVERINA]

pogged the results of having overeaten (or, to use the technically precise expression, as full as a goog).

[SOUTH COAST AND SOUTHERN TABLELANDS]

poler a slacker; someone not pulling their weight; especially in a team or communal activity. (According to one contributor, the term comes from the days of the bullock teams, where the beasts yoked at the rear of the team could give the appearance of pulling hard when all they were doing was supporting the pole.)

[CENTRAL WEST AUSTRALIA]

Pollyanna a girl's hairstyle (tied up in front, the back hanging loose). See also **half-up**, **half-down** and **waterfall**.

[HUNTER VALLEY AND NORTH COAST, SYDNEY REGION]

pollywaffle untreated faecal matter in the waterways. See also **blind mullet**, **blind trout**, **Bondi cigar**, **brown trout**, **King River prawn** and **Werribee trout**. [GIPPSLAND]

polony yet another *nom de culinaire* of that large, mild-flavoured, precooked sausage (usually sliced thinly and eaten cold). See also **beef Belgium**, **Belgium sausage**, **bung fritz**, **Byron sausage**, **devon**, **Empire sausage**, **fritz**, **German sausage**, **luncheon sausage**, **mystery meat**, **pork German**, **Strasburg**, **wheel meat** and **Windsor sausage**.

[PERTH REGION, CENTRAL WEST AUSTRALIA, WIMMERA AND MALLEE]

pony a small glass of beer (approximately 140 ml). In the dim and distant past it was the size most commonly served in the Ladies' Bar. See also **butcher**, **glass**, **handle**, **middy**, **pot**, **schooner**[1], **schooner**[2] and **seven**.

[WIMMERA AND MALLEE, CENTRAL HIGHLANDS VICTORIA, WESTERN DISTRICT, NORTHERN VICTORIA, GIPPSLAND, MELBOURNE REGION, EYRE AND YORKE PENINSULAS, ADELAIDE REGION, NORTHERN SOUTH AUSTRALIA, NORTHERN WEST AUSTRALIA, CENTRAL WEST AUSTRALIA, THE RIVERINA, PERTH REGION]

poofteenth a very small amount (approximately the equivalent of a nano-unit).

[MELBOURNE REGION, PERTH REGION, NORTHERN SOUTH AUSTRALIA, NORTH COAST QLD]

pools (or "the pool") the local swimming pool. See also **baths**.

[SOUTH COAST AND SOUTHERN TABLELANDS]

Popper a fruit-flavoured drink sealed in a small box and accessed with a straw. (From a brandname that, over time, became a generic term.) In other regions referred to as a **fruit box** or **Prima**.

[BRISBANE REGION, HUNTER VALLEY AND NORTH COAST, DARWIN AND NORTH COAST NT, SOUTH COAST AND SOUTHERN TABLELANDS, SYDNEY REGION, NORTH COAST QLD, THE RIVERINA]

porcupine an echidna. [TASMANIA]

pork fritz a type of continental meat sausage. [THE RIVERINA]

pork German a large, mild-flavoured, German sausage (usually sliced thinly and eaten cold). See also **baron sausage**, **beef Belgium**, **Belgium sausage**, **bung fritz**, **Byron sausage**, **devon**, **Empire sausage**, **fritz**, **German sausage**, **luncheon sausage**, **mystery meat**, **polony**, **Strasburg**, **wheel meat** and **Windsor sausage**. [MELBOURNE REGION, TASMANIA]

port 1. a suitcase. 2. a school bag or school case. (Shortened form of *portmanteau*.) It would, in theory, be possible to draw a "port line" across a map of Australia, distinguishing those areas where "suitcase" is spoken from those where only "port" is spoken (presumably with a grey area in between, in which baggage handlers are bilingual). This usage seems to have begun in Queensland and then, like the cane toad, spread more widely.

[BRISBANE REGION, CENTRAL COAST QLD, CENTRAL WEST NSW, FAR WEST NSW, HUNTER VALLEY AND NORTH COAST, NEW ENGLAND DISTRICT, NORTH COAST QLD, SOUTH COAST AND SOUTHERN TABLELANDS, THE RIVERINA, SYDNEY REGION]

Port contraction of any placename beginning with "Port", e.g. Port Macquarie, Port Adelaide, Port Hacking etc.

[SOUTH COAST AND SOUTHERN TABLELANDS, ADELAIDE REGION, SYDNEY REGION, HUNTER VALLEY AND NORTH COAST]

portable a school building consisting of one or two classrooms which can be removed from its foundations and relocated. See also **Bristol hut**, **demountable**, **dogbox**, **hot box**, **musset hut**, **pre-fab**, **relocatable**, **silver bullet**[1], **terrapin unit** and **transportable**.

[ADELAIDE REGION, CENTRAL HIGHLANDS VICTORIA, GIPPSLAND, MELBOURNE REGION, NORTHERN VICTORIA, TASMANIA, WESTERN DISTRICT, WIMMERA AND MALLEE, SYDNEY REGION]

port cart (obsolete) a light horse-drawn vehicle which once carried passengers between Adelaide and Port Adelaide.

[EYRE AND YORKE PENINSULAS, ADELAIDE REGION, NORTHERN SOUTH AUSTRALIA]

Port Melbourne piers rhyming slang: ears. Like all rhyming slang this is often abbreviated to just the first part of the expression as "Port Melbourne's" or just "Ports".

[CENTRAL HIGHLANDS VICTORIA, GIPPSLAND, MELBOURNE REGION, NORTHERN VICTORIA, WESTERN DISTRICT, WIMMERA AND MALLEE]

port rack a low shelf where schoolchildren store their **ports**.

[BRISBANE REGION, NORTH COAST QLD, WEST CENTRAL QLD]

possum knocker small rounded cakes/scones. (One contributor suggests that perhaps the term originally described cakes/scones that came out of the oven as hard as rocks.) [BRISBANE REGION]

pot a medium-sized glass of beer (approximately 285 ml). See also **butcher, glass, handle, middy, pony, schooner**[1], **schooner**[2] and **seven.**

[WIMMERA AND MALLEE, CENTRAL HIGHLANDS VICTORIA, WESTERN DISTRICT, NORTHERN VICTORIA, GIPPSLAND, MELBOURNE REGION, BRISBANE REGION, CENTRAL COAST QLD, NORTH COAST QLD, FAR NORTH QLD, WEST CENTRAL QLD, DARWIN AND NORTH COAST NT, THE CENTRE, NORTHERN WEST AUSTRALIA, CENTRAL WEST AUSTRALIA, PERTH REGION]

potato cake a thin slice of potato dipped in batter and deep-fried. This popular Australian comestible travels under a number of different aliases, including **potato fritter, potato scallop** and **scallop.**

[ADELAIDE REGION, CENTRAL HIGHLANDS VICTORIA, EYRE AND YORKE PENINSULAS, GIPPSLAND, MELBOURNE REGION, NORTHERN VICTORIA, TASMANIA, WESTERN DISTRICT, WIMMERA AND MALLEE, SYDNEY REGION]

potato flakes (now obsolete) name once used for potato crisps or chips. [BRISBANE REGION]

potato fritter the same thin slice of potato dipped in batter and deep fried. See also **potato cake, potato scallop** and **scallop.**

[TASMANIA, EYRE AND YORKE PENINSULAS, ADELAIDE REGION, NORTHERN SOUTH AUSTRALIA]

potato scallop our old friend the thin slice of potato dipped in batter and deep-fried (preferably eaten very hot on a cold winter's day with plenty of salt – thus pushing the blood pressure up just as the arteries are shutting down). See also **potato cake, potato fritter** and **scallop.**

[PERTH REGION, SYDNEY REGION, BRISBANE REGION, SOUTH COAST AND SOUTHERN TABLELANDS]

pov untrendy, cheap and nasty. (Abbreviation of "poverty stricken", it appears to have begun life as a derogatory term for an economically disadvantaged person.) Also called "povo".

[ADELAIDE REGION, NEW ENGLAND DISTRICT, BRISBANE REGION, SYDNEY REGION, THE RIVERINA, MELBOURNE REGION]

prairie oyster the discarded testicle of a castrated bull calf. These were invariably fed to the dogs, but visitors were often threatened with "prairie oysters in garlic butter for tea tonight". This is possibly an Americanisation of the Australian expression **mountain oyster**. [WEST CENTRAL QLD, NORTH COAST QLD]

pre-fab a portable classroom. See also **Bristol hut**, **demountable**, **dogbox**, **hot box**, **musset hut**, **portable**, **relocatable**, **silver bullet**[1], **terrapin unit** and **transportable**.
[EYRE AND YORKE PENINSULAS, ADELAIDE REGION, NORTHERN SOUTH AUSTRALIA, NORTHERN VICTORIA]

pregnant pastie a Volkswagen beetle. [ADELAIDE REGION]

preliminary historically significant term referring to land transactions made in England by pioneer settlers before they set out for South Australia.
[ADELAIDE REGION, EYRE AND YORKE PENINSULAS, NORTHERN SOUTH AUSTRALIA]

preliminary section the land selection sold in such a **preliminary** transaction.
[EYRE AND YORKE PENINSULAS, ADELAIDE REGION, NORTHERN SOUTH AUSTRALIA]

prep ("or preps") 1. a **preparatory class**. 2. a child attending a preparatory class. See also **kindergarten**, **reception class** and **transition**.
[CENTRAL HIGHLANDS VICTORIA, GIPPSLAND, MELBOURNE REGION, NORTHERN VICTORIA, WESTERN DISTRICT, WIMMERA AND MALLEE, TASMANIA]

preparatory class the first year in primary school. (Once common in Queensland, but now obsolete in that state.) See also **kindergarten**, **reception class** and **transition**.
[BRISBANE REGION, CENTRAL COAST QLD, NORTH COAST QLD, FAR NORTH QLD, WEST CENTRAL QLD, WIMMERA AND MALLEE, CENTRAL HIGHLANDS VICTORIA, WESTERN DISTRICT, NORTHERN VICTORIA, GIPPSLAND, MELBOURNE REGION, TASMANIA]

pre-primary the year during which five-year-olds attend school part-time, preceding the first full year of primary school.
[NORTHERN WEST AUSTRALIA, CENTRAL WEST AUSTRALIA, PERTH REGION]

press button a Presbyterian. See also **cattle tick**, **metholated spirits** and **mickey drip**. [BRISBANE REGION, SYDNEY REGION]

prickle 1. any prickly burr, including a **bindi-eye** (or **jo-jo**) and **double-gee** (or **three-corner jack**). [PERTH REGION] 2. (specifically) the bindi-eye (as opposed to a double-gee). [PERTH REGION, MELBOURNE REGION, FAR WEST NSW, BRISBANE REGION]

prickle annie a species of burr. A contributor explains: "It grows on a stem a little like a wheat head (only larger) from which each seed breaks off armed with dozens of spines." [FAR WEST NSW]

prickle jack a low-growing plant with hard spiky seeds. Also known as "prickly jack".

[ADELAIDE REGION, WIMMERA AND MALLEE, EYRE AND YORKE PENINSULAS]

prill ("or prill ore") rich copper ore. (From a Cornish source word.)

[EYRE AND YORKE PENINSULAS, ADELAIDE REGION, NORTHERN SOUTH AUSTRALIA]

Prima a boxed juice drink (from a brand name that, over time, has become generic). See also **fruit box** and **Popper**. [MELBOURNE REGION]

Prisoner of War nickname of the Prince of Wales Hospital (coined by the students of the nearby University of New South Wales).

[SYDNEY REGION]

probationary licence an initial driver's licence which stipulates a restricted speed and the use of P-plates (usually for one year). In other regions called a **provisional licence**.

[EYRE AND YORKE PENINSULAS, ADELAIDE REGION, NORTHERN SOUTH AUSTRALIA, WIMMERA AND MALLEE, CENTRAL HIGHLANDS VICTORIA, WESTERN DISTRICT, NORTHERN VICTORIA, GIPPSLAND, MELBOURNE REGION, NORTHERN WEST AUSTRALIA, CENTRAL WEST AUSTRALIA, PERTH REGION]

problem solvered a problem has been fixed (from an advertising slogan for Solver Paint). [ADELAIDE REGION]

provisional licence an initial driver's licence which stipulates a restricted speed and the use of P-plates (usually for one year). In other regions called a **probationary licence**.

[SOUTH COAST AND SOUTHERN TABLELANDS, SYDNEY REGION, HUNTER VALLEY AND NORTH COAST, NEW ENGLAND DISTRICT, THE RIVERINA, CENTRAL WEST NSW, FAR WEST NSW, DARWIN AND NORTH COAST NT, THE CENTRE, BRISBANE REGION, CENTRAL COAST QLD, NORTH COAST QLD, FAR NORTH QLD, WEST CENTRAL QLD, TASMANIA]

pug 1. to convey a second person on a horse, bicycle or motorcycle. 2. a ride obtained from being pugged. See **bar**², **dink**, **dinky**¹, **dinky-double**, **donkey**¹, **double** and **dub**.

[ADELAIDE REGION, WIMMERA AND MALLEE, EYRE AND YORKE PENINSULAS]

pughole 1. a hole in a dried-up watercourse, especially one in which rubbish collects. 2. a deep clay pit, once used in brick-making, now surrounded by urban development and used as a landfill site (often developed as parkland when filled).

[ADELAIDE REGION, EYRE AND YORKE PENINSULAS, WIMMERA AND MALLEE]

punch buggy a children's game in which the first child in a group to see a passing VW beetle would shout "punch buggy" and punch the others on the upper arm. [BRISBANE REGION, SYDNEY REGION]

pusher a light, collapsible chair on wheels for small children. (Abbreviation of "push chair".) Another name for a **stroller**.

[ADELAIDE REGION, CENTRAL HIGHLANDS VICTORIA, EYRE AND YORKE PENINSULAS, GIPPSLAND, MELBOURNE REGION, NORTHERN VICTORIA, PERTH REGION, TASMANIA, WESTERN DISTRICT, WIMMERA AND MALLEE]

pushie a pushbike.

[MELBOURNE REGION, CENTRAL COAST QLD, WEST CENTRAL QLD, BRISBANE REGION, NORTHERN VICTORIA]

pus pie (or "pus cake") 1. a vanilla slice. (See also **snot-block**.) [MELBOURNE REGION] 2. a custard tart. [BRISBANE REGION, MELBOURNE REGION, SYDNEY REGION]

pussy-in-the-corner a children's game played in a school **shelter shed**. The "in" group occupy the corners of the shed while the "out" group roams free. The object of the game is for pairs of "in" players to swap corners without losing their place to one of the "out" players. (The call between "in" players to attempt a corner swap is a whispered "pussy, pussy".) [CENTRAL HIGHLANDS VICTORIA]

Q

QG a Queensland government car (from the QG letters on their number plates). See also **red plate** and **Z car**.

[BRISBANE REGION, CENTRAL COAST QLD, FAR NORTH QLD, NORTH COAST QLD, WEST CENTRAL QLD]

quadrangle the bitumen area of the school grounds, normally surrounded by classroom buildings, and usually the place where the whole school assembles. See also **hard-play**.

[BRISBANE REGION, PERTH REGION, TASMANIA, NORTHERN SOUTH AUSTRALIA, ADELAIDE REGION, SOUTH COAST AND SOUTHERN TABLELANDS, SYDNEY REGION, GIPPSLAND]

Queenslander a old, highset weatherboard house surrounded by verandas. (Authentic examples can date back to the 1800s but nowadays the term is sometimes applied loosely to any older house that is up on stumps.) [NORTH COAST QLD]

Queensland nut macadamia nut. See also **bopple** and **macca**.

[BRISBANE REGION, CENTRAL COAST QLD, FAR NORTH QLD, NORTH COAST QLD, WEST CENTRAL QLD, NEW ENGLAND DISTRICT, HUNTER VALLEY AND NORTH COAST]

Queen Street bushie (alternative "Queen Street cocky" or "Queen Street cowboy") owner of a country property (often held for tax loss purposes) who lives and works in Brisbane (Queen Street being a major Brisbane thoroughfare). See also **Collins Street cocky** and **Pitt Street farmer**.

[BRISBANE REGION, CENTRAL COAST QLD, NORTH COAST QLD, FAR NORTH QLD, WEST CENTRAL QLD]

Queen Street ringer someone who dresses in ringer's clothes (moleskins, elastic-sided boots etc.) but couldn't shear sheep or muster cattle to save his life.

[WEST CENTRAL QLD]

quiz night a trivia quiz night held in a public place to raise money for charity.

[PERTH REGION, EYRE AND YORKE PENINSULAS, NORTHERN SOUTH AUSTRALIA, ADELAIDE REGION]

quokka soccer a (usually joking) threat to treat the cute quokkas of Rottnest Island as soccer balls. [PERTH REGION]

R

racehorse[1] a sand goanna.

racehorse[2] a very thin cigarette. See also **bulyu**, **bunger**, **busta**, **dar** and **darb**. [WEST CENTRAL QLD, SYDNEY REGION]

racers see **Speedos**. See also **ballhuggers**, **boasters**, **budgie-huggers**, **budgie-smugglers**, **cluster busters**, **cockchokers**, **cock jocks**, **codjocks**, **dick bathers**, **dick-pointers**, **dick-pokers**, **dick stickers**, **dick togs**, **dikdaks**, **dipsticks**, **fish frighteners**, **jammers**, **Jimmy clingers**, **knobbies**, **lolly-baggers**, **lolly bags**, **meat-hangers**, **nut huggers**, **nylon disgusters**, **racing bathers**, **scungies**[2], **sluggers**, **sluggos**, **slug huggers**, **tights**, **toolies**, **trunks** and **wog togs**.
[CENTRAL WEST AUSTRALIA, NORTHERN WEST AUSTRALIA, PERTH REGION]

racing bathers see **Speedos**. See also **ballhuggers**, **boasters**, **budgie-huggers**, **budgie-smugglers**, **cluster busters**, **cockchokers**, **cock jocks**, **codjocks**, **dick bathers**, **dick-pointers**, **dick-pokers**, **dick stickers**, **dick togs**, **dikdaks**, **dipsticks**, **fish frighteners**, **jammers**, **Jimmy clingers**, **knobbies**, **lolly-baggers**, **lolly bags**, **meat-hangers**, **nut huggers**, **nylon disgusters**, **racers**, **scungies**[2], **sluggers**, **sluggos**, **slug huggers**, **tights**, **toolies**, **trunks** and **wog togs**. [PERTH REGION]

racing chook Tasmanian native hen (from its distinctive and fast style of running). See also **bush chook**[2]. [TASMANIA]

racing tadpole, got a head like a an ugliness insult. [PERTH REGION]

rah rah a fanatical Rugby Union player or supporter. [SYDNEY REGION]

rain boots rubber boots for wet weather (equivalent of the British "gumboots"). [FAR WEST NSW]

rainbow dozen a mixture of the range of Cascade beers (blue, red and green). A contributor says this expression was more common in the days when beer was predominantly bought as "tall boys" rather than stubbies. [TASMANIA]

rally jack to run at high speed into inanimate suburban objects (such as garbage bins) late at night while drunk. [BRISBANE REGION]

ralph to vomit.
[MELBOURNE REGION, ADELAIDE REGION, BRISBANE REGION, SYDNEY REGION]

ramp a set of parallel steel bars set in the road (over a shallow pit) where it passes through a fence – which vehicles can drive across but which cattle will not walk over (making a gate unnecessary). See also **cattle grate**, **cattle grid**, **cattle ramp** and **grid**[2].
[FAR WEST NSW, NEW ENGLAND DISTRICT]

random 1. a non-local or outsider. 2. an idiot. (A piece of Californian slang that has caught on in some Australian regions, and not others.) See also **banger**, **minda**, **nuff nuff**, **oxygen thief** and **roo**.
[SOUTH COAST AND SOUTHERN TABLELANDS, SYDNEY REGION, MELBOURNE REGION]

ranga a person with red hair, either male or female. Possibly from orang-utan, but (according to contributors) not intended as derogatory See also **blood nut** and **copper-top**. [PERTH REGION]

rantan, to go on the to cut loose; to act wildly. [SYDNEY REGION]

ratter someone who enters your opal claim or mine to steal opal.
[FAR WEST NSW]

razzle the RSL. See also **rissole**. [CENTRAL WEST NSW]

reception class the first year in primary school. See also **kindergarten**, **preparatory class** and **transition**.
[ADELAIDE REGION, EYRE AND YORKE PENINSULAS, NORTHERN SOUTH AUSTRALIA]

recess 1. the mid-morning break in primary or high school. 2. a snack eaten then. See also **elevener**, **elevenses**, **levna**, **little lunch**, **little play**, **morning lunch**, **morning play**, **play lunch**, **playtime** and **snack**.
[DARWIN AND NORTH COAST NT, ADELAIDE REGION, CENTRAL HIGHLANDS VICTORIA, CENTRAL WEST NSW, EYRE AND YORKE PENINSULAS, FAR WEST NSW, GIPPSLAND, HUNTER VALLEY AND NORTH COAST, MELBOURNE REGION, NEW ENGLAND DISTRICT, NORTHERN VICTORIA, PERTH REGION, SOUTH COAST AND SOUTHERN TABLELANDS, SYDNEY REGION, TASMANIA, THE RIVERINA, WESTERN DISTRICT, WIMMERA AND MALLEE, PERTH REGION]

record a publication sold at football matches (containing information on the current round of footy). See also **budget**.
[MELBOURNE REGION, TASMANIA]

red back a twenty dollar note. See also **cray**[2], **crayfish**[2], **lobster**[3] and **rock lobster.** [WESTERN DISTRICT, SYDNEY REGION, BRISBANE REGION]

red can a can of Melbourne Bitter beer. See also **blue can**, **can of red**, **green can**, **white can** and **yellow can.**
[DARWIN AND NORTH COAST NT, MELBOURNE REGION]

redders tomato sauce. See also **train smash.**
[SOUTH COAST AND SOUTHERN TABLELANDS]

red handbag a cask of red wine. See also **bag of death**, **Balga handbag**, **Bellambi handbag**, **boxie**, **box monster**, **Broadmeadows briefcase**, **cardboard handbag**, **Coraki handbag**, **death bag**, **Dubbo handbag**, **gin's handbag**, **goon**, **goonbag**, **goonbox**, **goonie**, **goonsack**, **lady in the boat**, **sack** and **vino collapso.** [TASMANIA]

red hen (obsolete) railcars which once operated on the Adelaide suburban rail service (as distinct from **blue birds**, which operated long distance country services). See also **Barwell's bull** and **Brill car.** [ADELAIDE REGION]

red myrtle boiled corned beef. [TASMANIA]

rednut red-haired person. See also **blood nut** and **ranga.**
[SOUTH COAST AND SOUTHERN TABLELANDS]

red plate a Victorian government car (from the colour of their number plates). See also **QG** and **Z car.**
[MELBOURNE REGION, WIMMERA AND MALLEE, CENTRAL HIGHLANDS VICTORIA, WESTERN DISTRICT, NORTHERN VICTORIA, GIPPSLAND]

red rattler older suburban railway carriages (burgundy red in colour) not noted for their passenger comfort. They were draughty, noisy and (lacking automatically closing doors) they flew along with doors wide open (and schoolboys hanging out in the breeze). See also **blue rattler** and **silver rattler.**
[SYDNEY REGION, HUNTER VALLEY AND NORTH COAST, NEW ENGLAND DISTRICT, THE RIVERINA, SOUTH COAST AND SOUTHERN TABLELANDS, CENTRAL WEST NSW, FAR WEST NSW, WIMMERA AND MALLEE, CENTRAL HIGHLANDS VICTORIA, WESTERN DISTRICT, NORTHERN VICTORIA, GIPPSLAND, MELBOURNE REGION]

red rover a schoolyard game in which as many children as possible would run from one side of the asphalt to the other, trying to avoid being caught by whoever was "in". See also **British bulldog**, **bullrush** and **cockylora**.

[SYDNEY REGION, BRISBANE REGION, ADELAIDE REGION, WEST CENTRAL QLD, CENTRAL COAST QLD, PERTH REGION, TASMANIA, MELBOURNE REGION, FAR WEST NSW, HUNTER VALLEY AND NORTH COAST]

reefer jacket sports jacket (usually dark blue) with silver buttons. See also **Bermuda jacket**.

[MELBOURNE REGION, WIMMERA AND MALLEE, CENTRAL HIGHLANDS VICTORIA, WESTERN DISTRICT, NORTHERN VICTORIA, GIPPSLAND]

ref canteen or tuck shop (short for "refectory"). See **canteen**, **refec** and **tuck shop**. [TASMANIA, PERTH REGION]

refec canteen, bistro, hot food shop (short for "refectory"). See also **canteen**, **ref** and **tuck shop**.

[BRISBANE REGION, NORTH COAST QLD, SOUTH COAST AND SOUTHERN TABLELANDS, ADELAIDE REGION]

Referdex street directory. Compare **Melways** and **Gregory's**.

[BRISBANE REGION]

reg grundies or "reggies" underwear (rhyming slang for undies). See also **derps** and **underdungers**. [SYDNEY REGION, BRISBANE REGION]

relocatable a portable classroom. See also **Bristol hut**, **demountable**, **dogbox**, **hot box**, **musset hut**, **portable**, **pre-fab**, **silver bullet**[1], **terrapin unit** and **transportable**.

[MELBOURNE REGION]

revolving mallee root unruly hair (intended as an insult – but you'd worked that out, hadn't you?). See also **head like a busted sofa**. [EYRE AND YORKE PENINSULAS]

Richmond Clinic crazy as they come (the Richmond Clinic being the psychiatric ward at Lismore Base Hospital). See also **Baillie**, **crackadog**, **ward eight**, **ward twenty** and **womba**.

[HUNTER VALLEY AND NORTH COAST]

rig a big, dominant person. [SYDNEY REGION]

Ringwood Reeboks moccasins. See also **Broadmeadows wedding shoes**, **Corio work boots**, **moccas** and **Sunshine stilettos**.

[MELBOURNE REGION]

rio pie (pronounced rye-oh) a pie made from a gramma pumpkin. Also called "gramma pie". [SYDNEY REGION]

rissole RSL club. See also **razzle**. [SYDNEY REGION]

Riverina bluebell 1. a biennial herb, *Echium plantagineum*, native to the Mediterranean area, but widely naturalised in settled parts of Australia, having blue-purple flowers. See also **blue weed**, **Lachlan lilac**, **Murrumbidgee sweet pea**, **Paterson's curse** and **Salvation Jane**. 2. ladies of the Riverina who are Councillors of the Federation of Parents and Citizens Associations of New South Wales.

[SYDNEY REGION, HUNTER VALLEY AND NORTH COAST, NEW ENGLAND DISTRICT, THE RIVERINA, SOUTH COAST AND SOUTHERN TABLELANDS, CENTRAL WEST NSW, FAR WEST NSW]

rivulet a creek (used in official placenames from the early years of settlement in Tasmania). [TASMANIA]

roadie[1] a drink you consume in the car on the way home (usually a can/stubbie of beer).

[CENTRAL HIGHLANDS VICTORIA, GIPPSLAND, NORTHERN VICTORIA, WESTERN DISTRICT, WIMMERA AND MALLEE, MELBOURNE REGION, NORTHERN SOUTH AUSTRALIA, EYRE AND YORKE PENINSULAS, ADELAIDE REGION, PERTH REGION, BRISBANE REGION, CENTRAL COAST QLD, NORTH COAST QLD, FAR NORTH QLD, WEST CENTRAL QLD, SYDNEY REGION, NORTHERN WEST AUSTRALIA, CENTRAL WEST AUSTRALIA, PERTH REGION, SOUTH COAST AND SOUTHERN TABLELANDS]

roadie[2] the last drink you consume at the bar before heading for home. [SYDNEY REGION]

road maps bloodshot eyes. [THE RIVERINA]

robber the fluffy airborne seeds of various plants, such as the moth plant or Scotch thistle. See also **fairy**, **Father Christmas**, **Santa Claus** and **wish**.

[CENTRAL HIGHLANDS VICTORIA, GIPPSLAND, MELBOURNE REGION, NORTHERN VICTORIA, TASMANIA, WESTERN DISTRICT, WIMMERA AND MALLEE]

robber crab a person born on Christmas Island. [PERTH REGION]

rock and roll rhyming slang: the dole. [BRISBANE REGION]

rock ape now dated school slang implying lack of class or style in dress and a lack of sophistication in manners. [MELBOURNE REGION]

rock box a portable radio or CD player. (Perhaps the Australian equivalent of the American "boom box".)

[SYDNEY REGION, DARWIN AND NORTH COAST NT, NORTH COAST QLD]

rock doctor geologist. See also **geo**. [PERTH REGION]

rock lobster a twenty dollar note. See also **cray**², **crayfish**², **lobster**³ and **red back**. [BRISBANE REGION]

rockmelon the edible fruit of the melon *Cucumis melo* var. *cantalupensis*, having a hard, usually ribbed and netted rind, and orange-coloured flesh. For the full story see **cantaloupe**.

[SYDNEY REGION, HUNTER VALLEY AND NORTH COAST, NEW ENGLAND DISTRICT, THE RIVERINA, SOUTH COAST AND SOUTHERN TABLELANDS, CENTRAL WEST NSW, FAR WEST NSW, BRISBANE REGION, CENTRAL COAST QLD, NORTH COAST QLD, FAR NORTH QLD, WEST CENTRAL QLD, DARWIN AND NORTH COAST NT, THE CENTRE, NORTHERN WEST AUSTRALIA, CENTRAL WEST AUSTRALIA, PERTH REGION, TASMANIA, EYRE AND YORKE PENINSULAS, ADELAIDE REGION, NORTHERN SOUTH AUSTRALIA]

Rock Vegas nickname for Rockhampton. (Brisbane has been given the same treatment to become **Bris-Vegas**.) See also **Rocky**.

[BRISBANE REGION, NORTH COAST QLD]

Rocky nickname for Rockhampton. See also **Rock Vegas**.

[CENTRAL COAST QLD]

Roman sandals leather sandals with brown crisscross straps. Also known as **JCs**. [SOUTH COAST AND SOUTHERN TABLELANDS, SYDNEY REGION]

ronnie a stone or pebble. See also **boondie**², **brinnie**, **connie**², **gibber**, **gonnie**, **goolie** and **yonnie**.

[ADELAIDE REGION, WIMMERA AND MALLEE, EYRE AND YORKE PENINSULAS]

roo an idiot, fool or clumsy person. Mostly used on cattle stations. (Possibly from the old saying, "He's got kangaroos in his top paddock".) See also **banger**, **clumsy as a duck in a ploughed paddock**, **minda**, **nuff nuff**, **oxygen thief** and **random**.

[CENTRAL WEST AUSTRALIA]

roo bar heavy metal protection on the front of a car. See also **bull bar**. [PERTH REGION]

Rose Bay shopping trolley top-of-the-line four-wheel drive vehicles that have never seen a dirt road. See also **Balmain bulldozer**,

Bronte buggy, **Burnside bus**, **Kenmore tractor**, **North Shore tank**, **Toorak tractor** and **Turramurra tractor**. [SYDNEY REGION]

Rotto nickname for Rottnest Island. [PERTH REGION]

round a round of sandwiches is one sandwich. This is the expression used when placing a sandwich order in these regions, as in: "a round of ham and tomato, please".
[PERTH REGION, BRISBANE REGION]

rubbernut a dill, drongo, drip or boofhead (derogatory) Sometimes abbreviated to "rubber". See also **drap sack** and **woppett**.
[BRISBANE REGION]

rubber undercarriage footwear: your basic rubber thong.
[SYDNEY REGION]

rubbish bin a container for the disposal of household waste. Elsewhere this becomes **dirt bin** or **garbage bin**. However, in some regions all of these terms are known and used interchangeably. See also **dirt bin** and **garbage bin**.
[BRISBANE REGION, CENTRAL COAST QLD, NORTH COAST QLD, FAR NORTH QLD, WEST CENTRAL QLD, WIMMERA AND MALLEE, CENTRAL HIGHLANDS VICTORIA, WESTERN DISTRICT, NORTHERN VICTORIA, GIPPSLAND, MELBOURNE REGION, TASMANIA, EYRE AND YORKE PENINSULAS, ADELAIDE REGION, PERTH REGION]

rubbish collector a garbage collector. See also **bin man** and **garbo**.
[BRISBANE REGION, CENTRAL COAST QLD, NORTH COAST QLD, FAR NORTH QLD, WEST CENTRAL QLD, WIMMERA AND MALLEE, CENTRAL HIGHLANDS VICTORIA, WESTERN DISTRICT, NORTHERN VICTORIA, GIPPSLAND, MELBOURNE REGION, TASMANIA, EYRE AND YORKE PENINSULAS, ADELAIDE REGION, PERTH REGION]

rum 'un an odd person; a touch eccentric; a bit of a character. This comes from a British expression (in full "rum one") which seems to have survived in just two Australian regions. See also **cranky**.
[TASMANIA, ADELAIDE REGION]

run-away hole a contributor explains: "In the south-east of South Australia, which is limestone country with many underground caverns, there exist run-away holes – depressions in the ground that appear to be solid yet in heavy downpours run-off water floods in and drains rapidly away through the porous bottom of the hole. Very often a tree grows next to these holes."
[ADELAIDE REGION]

runners sports knickers: the pants girls wear over their knickers underneath their sport skirts. See also **bloomers**, **bum shorts** and **scungies**[1]. [BRISBANE REGION, MELBOURNE REGION, SYDNEY REGION]

rural a person living in a rural area, especially on a farm. [TASMANIA]

S

sack a cask of cheap wine. See also **bag of death**, **Balga handbag**, **Bellambi handbag**, **boxie**, **box monster**, **Broadmeadows briefcase**, **cardboard handbag**, **Coraki handbag**, **death bag**, **Dubbo handbag**, **gin's handbag**, **goon**, **goonbag**, **goonbox**, **goonie**, **goonsack**, **lady in the boat**, **red handbag** and **vino collapso**.
[HUNTER VALLEY AND NORTH COAST]

safety ramp a sharply rising side track leading off a steep roadway (used to bring a heavy vehicle to an emergency stop in the event of brake failure). See also **arrester bed.** [SYDNEY REGION]

salad dodger an obese person. [BRISBANE REGION]

saltpan a large, flat area of hard mud sometimes inundated by very high tides. [NORTH COAST QLD]

Salvation Jane a biennial herb, *Echium plantagineum*, native to the Mediterranean area but widely naturalised in settled parts of Australia, having blue-purple flowers. Also **blue weed**, **Lachlan lilac**, **Murrumbidgee sweet pea**, **Paterson's curse** and **Riverina bluebell**.
[ADELAIDE REGION, WIMMERA AND MALLEE, EYRE AND YORKE PENINSULAS, PERTH REGION, NORTHERN SOUTH AUSTRALIA]

sambo a sandwich. See also **piece**, **sanga** and **schnitter**.
[PERTH REGION, SYDNEY REGION, MELBOURNE REGION, CENTRAL WEST NSW]

sandshoe athletic shoe, running shoe. (In other regions they can be "joggers", "gym boots" or "trainers".) See also **tennis shoe**.
[PERTH REGION, FAR NORTH QLD, NORTH COAST QLD, SYDNEY REGION, ADELAIDE REGION, DARWIN AND NORTH COAST NT, THE CENTRE, THE RIVERINA, WIMMERA AND MALLEE, BRISBANE REGION, GIPPSLAND]

sandy a sand crab or blue swimmer crab. [BRISBANE REGION]

sanga a sandwich. See also **piece**, **sambo** and **schnitter**.
[PERTH REGION, NORTHERN WEST AUSTRALIA, ADELAIDE REGION, THE RIVERINA, NORTH COAST QLD, SYDNEY REGION, BRISBANE REGION]

Santa Claus the fluffy airborne seeds of various plants, such as the moth plant or Scotch thistle. See also **fairy**, **Father Christmas**, **robber** and **wish**.
[BRISBANE REGION, CENTRAL COAST QLD, CENTRAL WEST NSW, HUNTER VALLEY AND NORTH COAST, NEW ENGLAND DISTRICT, NORTH COAST QLD, SOUTH COAST AND SOUTHERN TABLELANDS, SYDNEY REGION, THE RIVERINA]

sarvey this afternoon. See also **arftie**, **arvo**[1] and **sarvo**.

[BRISBANE REGION, SYDNEY REGION, SOUTH COAST AND SOUTHERN TABLELANDS]

sarvo this afternoon. See also **arftie**, **arvo**[1], and **sarvey**.

[SYDNEY REGION, TASMANIA, BRISBANE REGION, NORTH COAST QLD, FAR NORTH QLD, MELBOURNE REGION]

savoury slice a pastry slice with savoury mince filling and topped with cheese and bacon. [ADELAIDE REGION]

scab to borrow items (either temporarily or permanently) from another. See also **cash**.

[MELBOURNE REGION, DARWIN AND NORTH COAST NT, THE CENTRE, SYDNEY REGION, NEW ENGLAND DISTRICT, BRISBANE REGION, ADELAIDE REGION]

scab duty school detention requiring the detainees to pick up rubbish around the schoolyard. See also **emu bob**, **emu parade**, **emu patrol**, **emu stalk** and **emu walk**.

[NORTH COAST QLD, PERTH REGION, THE RIVERINA, SYDNEY REGION, SOUTH COAST AND SOUTHERN TABLELANDS, NEW ENGLAND DISTRICT, DARWIN AND NORTH COAST NT]

Scabs nickname for the Perth suburb of Scarborough. [PERTH REGION]

scadgy looking untidy and grubby by choice. [TASMANIA]

scale to remove loose rocks from the walls of a mine as a safety measure. [CENTRAL WEST AUSTRALIA]

scallop a thin slice of potato dipped in batter and deep-fried. See also **potato cake**, **potato fritter** and **potato scallop**.

[BRISBANE REGION, CENTRAL COAST QLD, CENTRAL WEST NSW, HUNTER VALLEY AND NORTH COAST, NEW ENGLAND DISTRICT, NORTH COAST QLD, SOUTH COAST AND SOUTHERN TABLELANDS, SYDNEY REGION, THE RIVERINA, FAR WEST NSW, WESTERN DISTRICT]

scheme water mains water from WA's pipelines. Also known as being on **town water**. [PERTH REGION]

schluck a quick drink; a nip of alcohol; a friendly drink. (A bit of Barossa German.) [ADELAIDE REGION]

schmidee beer glass size: smaller than a **schooner** but bigger than a **middy**. [SYDNEY REGION]

schnitter a sandwich. (A Barossa German word.) See also **piece**, **round**, **sambo** and **sanga**. [ADELAIDE REGION]

schoolie a schoolteacher. [PERTH REGION]

schoolies 1. end of secondary schooling celebrations (short for "schoolies' week"). 2. the graduating students attending these celebrations.

[CENTRAL WEST NSW, FAR WEST NSW, HUNTER VALLEY AND NORTH COAST, NEW ENGLAND DISTRICT, SOUTH COAST AND SOUTHERN TABLELANDS, SYDNEY REGION, THE RIVERINA, BRISBANE REGION, MELBOURNE REGION, ADELAIDE REGION]

school milk the milk once supplied free by some state governments to all children in state primary schools (and, as a number of our contributors remembered, it was always left in the sun and had to be drunk warm. Yuk!). [TASMANIA, SYDNEY REGION, MELBOURNE REGION]

school port a child's school case. See also **port**.

[BRISBANE REGION, CENTRAL COAST QLD, NORTH COAST QLD, FAR NORTH QLD, WEST CENTRAL QLD, THE RIVERINA]

schooner[1] a large glass of beer (approximately 385 ml) served in New South Wales. See **butcher**, **glass**, **handle**, **middy**, **pony**, **pot**, **schooner**[2] and **seven**.

[SYDNEY REGION, HUNTER VALLEY AND NORTH COAST, NEW ENGLAND DISTRICT, THE RIVERINA, SOUTH COAST AND SOUTHERN TABLELANDS, CENTRAL WEST NSW, FAR WEST NSW]

schooner[2] a glass of beer (approximately 285 ml) served in South Australia; equivalent to a **pot**. See also **butcher**, **glass**, **handle**, **middy**, **pony**, **schooner**[1] and **seven**.

[EYRE AND YORKE PENINSULAS, ADELAIDE REGION, NORTHERN SOUTH AUSTRALIA]

scone gobbler a visiting minister or priest. [FAR WEST NSW]

scott a loner (someone who … "'s got no mates"). See also **neville**, **nigel** and **nof**. [SOUTH COAST AND SOUTHERN TABLELANDS]

scotty tired and irritable, cranky.

[SYDNEY REGION, WIMMERA AND MALLEE, NORTHERN SOUTH AUSTRALIA]

scozzer a dag; much the same, in other words, as a **bennie**, **bethan**, **bogan**, **bevan**, **bog**[2], **booner**, **boonie**, **chigger**, **chookie**, **feral**, **garry** or **westie**. [WESTERN DISTRICT]

Scozzie Scottish-born Aussie. [MELBOURNE REGION, SYDNEY REGION]

scrag an unkempt person of meagre means.
[ADELAIDE REGION, SYDNEY REGION, DARWIN AND NORTH COAST NT, THE CENTRE, PERTH REGION, HUNTER VALLEY AND NORTH COAST]

scrap a bicycle: short for "scrap iron". See also **deadly treadly**, **grid**[1], **grunter** and **treadly**. [PERTH REGION]

scratchie[1] a pre-purchased ticket for use on a train, tram or bus.
[MELBOURNE REGION]

scratchie[2] a scratch lottery ticket. [SYDNEY REGION]

scribble scrabble roast pork skin (or "crackling"). [ADELAIDE REGION]

scrubber nickname for a common type of kangaroo found in scrub country. [NORTHERN SOUTH AUSTRALIA]

scudge a damp, heavy mist, but not rain. [GIPPSLAND]

scunge 1. the act of bludging, cadging or scabbing something from someone. 2. the person who does this.
[CENTRAL HIGHLANDS VICTORIA, GIPPSLAND, MELBOURNE REGION]

scungies[1] the sports knickers girls wear under netball skirts. See also **bloomers**, **bum shorts** and **runners**.
[SYDNEY REGION, SOUTH COAST AND SOUTHERN TABLELANDS, CENTRAL WEST NSW]

scungies[2] see **Speedos**. See also **ballhuggers**, **boasters**, **budgie-huggers**, **budgie-smugglers**, **cluster busters**, **cockchokers**, **cock jocks**, **codjocks**, **dick bathers**, **dick-pointers**, **dick-pokers**, **dick stickers**, **dick togs**, **dikdaks**, **dipsticks**, **fish frighteners**, **jammers**, **Jimmy clingers**, **knobbies**, **lolly-baggers**, **lolly bags**, **meat-hangers**, **nut huggers**, **nylon disgusters**, **racers**, **racing bathers**, **sluggers**, **sluggos**, **slug huggers**, **tights**, **toolies**, **trunks** and **wog togs**.
[SOUTH COAST AND SOUTHERN TABLELANDS, CENTRAL WEST NSW, SYDNEY REGION]

scunted caught! busted; caught in the act; caught red-handed. (Especially of a teenager scunted by a parent or teacher.)
[PERTH REGION, NORTH COAST QLD, DARWIN AND NORTH COAST NT]

seagull[1] a worker employed on a **fly-in fly-out** basis.
[TASMANIA, SYDNEY REGION]

seagull[2] a visiting tourist (especially of the caravan or bus variety).
[HUNTER VALLEY AND NORTH COAST]

the season the sugar-crushing season. [NORTH COAST QLD]

secondary tops in those Queensland country towns where there
was no high school, a school called a secondary tops (grades eight
to ten) was attached to the local primary school. See also **area
school**, **central school**, **consolidated school**, **district school** and
high top.

[CENTRAL COAST QLD, NORTH COAST QLD, FAR NORTH QLD, WEST CENTRAL QLD]

SEC pole a power pole (from the initials of the State Electricity
Commission). See also **hydro pole**, **Stobie pole**, **telegraph pole**
and **telepole**.

[WIMMERA AND MALLEE, CENTRAL HIGHLANDS VICTORIA, WESTERN DISTRICT,
NORTHERN VICTORIA, GIPPSLAND, MELBOURNE REGION]

session the hours on Sunday during which a particular hotel may
open. (Sometimes as "the Sunday Sess" or "Sesh".) See also **Sunday
Session**.

[BRISBANE REGION, CENTRAL COAST QLD, CENTRAL WEST AUSTRALIA, FAR NORTH
QLD, NORTH COAST QLD, NORTHERN WEST AUSTRALIA, PERTH REGION, WEST
CENTRAL QLD]

seven a seven fluid ounce glass of beer served in a NSW hotel. See
also **butcher**, **glass**, **handle**, **middy**, **pony**, **pot**, **schooner**[1] and
schooner[2]. [HUNTER VALLEY AND NORTH COAST]

seven-course meal a six-pack of beer and a meat pie.
[SOUTH COAST AND SOUTHERN TABLELANDS]

seven o'clock wave a mythical wave released each day from the
dam up the Murrumbidgee River from Wagga Wagga. As a
contributor explains, "Newcomers would always be told to get a
surfboard and be at Wagga beach to catch the seven o'clock wave
which had been released earlier from the dam." (Ah, those
visitors, they'll fall for anything, won't they?) However, other
contributors insist that it was the "five o'clock wave". (This is what
I like: when people argue about the arrival time of something that
doesn't exist!) [THE RIVERINA]

Sevo the Sydney suburb of Seven Hills. [SYDNEY REGION]

shack a holiday house. See also **weekender**.

[ADELAIDE REGION, BRISBANE REGION, CENTRAL COAST QLD, CENTRAL HIGHLANDS VICTORIA, EYRE AND YORKE PENINSULAS, FAR NORTH QLD, GIPPSLAND, MELBOURNE REGION, NORTH COAST QLD, NORTHERN VICTORIA, PERTH REGION, TASMANIA, WEST CENTRAL QLD, WESTERN DISTRICT, WIMMERA AND MALLEE]

shaiack the nanny to act in a foolish and irresponsible manner; to "act the goat". (Note: sometimes spelled **chiack**.)

[SYDNEY REGION, THE RIVERINA]

shallow water swimmer someone who is easily frightened.

[SYDNEY REGION]

shame job an expression or exclamation used to describe an embarrassing situation. (According to one contributor, shame job is found in Aboriginal English across Australia.)

[DARWIN AND NORTH COAST NT, THE CENTRE, EYRE AND YORKE PENINSULAS, NORTHERN SOUTH AUSTRALIA]

shanghai (the "H" is not sounded: pronounced shang-eye) a slingshot or catapult made from a forked stick and a strong band of rubber (often cut from a bicycle tube). Now obsolete. See also **dong-eye**, **ging**, **gonk** and **slingshot**.

[BRISBANE REGION, NORTH COAST QLD, FAR NORTH QLD, TASMANIA, PERTH REGION, SYDNEY REGION, ADELAIDE REGION, WESTERN DISTRICT, MELBOURNE REGION, NORTHERN VICTORIA, HUNTER VALLEY AND NORTH COAST, FAR WEST NSW, SOUTH COAST AND SOUTHERN TABLELANDS]

shark biscuit a cheap surfboard made of foam (rather than fibreglass). According to one contributor, the term shark biscuit is sometimes applied to the second-rate surfers who use such boards.

[SYDNEY REGION]

shaver a boy or young lad (now largely obsolete).

[TASMANIA, MELBOURNE REGION, SYDNEY REGION]

Shazza generic name for a female **bogan** (adapted from such names as **Charlene** or **Charmaine**). [MELBOURNE REGION]

shellback a garden snail. [TASMANIA]

shelter shed a shed on school grounds, usually open on one side (and separate from the classrooms), in which children could play in wet weather. See also **lunch shed**, **play shed** and **weather shed**.

[WIMMERA AND MALLEE, CENTRAL HIGHLANDS VICTORIA, WESTERN DISTRICT, NORTHERN VICTORIA, GIPPSLAND, MELBOURNE REGION, PERTH REGION, BRISBANE REGION]

shifter an adjustable spanner.

[PERTH REGION, SYDNEY REGION, BRISBANE REGION]

Shire, The Sutherland Shire, in the southern suburbs of Sydney.

[SYDNEY REGION, SOUTH COAST AND SOUTHERN TABLELANDS]

Shire chick a Sutherland Shire girl. [SYDNEY REGION]

Shirley Temple a clear glass marble with a spiral of colour inside.

[PERTH REGION]

shmick (or "schmicko") good, or very good.

[PERTH REGION, HUNTER VALLEY AND NORTH COAST, SYDNEY REGION]

Shooter's Ditch an imaginary remote country town. (Because of the vagaries of mythical cartography, Shooter's Ditch may well share a common border with **Bundiwallop**, **Kickastickalong**, **Oodnagalahbi** and **Wheelyabarraback**.) [SYDNEY REGION, TASMANIA]

shoot through like a Bondi tram to depart in haste. (Sadly, long obsolete – like the tram it's named after.) [SYDNEY REGION]

shopping trolley any four-wheel drive, especially one used primarily to carry the kids to school and do the shopping.

[SYDNEY REGION]

show[1] a party. [ADELAIDE REGION]

show[2] a small gold mine run by a prospector. [CENTRAL WEST AUSTRALIA]

side (or "side of paper") a page. [TASMANIA]

sidecut the gully, dip or gravel on the edge of the road.

[NORTHERN VICTORIA]

sieve door flyscreen door. [EYRE AND YORKE PENINSULAS]

silent cop a circular steel plate (embedded with reflective **cat's eyes**) set into the asphalt in the centre of intersections without traffic lights (in the days before roundabouts), originally painted bright yellow.

[ADELAIDE REGION, PERTH REGION, WIMMERA AND MALLEE, CENTRAL HIGHLANDS VICTORIA, WESTERN DISTRICT, NORTHERN VICTORIA, GIPPSLAND, HUNTER VALLEY AND NORTH COAST, SYDNEY REGION, MELBOURNE REGION, TASMANIA, NORTHERN SOUTH AUSTRALIA]

silver beet the plant *Beta vulgaris cicla*, having large, crisp, crinkly, strongly veined dark green leaves and a long fleshy stalk, used as a vegetable. ("English spinach", the plant *Spinacia oleracea* , has light green leaves, and is also used as a vegetable). See also **spinach**.

[CENTRAL HIGHLANDS VICTORIA, GIPPSLAND, MELBOURNE REGION, NORTHERN VICTORIA, WESTERN DISTRICT, WIMMERA AND MALLEE, ADELAIDE REGION]

silver bullet[1] a portable classroom. See also **Bristol hut**, **demountable**, **dogbox**, **hot box**, **musset hut**, **portable**, **pre-fab**, **relocatable**, **terrapin unit** and **transportable**.

[DARWIN AND NORTH COAST NT]

silver bullet[2] a can of Resch's Pilsener. [SYDNEY REGION]

silver licence a full driver's licence, issued on successful completion of the **provisional licence** period.

[SYDNEY REGION, HUNTER VALLEY AND NORTH COAST, NEW ENGLAND DISTRICT, THE RIVERINA, SOUTH COAST AND SOUTHERN TABLELANDS, CENTRAL WEST NSW, FAR WEST NSW]

silver rattler Melbourne suburban trains (Hitachi trains, introduced in the 1970s). See also **blue rattler** and **red rattler**.

[MELBOURNE REGION]

sinker a solid square of dried, mixed fruit of about 7–8 cm square and some 2 cm thick, with flaky pastry on the top and bottom and topped with (usually pink) icing (also called a "Chester square"). Another of Adelaide's contributions to world gastronomy (along with the **pie floater**, the **savoury slice** and the **frog cake**). [ADELAIDE REGION]

sitdown period prior to expected delivery when pregnant Aboriginal women come to Alice Springs to sit down and wait for the commencement of labour. [THE CENTRE]

six and out in the rules of backyard cricket if you hit a six (over the fence) you've also lost your wicket: you are six and out (*and* you have to climb over the fence and get the ball!).
[SOUTH COAST AND SOUTHERN TABLELANDS, SYDNEY REGION]

six-pointer two sandwiches consisting of three slices of bread cut diagonally (that is, one and a half **rounds**). When ordering sandwiches in a Tasmania café you may be asked if you want a **four-pointer** or a **six-pointer**. [TASMANIA]

skeetie abbreviation of mosquito. [MELBOURNE REGION]

skeg (derogatory) a surfer (the fins on surfboards are called skegs).
[HUNTER VALLEY AND NORTH COAST, BRISBANE REGION]

skidder a piece of heavy machinery used in logging operations to move fallen trees. [TASMANIA]

skid lid crash helmet. [BRISBANE REGION, MELBOURNE REGION, SYDNEY REGION]

skinny ("or skinnyfish") a queenfish (genus *Scomberoides*).
[DARWIN AND NORTH COAST NT]

skinny park the grassed area on a traffic island, especially when planted with trees. [CENTRAL WEST AUSTRALIA]

skip the name non-Anglo Australians (of Italian, Greek etc. background) give to Anglo Australians. (From the popular television series *Skippy, the Bush Kangaroo*.)
[SYDNEY REGION, PERTH REGION, MELBOURNE REGION]

skipjack ("or skippy") a type of fish.
[PERTH REGION, SOUTH COAST AND SOUTHERN TABLELANDS]

skipper the designated driver in a group (the one who'll stay sober to drive them all home). [PERTH REGION]

skite a conversation between two or more people. [TASMANIA]

slab a pack of 24 stubbies or cans of beer. See also **block**[2], **box**, **carton** and **case**[2].

[CENTRAL WEST NSW, CENTRAL WEST AUSTRALIA, FAR WEST NSW, HUNTER VALLEY AND NORTH COAST, NEW ENGLAND DISTRICT, NORTHERN WEST AUSTRALIA, PERTH REGION, SOUTH COAST AND SOUTHERN TABLELANDS, SYDNEY REGION, THE RIVERINA, MELBOURNE REGION, TASMANIA]

Slack, The the off season, or maintenance season, in sugar growing areas. [NORTH COAST QLD]

sleep-out an enclosed veranda, or an annexe to a house, providing extra sleeping accommodation. (Occasionally an out-building separate from the house.) Many contributors remembered the sleep-out being enclosed with glass louvres.

[WIMMERA AND MALLEE, CENTRAL HIGHLANDS VICTORIA, WESTERN DISTRICT, NORTHERN VICTORIA, GIPPSLAND, MELBOURNE REGION, ADELAIDE REGION, TASMANIA, BRISBANE REGION, CENTRAL COAST QLD, HUNTER VALLEY AND NORTH COAST]

slide a piece of children's playground equipment consisting principally of a slope for children to slide down. See also **slippery dip** and **slippery slide**.

[PERTH REGION, WIMMERA AND MALLEE, CENTRAL HIGHLANDS VICTORIA, WESTERN DISTRICT, NORTHERN VICTORIA, GIPPSLAND, MELBOURNE REGION, TASMANIA]

slik pick a computer-generated lottery ticket. [PERTH REGION]

slingshot a catapult made from a forked stick and a strong band of rubber (often cut from a bicycle tube). See also **dong-eye**, **ging**, **gonk** and **shanghai**.

[CENTRAL WEST NSW, FAR WEST NSW, HUNTER VALLEY AND NORTH COAST, NEW ENGLAND DISTRICT, SOUTH COAST AND SOUTHERN TABLELANDS, SYDNEY REGION, MELBOURNE REGION, THE RIVERINA]

slippery dip a piece of children's playground equipment consisting principally of a slope for children to slide down. Some contributors reported knowing a slippery dip as a different piece of equipment from a slide or slippery slide. For them a slippery dip was a fairground ride involving a long, and bumpy, ride on a mat. See also **slide** and **slippery slide**.

[EYRE AND YORKE PENINSULAS, ADELAIDE REGION, NORTHERN SOUTH AUSTRALIA, SYDNEY REGION, HUNTER VALLEY AND NORTH COAST, NEW ENGLAND DISTRICT, THE RIVERINA, SOUTH COAST AND SOUTHERN TABLELANDS, CENTRAL WEST NSW, FAR WEST NSW]

slippery slide an item of children's playground equipment consisting principally of a slope for children to slide down. And there are regional disagreements over what to call it: if not this, then **slide** or **slippery dip**.

[BRISBANE REGION, CENTRAL COAST QLD, NORTH COAST QLD, FAR NORTH QLD, WEST CENTRAL QLD, THE RIVERINA, SOUTH COAST AND SOUTHERN TABLELANDS, MELBOURNE REGION]

sloppy joe a long-sleeved sweatshirt. (Sometimes applied to any loose-fitting overgarment.)

[SYDNEY REGION, HUNTER VALLEY AND NORTH COAST, NEW ENGLAND DISTRICT, THE RIVERINA, SOUTH COAST AND SOUTHERN TABLELANDS, CENTRAL WEST NSW, FAR WEST NSW, BRISBANE REGION, CENTRAL COAST QLD, NORTH COAST QLD, FAR NORTH QLD, MELBOURNE REGION, WEST CENTRAL QLD]

slubberdegullion a meal made up from leftovers or unlikely ingredients from the fridge. [MELBOURNE REGION]

sluggers see **Speedos**. See also **ballhuggers**, **boasters**, **budgie-huggers**, **budgie-smugglers**, **cluster busters**, **cockchokers**, **cock jocks**, **codjocks**, **dick bathers**, **dick-pointers**, **dick-pokers**, **dick stickers**, **dick togs**, **dikdaks**, **dipsticks**, **fish frighteners**, **jammers**, **Jimmy clingers**, **knobbies**, **lolly-baggers**, **lolly bags**, **meat-hangers**, **nut huggers**, **nylon disgusters**, **racers**, **racing bathers**, **scungies**[2], **sluggos**, **slug huggers**, **tights**, **toolies**, **trunks** and **wog togs**.

[CENTRAL WEST AUSTRALIA, PERTH REGION]

sluggos see **Speedos**. See also **ballhuggers**, **boasters**, **budgie-huggers**, **budgie-smugglers**, **cluster busters**, **cockchokers**, **cock jocks**, **codjocks**, **dick bathers**, **dick-pointers**, **dick-pokers**, **dick stickers**, **dick togs**, **dikdaks**, **dipsticks**, **fish frighteners**, **jammers**, **Jimmy clingers**, **knobbies**, **lolly-baggers**, **lolly bags**, **meat-hangers**, **nut huggers**, **nylon disgusters**, **racers**, **racing bathers**, **scungies**[2], **sluggers**, **slug huggers**, **tights**, **toolies**, **trunks** and **wog togs**.

[SYDNEY REGION, HUNTER VALLEY AND NORTH COAST, NEW ENGLAND DISTRICT, BRISBANE REGION]

slug huggers see **Speedos**. See also **ballhuggers**, **boasters**, **budgie-huggers**, **budgie-smugglers**, **cluster busters**, **cockchokers**, **cock jocks**, **codjocks**, **dick bathers**, **dick-pointers**, **dick-pokers**, **dick stickers**, **dick togs**, **dikdaks**, **dipsticks**, **fish frighteners**, **jammers**, **Jimmy clingers**, **knobbies**, **lolly-baggers**, **lolly bags**, **meat-hangers**, **nut huggers**, **nylon disgusters**, **racers**, **racing bathers**, **scungies**[2], **sluggers**, **sluggos**, **tights**, **toolies**, **trunks** and **wog togs**.

[BRISBANE REGION]

Slurry Hills the Sydney suburb of Surry Hills. [SYDNEY REGION]

slushies those rostered to do the dishes, particularly when camping (at Scouts, school cadets and church youth group camps). [MELBOURNE REGION, BRISBANE REGION, CENTRAL COAST QLD, NORTH COAST QLD, FAR NORTH QLD, WEST CENTRAL QLD]

smiley fritz sliced pressed meat with a smiley face pattern. See also **fritz.** [ADELAIDE REGION]

snack the mid-morning break at school. See also **elevener**, **elevenses, levna, little lunch, little play, morning lunch, morning play, play lunch, playtime** and **recess.** [WESTERN DISTRICT, MELBOURNE REGION]

snatch it to resign from a job (coal mining and construction industry jargon). [CENTRAL WEST AUSTRALIA, NORTH COAST QLD]

snick-and-run a form of cricket in which the person batting must run if he or she hits the ball. Also known as "tippety cricket", "tippety runs", and "tippety". See also **hit-and-run, tip-and-go, tip-and-run, tippy cricket, tippy-go-run, tippy-runs, tipsy** and **tipsy-run.** [TASMANIA]

snicker-snacks cooking tongs (especially barbecue tongs). See also **gotchas** and **nickernackers.** [TASMANIA]

snig (timber industry jargon) to pull or drag logs. [HUNTER VALLEY AND NORTH COAST]

snip 1. to latch (a door or window). 2. the latch itself. [WIMMERA AND MALLEE, CENTRAL HIGHLANDS VICTORIA, WESTERN DISTRICT, NORTHERN VICTORIA, GIPPSLAND, MELBOURNE REGION, TASMANIA]

Snives the Sydney suburb of St Ives in Sydney. (This name was "intended", a contributor explains, "to bring the snooty Snives people down a peg or two".) [SYDNEY REGION]

snoozer 1. a person (usually male); a bloke; a chap; a guy. [TASMANIA] 2. a derogatory term for a man. [BRISBANE] 3. a senior citizen. [MELBOURNE REGION]

snorker a sausage. See also **tube steak.** [BRISBANE REGION]

snot-block (or "snot-box" or "snot-brick" or "snotty") a vanilla slice. "Disgusting!" (signed) Mother of Five, Hurstville. See also **phlegm cake**, **pus pie** and **wet Nellie**.

[CENTRAL HIGHLANDS VICTORIA, GIPPSLAND, MELBOURNE REGION, NORTHERN VICTORIA, WESTERN DISTRICT, WIMMERA AND MALLEE, ADELAIDE REGION, SOUTH COAST AND SOUTHERN TABLELANDS, PERTH REGION, TASMANIA]

snotty gobble 1. a climbing plant that grows on mallee scrub (sometimes producing small whitish flowers). One contributor says, "Thick enough so that it could be used for a hammock when we were kids." [ADELAIDE REGION, PERTH REGION, WIMMERA AND MALLEE] 2. the persoonia tree. [PERTH REGION]

snowbird a caravanning tourist who arrives in Darwin (or the Top End generally) at the start of the dry season and who leaves before the **build-up**. [DARWIN AND NORTH COAST NT]

soap box a billy cart; a home-made downhill racer. See also **billy cart**, **go-cart** and **hill trolley**.

[ADELAIDE REGION, EYRE AND YORKE PENINSULAS]

SOG acronym for the Victoria Police Special Operations Group. Also known as "soggies".

[WIMMERA AND MALLEE, CENTRAL HIGHLANDS VICTORIA, WESTERN DISTRICT, NORTHERN VICTORIA, GIPPSLAND, MELBOURNE REGION]

sonny boy frozen ice treat in the shape of a pyramid that could be either eaten as an ice block or drunk as a cool drink. (Originally a brand name.) See also **pyramid**.

[MELBOURNE REGION, GIPPSLAND, SYDNEY REGION]

soup, I'll see you in the a form of farewell; a more elaborate way of saying "goodbye". See also **cheerio**, **cheery**, **hooray**, **hooroo**, **hurrah** and **oo-roo**.

[SYDNEY REGION, SOUTH COAST AND SOUTHERN TABLELANDS]

sourgrass the yellow-flowered herb *Oxalis pes caprae*. See also **soursob**.

[WIMMERA AND MALLEE, CENTRAL HIGHLANDS VICTORIA, WESTERN DISTRICT, NORTHERN VICTORIA, GIPPSLAND, MELBOURNE REGION, TASMANIA, THE RIVERINA, PERTH REGION]

soursob 1. the yellow-flowered herb *Oxalis pes caprae*. (See also **sourgrass**.) 2. a stem of this plant, often sucked or chewed for its sour taste. (One contributor writes: "As children in Adelaide, we dipped the broken stalks of soursobs into sand and rubbed them vigorously on penny coins. This rapidly removed any tarnish and restored the pennies to a shiny new condition. Whatever the mystery chemical in soursobs, I wonder what it did to our teeth when we sucked them for the delicious sour taste?")
[WIMMERA AND MALLEE, CENTRAL HIGHLANDS VICTORIA, WESTERN DISTRICT, NORTHERN VICTORIA, GIPPSLAND, MELBOURNE REGION, TASMANIA, ADELAIDE REGION, EYRE AND YORKE PENINSULAS, PERTH REGION]

South, The 1. the southern states of Australia (especially Victoria and New South Wales). [BRISBANE REGION, CENTRAL COAST QLD, FAR NORTH QLD, NORTH COAST QLD, WEST CENTRAL QLD] 2. southern Queensland. [FAR NORTH QLD, NORTH COAST QLD]

South African fillet smoked cod.
[ADELAIDE REGION, WIMMERA AND MALLEE, EYRE AND YORKE PENINSULAS, PERTH REGION]

southerly buster a cool southerly wind in the afternoon or evening of a hot Sydney summer day. [SYDNEY REGION]

southerner a derogatory term used in north Queensland to label those living south of the Tropic of Capricorn (the implication being that they are ignorant and/or self-important – especially applied to politicians based in Canberra or Brisbane). See also **Mexican**. [NORTH COAST QLD, FAR NORTH QLD]

spadger a sparrow. See also **spagger** and **spoggy**.
[MELBOURNE REGION]

spagger a sparrow. See **spadger** and **spoggy**.
[CENTRAL WEST NSW]

spanner water very cold water (because a spanner tightens nuts). Also the source of the surfing expression "spanner wave".
[SOUTH COAST AND SOUTHERN TABLELANDS]

sparrow's very early in the morning; dawn; abbreviation of "sparrow's fart" – although why it's assumed that sparrows begin the day by breaking wind is unclear. (The shortened version was

put into circulation by ABC NewsRadio sports commentator
David Lord.)

[PERTH REGION, SYDNEY REGION, MELBOURNE REGION, SOUTH COAST AND
SOUTHERN TABLELANDS, NORTH COAST QLD]

speckie a very high mark (Aussie Rules jargon).

[WIMMERA AND MALLEE, CENTRAL HIGHLANDS VICTORIA, WESTERN DISTRICT, NORTHERN
VICTORIA, GIPPSLAND, MELBOURNE REGION, SOUTH COAST AND SOUTHERN TABLELANDS]

Speedos registered brand name of Australian swimwear
manufacturing company first established in 1928 when the
McRae Knitting Mills manufactured the world's first swimsuit
made from silk and joined in the middle of the back (the
"Razorback"). Speedo introduced the world's first nylon swimsuit
in 1957. To understand the many nicknames for Speedos you
simply need to understand that they all refer to a form of men's
nylon, legless swimming costume that is *very* snug fitting! Hence
the following range of inventive labels: **ballhuggers**, **boasters**,
budgie-huggers, **budgie-smugglers**, **dick bathers** (or DBs), **dick-
pointers** (or DPs), **dick-pokers** (or DPs), **dick stickers**, **dick togs**
(or DTs), **dikdaks**, **dipsticks**, **cluster busters**, **cockchokers**, **cock
jocks**, **codjocks**, **fish frighteners**, **jammers**, **Jimmy clingers**,
knobbies, **lolly-baggers**, **lolly bags**, **meat-hangers**, **nut huggers**,
nylon disgusters, **racers**, **racing bathers**, **scungies**, **sluggers**,
sluggos, **slug huggers**, **tights**, **toolies** and **wog togs**.

For the regions where these various labels are used see their
individual entries. The term Speedos appears in the following
regions:

[PERTH REGION, SOUTH COAST AND SOUTHERN TABLELANDS, BRISBANE REGION,
WESTERN DISTRICT, NORTHERN WEST AUSTRALIA, SYDNEY REGION, HUNTER VALLEY
AND NORTH COAST, NORTH COAST QLD, THE RIVERINA, NORTHERN SOUTH
AUSTRALIA, CENTRAL WEST AUSTRALIA, NORTHERN WEST AUSTRALIA]

spider a tall glass of soft drink with a scoop of ice-cream added;
what the Americans would call an ice-cream soda. (Several
contributors suggested that the best spiders are made with ginger
beer. I just thought you'd like to know.)

[WIMMERA AND MALLEE, CENTRAL HIGHLANDS VICTORIA, WESTERN DISTRICT,
NORTHERN VICTORIA, GIPPSLAND, MELBOURNE REGION, TASMANIA, EYRE AND YORKE
PENINSULAS, ADELAIDE REGION, PERTH REGION, SYDNEY REGION, HUNTER VALLEY AND
NORTH COAST, NEW ENGLAND DISTRICT, THE RIVERINA, SOUTH COAST AND
SOUTHERN TABLELANDS, CENTRAL WEST NSW, FAR WEST NSW, BRISBANE REGION]

spinach the edible plant *Beta vulgaris cicla*, having large, crisp, crinkly, strongly veined dark green leaves and a long fleshy stalk, used as a vegetable. As opposed to "English spinach" (the plant *Spinacia oleracae* with light green leaves, also used as a vegetable). See also **silver beet**.

[CENTRAL WEST NSW, FAR WEST NSW, HUNTER VALLEY AND NORTH COAST, NEW ENGLAND DISTRICT, SOUTH COAST AND SOUTHERN TABLELANDS, SYDNEY REGION, THE RIVERINA, PERTH REGION]

spinifex grasshopper a kangaroo. [CENTRAL WEST AUSTRALIA]

spinning jenny a device used to unroll coils of fencing wire.

[WEST CENTRAL QLD]

spoggy a sparrow. See also **spadger** and **spagger**.

[FAR WEST NSW, NORTHERN SOUTH AUSTRALIA, ADELAIDE REGION, EYRE AND YORKE PENINSULAS, SYDNEY REGION]

spondonicals pot holders; any tool used to pick up a hot pot (usually from a fuel stove or campfire). Sometimes as "spongs" or "sponies" for short. See also **billy grips** and **spondoolikan**.

[SYDNEY REGION, PERTH REGION]

spondoolikan pot holders; any tool used to pick up a hot pot. See also **billy grips** and **spondonicals**. [SYDNEY REGION]

spouting metal guttering for carrying rainwater.

[CENTRAL HIGHLANDS VICTORIA, GIPPSLAND, MELBOURNE REGION, NORTHERN VICTORIA, TASMANIA, WESTERN DISTRICT, WIMMERA AND MALLEE]

sprigs studs or spikes on the soles of footy boots. See also **stops**, **studs** and **tags**. [ADELAIDE REGION, PERTH REGION]

spud a hole in a sock.

[TASMANIA, SYDNEY REGION, CENTRAL WEST NSW, THE RIVERINA]

Spud Buster nickname for the (Queenstown) *Advocate* newspaper.

[TASMANIA]

spud cake a battered slice of potato. See **potato cake**, **potato scallop**, **scallop**. [MELBOURNE REGION]

spuds[1] 1. dirt behind the ears. 2. nickname for a child with this particular hygiene problem. [THE RIVERINA]

spuds[2] 1. fists. 2. schoolyard rhyming game (involving counting off the fists, or spuds, of a group of children to determine who would be **in** or **it** or **he** in the chasing or ball game to follow).
[ADELAIDE REGION, PERTH REGION]

square ball schoolyard ball game (also known as "four-square"). See also **handball**, **king ping** and **two-square**. [PERTH REGION]

square bear a 700 ml bottle of Bundaberg rum.
[BRISBANE REGION, CENTRAL COAST QLD, NORTH COAST QLD, FAR NORTH QLD, WEST CENTRAL QLD]

square hook a fishing net set illegally in an area reserved for rod and line fishing. [TASMANIA]

squib a person who refuses to honour an undertaking; one who withdraws from an undertaking without adequate reason.
[THE RIVERINA]

Starlight Hotel sleeping in the open. [SYDNEY REGION]

stay to reside; to take up residence. See **stop**.
[HUNTER VALLEY AND NORTH COAST, NEW ENGLAND DISTRICT, THE RIVERINA, SOUTH COAST AND SOUTHERN TABLELANDS, CENTRAL WEST NSW, FAR WEST NSW]

steak florentina or **steak florrie** ham, cheese and steak, crumbed and deep-fried. [WIMMERA AND MALLEE]

steel post breeder agricultural research station workers (because of the high quality of fencing on such research stations – with the implication, by "real" farmers, that fences are all they can grow).
[THE RIVERINA]

steep creekin' white-water rafting. [BRISBANE REGION]

stem a 1950s/60s derogatory term used by kids about other kids (meaning "dork", "nerd" etc.) Sometimes as "stemmy".
[FAR WEST NSW, SOUTH COAST AND SOUTHERN TABLELANDS]

St Georges Terrace cocky one who lives and works in Perth and who owns a country property (perhaps for tax loss purposes). See also **Collins Street cocky**, **Pitt Street farmer** and **Queen Street bushie**. [PERTH REGION, CENTRAL WEST AUSTRALIA]

sticker licker a parking inspector. See also **brown bomber**, **blue bomber**, **grey ghost** and **grey meanie**.
[ADELAIDE REGION, WIMMERA AND MALLEE, EYRE AND YORKE PENINSULAS]

stickybeak a black grass seed which sticks to clothing.
[SOUTH COAST AND SOUTHERN TABLELANDS]

sticky bun a sweet white roll with pink icing and coconut (elsewhere known as a finger bun). [BRISBANE REGION, PERTH REGION]

sticky mickey a creeping or climbing plant with many small hairs and prickles that stick to clothing. [TASMANIA]

stinger net a mesh enclosure excluding box jellyfish and other marine nasties from a swimming area. [NORTH COAST QLD]

stink-boat derogatory term for a powerboat (employed by crews on sailing craft). [BRISBANE REGION]

stink bomb acacia seeds that give off a foul smell when crushed and wet. [MELBOURNE REGION]

stinker a black eye. [SYDNEY REGION]

stinkerkaese quark cheese, a white smelly cheese made from curdled skim milk (a Barossa German word). [ADELAIDE REGION]

stinkfish a small shore fish, the dragonet.
[EYRE AND YORKE PENINSULAS, ADELAIDE REGION, NORTHERN SOUTH AUSTRALIA]

stir the possum to hurry up. [TASMANIA]

Stobie pole a power pole. In South Australia these are concrete with sides of steel. They take their name from engineer James Cyril Stobie (1895-1953), who designed them for the Adelaide Electric Supply Company in 1924 to compensate for the lack of hardwood and the widespread presence of termites in South Australia. See also **hydro pole**, **SEC pole**, **telegraph pole** and **telepole**.
[EYRE AND YORKE PENINSULAS, ADELAIDE REGION, NORTHERN SOUTH AUSTRALIA, DARWIN AND NORTH COAST NT, THE CENTRE]

stoner a druggie; someone who acts as if they're on drugs.
[ADELAIDE REGION, PERTH REGION]

stonkered in the condition of having eaten an elegant sufficiency; as full as a goog. [HUNTER VALLEY AND NORTH COAST]

stop to reside temporarily; to take up temporary residence. See also **stay.** [HUNTER VALLEY AND NORTH COAST]

stope the work area of an underground mine. [FAR WEST NSW]

stops the spikes (or **sprigs** or **studs** or **tags**) on the bottom of footy boots.

[WIMMERA AND MALLEE, CENTRAL HIGHLANDS VICTORIA, WESTERN DISTRICT, NORTHERN VICTORIA, GIPPSLAND, MELBOURNE REGION]

storm bird any migratory bird that arrives in a region close to the beginning of the storm season. [BRISBANE REGION, NORTH COAST QLD]

Straddie Stradbroke Island, Queensland, [BRISBANE REGION]

stranglers trousers worn too high on the waist. [MELBOURNE REGION]

Strasburg a large, mild-flavoured, precooked sausage usually sliced thinly and eaten cold. Sometimes known as "Stras" or "Straz" for short. (Like hamburgers and frankfurts this is a food bearing a placename, Strasbourg being a town in north-eastern France, which was under German rule from 1870 to 1918.) See also **baron sausage**, **beef Belgium**, **Belgium sausage**, **bung fritz**, **Byron sausage**, **devon**, **Empire sausage**, **fritz**, **German sausage**, **luncheon sausage**, **mystery meat**, **polony**, **pork German**, **wheel meat** and **Windsor sausage**.

[WIMMERA AND MALLEE, CENTRAL HIGHLANDS VICTORIA, WESTERN DISTRICT, NORTHERN VICTORIA, GIPPSLAND, MELBOURNE REGION, BRISBANE REGION]

strawberry fete a country concert with strawberries-and-cream for supper – usually run as a fundraiser.

[EYRE AND YORKE PENINSULAS, NORTHERN SOUTH AUSTRALIA]

street lawn a roadside strip of grass; the grassed area of the footpath. See also **berm**, **nature strip**, **verge**. [PERTH REGION]

Streuselkuchen (or "Streusel cake") German cake; a yeast cake common in the Barossa Valley and other areas settled by Germans in the 1800s. [ADELAIDE REGION]

strike me roan! "I'm very surprised!" (Now possibly obsolete.) See also **bulltwang!**; **bunnies to that!**; **chowoon**; **eh**; **gammon**; **hells, bells and bootlaces** and **Himmel**. [TASMANIA]

strip to harvest grain with a mechanical header. (Strip is used, in fact, throughout much of eastern Australia, where "reap" would be used in South Australia). [CENTRAL WEST NSW]

stroller a light collapsible chair on wheels for carrying small children. See also **pusher**. [SYDNEY REGION, PERTH REGION]

studs another name for those spikes on the bottom of football boots. See also **sprigs**, **stops** and **tags**.
[MELBOURNE REGION, FAR WEST NSW]

stump a tall hardwood (commonly jarrah) support holding a high-set building off the ground (usually at least one and half metres off the ground).
[BRISBANE REGION, CENTRAL COAST QLD, FAR NORTH QLD, NORTH COAST QLD, WEST CENTRAL QLD]

stu vac study vacation (the period of the university term just before exams). See also **swat vac**. [SYDNEY REGION]

sugarloaf a placename given to almost any conical hill (from the conical shape in which loaf sugar was imported to the colony in the early 19th century). [TASMANIA]

suicide season the period just before the wet season (the **build-up**); an extreme case of "going troppo".
[DARWIN AND NORTH COAST NT, THE CENTRE]

sulo bin a large rubbish bin on wheels. From the name of one of the more common manufacturers of such bins. See also **otto bin** and **wheely bin**.
[NEW ENGLAND DISTRICT, CENTRAL HIGHLANDS VICTORIA, SYDNEY REGION, ADELAIDE REGION, PERTH REGION]

Sunday Session the Sunday afternoon opening hours for pubs.
[MELBOURNE REGION]

Sunnie Coast abbreviation of Sunshine Coast. [BRISBANE REGION]

Sunshine stilettos moccasins. From the Melbourne suburb of
Sunshine. See also **Broadmeadows wedding shoes**, **Corio work
boots**, **moccas** and **Ringwood Reeboks**. [MELBOURNE REGION]

super full strength beer on tap in a bar. See also **gilgie's piss** and
unleaded. [PERTH REGION]

Super Chook a refurbished Red Hen railcar (of the type that ran on
the Adelaide suburban system). [ADELAIDE REGION]

supply teacher a relief teacher. See also **CRT** and **emergency
teacher**.
[BRISBANE REGION, CENTRAL COAST QLD, NORTH COAST QLD, FAR NORTH QLD, WEST
CENTRAL QLD]

swampy 1. a wanna-be surfer who populates areas of a beach that
are not good for surfing (the term is reported to be common on
the north-west coast of Tasmania). 2. a person born or raised in
Invermay, a suburb of Launceston (possibly the same hapless
surfer). [TASMANIA]

Swan and Coke a mix of Royal Swan Rum and Coca-Cola. (This is
only safe to order in Tasmania. If ordered on the mainland you're
likely to end up with a very odd mixture of Swan Lager and
Coke!)
[TASMANIA]

swat vac the period between the end of term and the start of exams
during which students try to cram in all the knowledge they have
ignored throughout the term. Applies to later years of secondary
school and university. Sometimes spelled "swot vac". See also **stu
vac**. [MELBOURNE REGION, TASMANIA]

swimmers a swimming costume. See also **bathers**, **clubbies**[1], **cossie**,
cozzie, **costume**, **swimsuit**, **togs** and **trunks**.
[SYDNEY REGION, HUNTER VALLEY AND NORTH COAST, NEW ENGLAND DISTRICT, THE
RIVERINA, SOUTH COAST AND SOUTHERN TABLELANDS, CENTRAL WEST NSW, FAR
WEST NSW, MELBOURNE REGION, BRISBANE REGION, NORTH COAST QLD]

swimsuit a swimming costume. See also **bathers**, **clubbies**[1], **cossie**,
cozzie, **costume**, **swimmers**, **togs** and **trunks**.
[SYDNEY REGION, HUNTER VALLEY AND NORTH COAST, NEW ENGLAND DISTRICT, THE
RIVERINA, SOUTH COAST AND SOUTHERN TABLELANDS, CENTRAL WEST NSW, FAR
WEST NSW]

SWOS acronym for the Special Weapons and Operations Section of the NSW Police Department.

[SYDNEY REGION, HUNTER VALLEY AND NORTH COAST, NEW ENGLAND DISTRICT, THE RIVERINA, SOUTH COAST AND SOUTHERN TABLELANDS, CENTRAL WEST NSW, FAR WEST NSW]

T

table drain open drain beside a bitumen road.
[FAR WEST NSW, NEW ENGLAND DISTRICT, TASMANIA, NORTHERN VICTORIA, SYDNEY REGION]

taddipum a mixture of potatoes and pumpkin. Some contributors recalled eating this dish while calling it "bubble-and-squeak". However, traditional bubble-and-squeak (an English dish) consisted of cold meat and cabbage (sometimes with potato or other vegetables substituted) fried together in butter.
[NORTH COAST QLD]

tags the protuberances on the bottom of your footy boots. See also **sprigs**, **stops** and **studs**.
[WIMMERA AND MALLEE, CENTRAL HIGHLANDS VICTORIA, WESTERN DISTRICT, NORTHERN VICTORIA, GIPPSLAND, MELBOURNE REGION, BRISBANE REGION, CENTRAL COAST QLD, NORTH COAST QLD, FAR NORTH QLD, WEST CENTRAL QLD]

tallie a 750 ml bottle of beer. Also spelled "tally". See also **big bot**, **big bud**, **Corinna stubby**, **longie** and **long neck**.
[BRISBANE REGION, HUNTER VALLEY AND NORTH COAST]

tall timber unusually tall, solidly built AFL footballers (usually ruckmen or backs). [MELBOURNE REGION]

tamma low, thick, shrubby vegetation, especially dominated by species of Casuarina. (Possibly from an Aboriginal word.)
[NORTHERN WEST AUSTRALIA, CENTRAL WEST AUSTRALIA, PERTH REGION]

tank dam; stock watering dam. According to one contributor a "dam" is formed by building an earth wall across a natural watercourse, while a "tank" is a depression that has been dug, or bulldozed, into which water is diverted. See also **dam**.
[HUNTER VALLEY AND NORTH COAST, NEW ENGLAND DISTRICT, THE RIVERINA, SOUTH COAST AND SOUTHERN TABLELANDS, CENTRAL WEST NSW, FAR WEST NSW]

tank loaf a loaf of bread baked in an enclosed, round corrugated tin giving the baked loaf that emerges the shape of a piece of corrugated pipe. See also **pipe loaf**.
[SYDNEY REGION, BRISBANE REGION, ADELAIDE REGION, PERTH REGION]

tappet a **bevan** with an interest in cars. [BRISBANE REGION]

tarrydiddlum (or "taradiddle") a small fib. [BRISBANE REGION, TASMANIA]

ta-ta flaps flabby down-hanging triceps. More detail on this physical condition will be found in the entries on **aunty arms**, **bingo wings**, **bye-nows**, **good-bye muscle**, **nannas**, **piano arms**, **reverse biceps**, **tuckshop arm** and **widow's curtain**.
[SYDNEY REGION, HUNTER VALLEY AND NORTH COAST]

tax 1. to steal from somebody. See also **gang** and **thump**. 2. to claim a share in something (usually food) that someone else has.
[TASMANIA, HUNTER VALLEY AND NORTH COAST, BRISBANE REGION, NORTH COAST QLD, PERTH REGION]

taxi a cry chorused in unison when a crash or breakage occurs at a party (indicating that the perpetrator has had too much to drink and needs a taxi to take them home).
[SOUTH COAST AND SOUTHERN TABLELANDS, MELBOURNE REGION, SYDNEY REGION]

teacake iced plain or fruit bun. See also **boston bun**.
[SOUTH COAST AND SOUTHERN TABLELANDS]

teasy (of a baby) irritable (possibly now obsolete).
[ADELAIDE REGION, EYRE AND YORKE PENINSULAS]

Teetulpa weed the perennial herb Lincoln weed (*Diplotaxis tenuifolia*) used in the northern agricultural areas of South Australia. From the place name Teetulpa, north of Peterborough, South Australia. [ADELAIDE REGION]

telegraph pole a utility pole for carrying overhead power and telephone cables; a power pole. (The name refuses to die, despite the death, long ago, of telegraph as a form of communication. Possibly the use of "Telegraph" on newspaper mastheads helps to keep the word alive.) See also **hydro pole**, **SEC pole**, **Stobie pole** and **telepole**.
[TASMANIA, SYDNEY REGION, HUNTER VALLEY AND NORTH COAST, BRISBANE REGION]

telepole a utility pole for carrying overhead power and telephone cables; a power pole. See also **hydro pole**, **SEC pole**, **Stobie pole** and **telegraph pole**. [FAR WEST NSW]

temporary Australian a bike rider not wearing protective headgear.
[NORTH COAST QLD, SYDNEY REGION]

tennis shoe a sandshoe. Elsewhere known as "runners", "sneakers" or "gym boots".
[WIMMERA AND MALLEE, CENTRAL HIGHLANDS VICTORIA, WESTERN DISTRICT, NORTHERN VICTORIA, GIPPSLAND, MELBOURNE REGION, TASMANIA]

TER acronym for Tertiary Entrance Rank: a number out of 100 calculated from the HSC examination, determining a student's eligibility for entrance to a particular tertiary institution.
[SYDNEY REGION, HUNTER VALLEY AND NORTH COAST, NEW ENGLAND DISTRICT, THE RIVERINA, SOUTH COAST AND SOUTHERN TABLELANDS, CENTRAL WEST NSW, FAR WEST NSW]

terrapin unit a portable classroom. See also **Bristol hut**, **demountable**, **dogbox**, **hot box**, **musset hut**, **portable**, **pre-fab**, **relocatable**, **silver bullet**[1] and **transportable**. [TASMANIA]

Territory rig long trousers, shirt and tie (male dress code for formal occasions in the Northern Territory). The tie, one contributor explained, is optional but expected. Also known as **Darwin rig**.
[DARWIN AND NORTH COAST NT, THE CENTRE]

testipop abrupt changes in voice pitch experienced by boys during puberty. [SYDNEY REGION]

thank you, Deanna response to someone who states the bleeding obvious. From Counsellor Deanna Troy, a character on *Star Trek: The Next Generation*. [ADELAIDE REGION]

thank you, Wally May response to someone who offers a comment on something that has just happened (regardless of whether the comment was witty, apt or plain embarrassing). From a football caller of that name, to whom the other commentators would throw with the words: "Comment, Wally May". [ADELAIDE REGION]

thank your mother for the rabbits an expression of farewell. (This possibly originated in the Depression era of the 1930s when rabbit became a predominant source of cheap meat. Kept alive today by Rex Hunt and Derryn Hinch.) [MELBOURNE REGION]

things are crook in ... (rhyming placename) the situation is grim. Nowadays used only as a deliberate archaism for comic effect. Of the three rhyming placenames suggested by contributors, Tallarook is probably the most common (Jack O'Hagan wrote a song called *Things is Crook in Tallarook* in 1952). The three rhyming place-names (and their language regions) are: Cooloongolook [CENTRAL WEST NSW, FAR WEST NSW, HUNTER VALLEY AND NORTH COAST, NEW ENGLAND DISTRICT, SOUTH COAST AND SOUTHERN TABLELANDS, SYDNEY REGION, THE RIVERINA]; Muswellbrook [CENTRAL WEST NSW, FAR WEST NSW, HUNTER VALLEY AND NORTH COAST, NEW ENGLAND DISTRICT, SOUTH COAST AND SOUTHERN TABLELANDS, SYDNEY REGION, THE RIVERINA]; and Tallarook. [CENTRAL HIGHLANDS VICTORIA, CENTRAL WEST NSW, FAR WEST NSW, GIPPSLAND, HUNTER VALLEY AND NORTH COAST, MELBOURNE REGION, NEW ENGLAND DISTRICT, NORTHERN VICTORIA, SOUTH COAST AND SOUTHERN TABLELANDS, SYDNEY REGION, THE RIVERINA, WESTERN DISTRICT, WIMMERA AND MALLEE]

three-corner jack 1. a low-growing plant (*Emex australis*) having many hard, sharp, spiny seeds that are extremely painful to step on and which will sometimes even puncture through shoe soles. 2. one of these seeds. See also **bullhead**, **California puncture weed**, **caltrop**, **cat head**¹, **cat's eye**¹, **double-gee** and **goat's head**. [ADELAIDE REGION, WIMMERA AND MALLEE, EYRE AND YORKE PENINSULAS, NORTHERN SOUTH AUSTRALIA, WESTERN DISTRICT]

throw a reggie throwing a temper tantrum; chucking a wobbly; spitting the dummy. [TASMANIA]

thugby the standard AFL or soccer fan's word for rugby. [PERTH REGION, SYDNEY REGION]

thumbs in an expression of agreement to join in a game or participate in a group activity (schoolyard slang). [PERTH REGION]

thump to steal. See also **gang** and **tax**. [PERTH REGION, SOUTH COAST AND SOUTHERN TABLELANDS]

thumper a thief. [PERTH REGION]

thunder and lightning an open sandwich of toast with treacle and cream drizzled on top. (Another astonishing Adelaidian contribution to world gastronomy.) [ADELAIDE REGION]

tick tock children's name for the small black-and-orange cicadas found in Western Australia. See also **black prince**, **brown baker**, **brown bomber**², **cicada**, **floury baker**, **greengrocer**², **pisswhacker** and **yellow Monday**. [CENTRAL WEST AUSTRALIA, NORTHERN WEST AUSTRALIA, PERTH REGION]

tier a mountain range.

[ADELAIDE REGION, BRISBANE REGION, MELBOURNE REGION, TASMANIA]

tiersman a timber-getter who works in the Tiers (the Mount Lofty
  Ranges).

[EYRE AND YORKE PENINSULAS, ADELAIDE REGION, NORTHERN SOUTH AUSTRALIA]

tig a schoolyard chasing game. See also **chasey**, **chasings**, **tag**, **tiggy**
  and **tip**[2]. [BRISBANE REGION]

tiggy the same schoolyard chasing game as above. See also **chasey**,
  chasings, **tag**, **tig** and **tip**[2].

[BRISBANE REGION, MELBOURNE REGION, WESTERN DISTRICT, PERTH REGION, CENTRAL
HIGHLANDS VICTORIA]

tights see **Speedos**. See also **ballhuggers**, **boasters**, **budgie-
  huggers**, **budgie-smugglers**, **cluster busters**, **cockchokers**, **cock
  jocks**, **codjocks**, **dick bathers**, **dick-pointers**, **dick-pokers**, **dick
  stickers**, **dick togs**, **dikdaks**, **dipsticks**, **fish frighteners**,
  jammers, **Jimmy clingers**, **knobbies**, **lolly-baggers**, **lolly bags**,
  meat-hangers, **nut huggers**, **nylon disgusters**, **racers**, **racing
  bathers**, **scungies**[2], **sluggers**, **sluggos**, **slug huggers**, **toolies**,
  trunks and **wog togs**.

[HUNTER VALLEY AND NORTH COAST]

tilly 1. utility (or ute). See also **buckboard**. 2. a kerosene lantern. 3.
  army slang for a Tracked Load Carrier (TLC).

[BRISBANE REGION, CENTRAL COAST QLD, FAR NORTH QLD, NORTH COAST QLD, WEST
CENTRAL QLD]

tin kettling a traditional pre-wedding celebration brought to the
  Barossa Valley by early Lutheran settlers. Originally this was a
  noisy event (*der Polter Abend* in Barossa German) held on the
  night before the wedding when friends would gather outside the
  home of the bride-to-be banging tins, blowing horns and
  generally making a lot of noise. They were then usually invited in
  for *streuselkuchen* (German cake), beer or wine. According to
  some contributors this old custom is quite possibly in the process
  of being revived. [ADELAIDE REGION, PERTH REGION]

tinnie a small aluminium (flat-bottomed) boat with an
  outboard motor. Also spelled "tinny". Elsewhere (universally

around Australia, not restricted to any region) a **tinnie** is a can of beer.

[FAR NORTH QLD, ADELAIDE REGION, BRISBANE REGION, SYDNEY REGION, SOUTH COAST AND SOUTHERN TABLELANDS]

tip[1] the local council rubbish dump. See also **depot** and **dump**.

[CENTRAL WEST NSW, FAR WEST NSW, HUNTER VALLEY AND NORTH COAST, NEW ENGLAND DISTRICT, SOUTH COAST AND SOUTHERN TABLELANDS, SYDNEY REGION, THE RIVERINA, BRISBANE REGION, TASMANIA]

tip[2] a schoolyard chasing game. (Sometimes in the plural as "tips".) See also **chasey**, **chasings**, **tag**, **tig** and **tiggy**. [SYDNEY REGION]

tip-and-go a form of cricket in which the person batting *must* run if he or she hits the ball. See also **hit-and-run**, **tip-and-run**, **tippety**, **tippety-run**, **tippy cricket**, **tippy-go-run**, **tippy-runs**, **tipsy** and **tipsy-run**. [ADELAIDE REGION]

tip-and-run see **tip-and-go**. See also **hit-and-run**, **tippety**, **tippety-run**, **tippy cricket**, **tippy-go-run**, **tippy-runs**, **tipsy** and **tipsy-run**.

[SYDNEY REGION, HUNTER VALLEY AND NORTH COAST, NEW ENGLAND DISTRICT, THE RIVERINA, SOUTH COAST AND SOUTHERN TABLELANDS, CENTRAL WEST NSW, FAR WEST NSW, CENTRAL WEST AUSTRALIA, PERTH REGION, CENTRAL COAST QLD, NORTH COAST QLD, FAR NORTH QLD]

tippety see **hit-and-run**, **tip-and-go**, **tip-and-run**, **tippy cricket**, **tippy-go-run**, **tippy-runs**, **tipsy** and **tipsy-run**.

[WIMMERA AND MALLEE, CENTRAL HIGHLANDS VICTORIA, WESTERN DISTRICT, NORTHERN VICTORIA, GIPPSLAND, MELBOURNE REGION]

tippety cricket see **hit-and-run**, **tip-and-go**, **tip-and-run**, **tippety-run**, **tippy-go-run**, **tippy-runs**, **tipsy** and **tipsy-run**.

[THE RIVERINA, NORTHERN SOUTH AUSTRALIA]

tippety-run see **hit-and-run**, **tip-and-go**, **tip-and-run**, **tippy cricket**, **tippy-go-run**, **tippy-runs**, **tipsy** and **tipsy-run**, **tippety cricket** and **tippety**.

[WIMMERA AND MALLEE, CENTRAL HIGHLANDS VICTORIA, WESTERN DISTRICT, NORTHERN VICTORIA, GIPPSLAND, MELBOURNE REGION, TASMANIA]

tippy cricket see **hit-and-run**, **tip-and-go**, **tip-and-run**, **tippety-run**, **tippy-go-run**, **tippy-runs**, **tipsy** and **tipsy-run**. [MELBOURNE REGION]

tippy-go see **hit-and-run**, **tip-and-go**, **tip-and-run**, **tippety-run**, **tippy cricket**, **tippy-go-run**, **tippy-runs**, **tipsy** and **tipsy-run**.

[EYRE AND YORKE PENINSULAS, ADELAIDE REGION]

tippy-go-run see **hit-and-run**, **tip-and-go**, **tip-and-run**, **tippety-run**, **tippy cricket**, **tippy-go**, **tippy-runs**, **tipsy** and **tipsy-run**.
[ADELAIDE REGION]

tippy-runs see **hit-and-run**, **tip-and-go**, **tip-and-run**, **tippety-run**, **tippy cricket**, **tippy-go**, **tippy-go-run**, **tipsy** and **tipsy-run**.
[FAR WEST NSW]

tipsy see **hit-and-run**, **tip-and-go**, **tip-and-run**, **tippety-run**, **tippy cricket**, **tippy-go**, **tippy-go-run**, **tippy runs** and **tipsy-run**.
[BRISBANE REGION, CENTRAL COAST QLD, NORTH COAST QLD, FAR NORTH QLD, WEST CENTRAL QLD]

tipsy-run see **hit-and-run**, **tip-and-go**, **tip-and-run**, **tippety-run**, **tippy cricket**, **tippy-go**, **tippy-go-run**, **tippy runs** and **tipsy**.
[BRISBANE REGION, CENTRAL COAST QLD, NORTH COAST QLD, FAR NORTH QLD, WEST CENTRAL QLD]

tissues cigarette papers (for making roll-your-owns). [TASMANIA]

toad burners powerful driving lights. [BRISBANE REGION]

toastie-toastie 1. a sealed sandwich with a sweet or savoury filling cooked in a buttered jaffle iron; (in other words) a jaffle. 2. the jaffle iron in which this was made. See also **Breville**.
[GIPPSLAND, PERTH REGION, ADELAIDE REGION]

togs swimming costume. There seemed to be wide agreement among contributors that this is a predominantly Queensland term (and has spread to other regions from there). The only other place where this label is dominant is (according to contributors) the Eastern Islands (aka New Zealand). See also **bathers**, **clubbies**[1], **cossie**, **cozzie**, **costume**, **swimmers**, **swimsuit** and **trunks**.
[BRISBANE REGION, CENTRAL COAST QLD, CENTRAL HIGHLANDS VICTORIA, FAR NORTH QLD, GIPPSLAND, MELBOURNE REGION, NORTH COAST QLD, NORTHERN VICTORIA, WEST CENTRAL QLD, WESTERN DISTRICT, WIMMERA AND MALLEE, DARWIN AND NORTH COAST NT, CENTRAL WEST AUSTRALIA, ADELAIDE REGION, PERTH REGION, HUNTER VALLEY AND NORTH COAST, CENTRAL WEST NSW, THE RIVERINA, TASMANIA]

tombola a large playing marble. Various other spellings are suggested: "tombowler", "tomboller" and so on. Tombolas were banned from many marbles games as the biggest marble and (therefore) giving the user of the tombola an unfair advantage. (There is an older English word "tombola" meaning a kind of lottery – so perhaps this large marble was originally meant to suggest the kind of numbered marbles used in lottery draws.)

[CENTRAL HIGHLANDS VICTORIA, GIPPSLAND, MELBOURNE REGION, NORTHERN VICTORIA, WESTERN DISTRICT, WIMMERA AND MALLEE, NORTH COAST QLD, CENTRAL WEST AUSTRALIA, PERTH REGION, ADELAIDE REGION, FAR WEST NSW]

tomboy stitch French knitting.

[WIMMERA AND MALLEE, CENTRAL HIGHLANDS VICTORIA, WESTERN DISTRICT, NORTHERN VICTORIA, GIPPSLAND, MELBOURNE REGION, TASMANIA, ADELAIDE REGION, DARWIN AND NORTH COAST NT]

tommy roundhead name given to small lizard with large head found in the Cooktown region; by extension applied to a small or shifty person. [FAR NORTH QLD]

toolies see **Speedos**. See also **ballhuggers**, **boasters**, **budgie-huggers**, **budgie-smugglers**, **cluster busters**, **cockchokers**, **cock jocks**, **codjocks**, **dick bathers**, **dick-pointers**, **dick-pokers**, **dick stickers**, **dick togs**, **dikdaks**, **dipsticks**, **fish frighteners**, **jammers**, **Jimmy clingers**, **knobbies**, **lolly-baggers**, **lolly bags**, **meat-hangers**, **nut huggers**, **nylon disgusters**, **racers**, **racing bathers**, **scungies**[2], **sluggers**, **sluggos**, **slug huggers**, **tights**, **trunks** and **wog togs**.

[NORTH COAST QLD]

toomba the Queensland city of Toowoomba. (A contributor suggests the word is used sarcastically, and is intended as a play on the Toowoomba accent.) [BRISBANE REGION]

Toonie the western Sydney suburb of Toongabbie. [SYDNEY REGION]

Toorak'n'ruin the Melbourne suburb of Toorak. [MELBOURNE REGION]

Toorak tractor a city-only four-wheel drive. See **Balmain bulldozer**, **Bronte buggy**, **Burnside bus**, **Kenmore tractor**, **North Shore tank**, **Rose Bay shopping trolley** and **Turramurra tractor**.

[MELBOURNE REGION, NORTHERN VICTORIA, ADELAIDE REGION]

tooth-to-tatt ratio hospital slang used to identify a patient who is on social security *and* a drug user (they have lots of tattoos and few teeth). [SYDNEY REGION]

top of the wozza number one in a given field. One contributor, drawing on information supplied by their grandfather (a First

World War veteran), suggests this may be an expression brought home from Cairo by the troops after 1918. [PERTH REGION]

torpedo a long bun with icing, that narrows at each end.
[ADELAIDE REGION, EYRE AND YORKE PENINSULAS, NORTHERN SOUTH AUSTRALIA]

Torri nickname for a Holden Torana.
[MELBOURNE REGION, PERTH REGION, ADELAIDE REGION]

t'other sider to a West Australian the label for all non-West Australians. [PERTH REGION]

town the city centre; the CBD.
[ADELAIDE REGION, SYDNEY REGION, MELBOURNE REGION]

townie someone who lives in a country town as opposed to someone who lives on a property. [THE RIVERINA, CENTRAL WEST NSW]

town water water from the mains (as opposed to tank water). See also **scheme water**.
[WIMMERA AND MALLEE, CENTRAL HIGHLANDS VICTORIA, WESTERN DISTRICT, NORTHERN VICTORIA, GIPPSLAND, MELBOURNE REGION, SYDNEY REGION, BRISBANE REGION]

Track, the the Stuart Highway that runs between Darwin and Alice Springs.
[DARWIN AND NORTH COAST NT, THE CENTRE, NORTHERN SOUTH AUSTRALIA]

train dog a ticket inspector. See also **Gestapo**, **Met cop**, **Metcard Mafia**, **train fascist**, **train Nazi** and **tram fascist**. [MELBOURNE REGION]

train fascist a ticket inspector. See also **Gestapo**, **Met cop**, **Metcard Mafia**, **train dog**, **train Nazi** and **tram fascist**. [SYDNEY REGION]

train Nazi a ticket inspector. See also **Gestapo**, **Met cop**, **Metcard Mafia**, **train dog**, **train fascist** and **tram fascist**. [SYDNEY REGION]

train smash 1. a hastily prepared meal consisting of a variety of ingredients, stewed together, and often served on toast. Contributors mentioned many possible ingredients, but the most common were scrambled eggs and tomatoes. The expression may have begun as rhyming slang for "hash" or as a description of the mangled mixture of ingredients, or both. It has also been suggested that it may have begun as navy slang for cooked tinned tomatoes served with bacon. [THE RIVERINA, BRISBANE REGION, SYDNEY REGION, PERTH REGION] 2. tomato sauce. See also **redders**. [TASMANIA, SYDNEY REGION]

train station an Americanism, heralding the death of the older Australian expression "railway station".

[PERTH REGION, SYDNEY REGION, MELBOURNE REGION, ADELAIDE REGION]

tram fascist ticket inspector. See also **Gestapo**, **Met cop**, **Metcard Mafia**, **train dog**, **train fascist** and **train Nazi**. [MELBOURNE REGION]

transition the first year in primary school. See also **kindergarten**, **preparatory class** and **reception class**.

[DARWIN AND NORTH COAST NT, THE CENTRE, HUNTER VALLEY AND NORTH COAST]

Transperth the Perth public transport network. [PERTH REGION]

transport a semi-trailer; sometimes with an adjective as in a "cattle transport" or a "sheep transport".

[CENTRAL WEST NSW, FAR WEST NSW, WIMMERA AND MALLEE]

transportable a portable classroom. See also **Bristol hut**, **demountable**, **dogbox**, **hot box**, **musset hut**, **portable**, **pre-fab**, **relocatable**, **silver bullet**[1] and **terrapin unit**.

[EYRE AND YORKE PENINSULAS, ADELAIDE REGION, NORTHERN SOUTH AUSTRALIA, BRISBANE REGION, PERTH REGION]

traymobile a small table on castors for carrying teapot, cups, dishes, food etc. See also **autotray**.

[SYDNEY REGION, HUNTER VALLEY AND NORTH COAST, NEW ENGLAND DISTRICT, THE RIVERINA, SOUTH COAST AND SOUTHERN TABLELANDS, CENTRAL WEST NSW, BRISBANE REGION, CENTRAL COAST QLD, NORTH COAST QLD, ADELAIDE REGION, WIMMERA AND MALLEE, EYRE AND YORKE PENINSULAS, PERTH REGION, TASMANIA]

treadly a pushbike (abbreviation of **deadly treadly**). Sometimes spelled "treddly". See also **deadly treadly**, **grid**[1], **grunter** and **scrap**.

[SYDNEY REGION, HUNTER VALLEY AND NORTH COAST, NEW ENGLAND DISTRICT, THE RIVERINA, SOUTH COAST AND SOUTHERN TABLELANDS, CENTRAL WEST NSW, FAR WEST NSW, BRISBANE REGION, CENTRAL COAST QLD, NORTH COAST QLD, FAR NORTH QLD, WEST CENTRAL QLD, CENTRAL WEST AUSTRALIA, PERTH REGION, WIMMERA AND MALLEE, CENTRAL HIGHLANDS VICTORIA, WESTERN DISTRICT, NORTHERN VICTORIA, GIPPSLAND, MELBOURNE REGION, EYRE AND YORKE PENINSULAS, ADELAIDE REGION, NORTHERN SOUTH AUSTRALIA, DARWIN AND NORTH COAST NT]

TRG a specialised police unit: the Tactical Response Group.

[SYDNEY REGION, HUNTER VALLEY AND NORTH COAST, NEW ENGLAND DISTRICT, THE RIVERINA, SOUTH COAST AND SOUTHERN TABLELANDS, CENTRAL WEST NSW, FAR WEST NSW, NORTHERN WEST AUSTRALIA, CENTRAL WEST AUSTRALIA, PERTH REGION, DARWIN AND NORTH COAST NT, THE CENTRE]

triamble a type of pumpkin. [ADELAIDE REGION]

triantelope a big hairy, fearsome-looking spider (such as a huntsman spider, the *Sparassidae isopoda*). The word is probably a variation on "tarantula" (possibly combined with elements from "antelope".) See also **Clarence**.

[NORTHERN SOUTH AUSTRALIA, NORTHERN VICTORIA, SYDNEY REGION]

triantiwontygong a mythical creature presumably related to a bunyip. One contributor writes that it was "used in central Victoria in the early 1940s to scare/embarrass/confuse city children sent to the country to 'escape the bombing'". The word is probably simplified from the creature invented by C. J. Dennis.

[CENTRAL HIGHLANDS VICTORIA, BRISBANE REGION, MELBOURNE REGION, ADELAIDE REGION, PERTH REGION, NORTHERN SOUTH AUSTRALIA]

Tryantiwontygongolope a mystical creature invented by poet C. J. Dennis (probably a poet's play upon the word **triantelope**) and recorded in his *A Book for Kids* (1921) in the following terms:

> *It is something like a beetle, and a little like a bee,*
> *But nothing like a woolly grub that climbs upon a tree.*
> *Its name is quite a hard one, but you'll learn it soon, I hope.*
> *So try, try, try: Triantiwontigongolope.*

[CENTRAL HIGHLANDS VICTORIA, BRISBANE REGION, MELBOURNE REGION, ADELAIDE REGION, PERTH REGION, NORTHERN SOUTH AUSTRALIA]

Trono slurred nickname for Toronto, New South Wales.

[HUNTER VALLEY AND NORTH COAST]

troppo 1. the madness brought on by hot, humid, tropical weather; for example, in the title of *Gone Troppo* by John O'Grady (1968). 2. a form of architecture designed for the hot, humid conditions.

[DARWIN AND NORTH COAST NT, NORTH COAST QLD, NORTHERN WEST AUSTRALIA]

trough a large sink installed in a laundry. Sometimes as "laundry trough" or "wash trough". (Note: some contributors tell us that in parts of Tasmania this word is pronounced to rhyme with "cow".)

See also **laundry trough**, **laundry tub**, **trove**, **wash trough** and **wash tub**.

[ADELAIDE REGION, CENTRAL HIGHLANDS VICTORIA, EYRE AND YORKE PENINSULAS, GIPPSLAND, MELBOURNE REGION, NORTHERN VICTORIA, PERTH REGION, TASMANIA, WESTERN DISTRICT, WIMMERA AND MALLEE]

trove a large sink installed in a laundry. See also **laundry trough**, **laundry tub**, **trough**, **wash trough** and **wash tub**.

[WIMMERA AND MALLEE, CENTRAL HIGHLANDS VICTORIA, WESTERN DISTRICT, NORTHERN VICTORIA, GIPPSLAND, MELBOURNE REGION, TASMANIA, THE RIVERINA]

true? A conversational response meaning something like "is it?" or "really?"; sometimes used as a sentence terminator, in much the same way as **but** and **eh**.

[DARWIN AND NORTH COAST NT, NORTHERN WEST AUSTRALIA, CENTRAL WEST AUSTRALIA, PERTH REGION, THE CENTRE]

trundler a shopping trolley. This expression appears to have been imported from the Eastern Islands (aka New Zealand).

[SYDNEY REGION]

trunks male swimming costume, either **Speedos** or board shorts. See also **bathers**, **clubbies**[1], **cossie**, **costume**, **cozzie**, **swimmers**, **swimsuit** and **togs**. [BRISBANE REGION, MELBOURNE REGION, SYDNEY REGION]

tube steak a sausage. See also **snorker**. [SYDNEY REGION]

tuck shop the school lunch shop (usually staffed by volunteers). Not an Australian term (English in origin), but a regionalism in that it is used differently in different parts of the country. (Note: some contributors report that the lunch shop in their primary school was called a tuck shop while in their high school it was called a canteen. Perhaps canteen was thought to be the more "grown-up" word.) See also **canteen**.

[BRISBANE REGION, WIMMERA AND MALLEE, CENTRAL HIGHLANDS VICTORIA, WESTERN DISTRICT, NORTHERN VICTORIA, GIPPSLAND, MELBOURNE REGION, CENTRAL COAST QLD, NORTH COAST QLD, FAR NORTH QLD, SYDNEY REGION, HUNTER VALLEY AND NORTH COAST, SOUTH COAST AND SOUTHERN TABLELANDS, NEW ENGLAND DISTRICT, THE RIVERINA, TASMANIA]

tuckshop arm the flabby triceps area of an overweight woman. (One contributor writes: "most of the mothers that ran the tuck shop had this affliction".) See also **aunty arms**, **bingo wings**,

bye-nows, **good-bye muscle**, **nannas**, **piano arms**, **reverse biceps**, **ta-ta flaps** and **widow's curtain**.

[BRISBANE REGION, ADELAIDE REGION, MELBOURNE REGION]

Tuggers nickname for Tuggeranong (South Canberra).

[SOUTH COAST AND SOUTHERN TABLELANDS]

tullawong a medium-sized black-and-white bird (elsewhere known as a currawong). [HUNTER VALLEY AND NORTH COAST]

tumbler mosquito pupal stage; roughly spherical when curled up, very active tumbling motion if disturbed in water. Also known as "wriggler". [ADELAIDE REGION]

tune-up corporal punishment.

[CENTRAL WEST NSW, BRISBANE REGION, CENTRAL COAST QLD, NORTH COAST QLD, FAR NORTH QLD, WEST CENTRAL QLD]

tuning "chatting up" someone at a social function (from the notion of tuning in to the right radio station).

[HUNTER VALLEY AND NORTH COAST, DARWIN AND NORTH COAST NT, MELBOURNE REGION]

turkey's nest a small dam. See also **dam** and **tank**.

[PERTH REGION, WEST CENTRAL QLD, NORTHERN SOUTH AUSTRALIA]

turks wethers (castrated male sheep); rhyming slang: "turkey feathers" for "wethers". [NORTHERN SOUTH AUSTRALIA]

Turramurra tractor a city-only four-wheel drive. It also travels under the following aliases: **Balmain bulldozer**, **Bronte buggy**, **Burnside bus**, **Kenmore tractor**, **North Shore tank**, **Rose Bay shopping trolley** and **Toorak tractor**. [SYDNEY REGION]

Tweed, the Tweed Heads (northern New South Wales).

[SYDNEY REGION, HUNTER VALLEY AND NORTH COAST]

twenty-eight a subspecies of the Australian ringneck parrot *Barnardius zonarius*. [PERTH REGION]

twig a friendly gathering around a campfire, usually alongside a **dam** on a farm. See also **twiggy**. [WIMMERA AND MALLEE]

twiggy a social event held around an open fire in a backyard or in the scrub. See also **twig**. [WIMMERA AND MALLEE]

two-bob now-obsolete term for the roughly circular track left by the tyres of a vehicle when floored on full lock. Also known as "circlework", "doughnut" and "doughies". See also **doing hoops**. [PERTH REGION]

two kilometre law a law which prohibits the consumption of alcoholic beverages out of doors within two kilometres of licensed premises. [DARWIN AND NORTH COAST NT, THE CENTRE]

2SM a tea or coffee order: "two sugars and milk". (From the call-sign of a Sydney radio station.) [SYDNEY REGION]

two-square a schoolyard game played with a tennis ball in a make-shift court of two squares chalked on the playground. See also **handball**, **four-square** and **king ping**. [PERTH REGION]

U

ugly tree mythical source of all ugly people. As in: "Just look at that bloke – he must've fallen out of the ugly tree." "Yeah, and got hit by all the branches on the way down!" [NORTH COAST QLD]

Uncle Bob okay. A variation on the more common (non-Aussie) expression "Bob's your uncle". [PERTH REGION]

Uncle David an Australian fifty dollar note. Expression used by the Aboriginal community at Point McLeay, South Australia. David Unaipon, a member of that community, is featured on the fifty dollar note, along with the church at Point McLeay and some of his inventions. See also **fiddy**, **golden drinking voucher**, **olive leaf**, **peacemaker**, **pineapple** and **yellow belly**[3]. [ADELAIDE REGION]

Uncle Rus rhyming slang: a bus. As with all rhyming slang this is often expressed using only the first half of the expression, making a bus "an uncle". [SYDNEY REGION]

underdungers underwear. Also as "underchungers" or simply "chungers". See also **derps** and **reg grundies**.
[GIPPSLAND, TASMANIA, BRISBANE REGION]

underground mutton rabbit.
[MELBOURNE REGION, EYRE AND YORKE PENINSULAS, ADELAIDE REGION, NORTHERN SOUTH AUSTRALIA, PERTH REGION, CENTRAL WEST NSW, FAR WEST NSW, BRISBANE REGION]

unleaded medium alcohol beer. [PERTH REGION]

unna uttered as a tag question, in place of "You agree?" or "Whaddaya reckon?" As in, "Looks a bit like rain, unna?"
[PERTH REGION]

up used in children's games to indicate the central player; for example, the player who is **in** or **it** or **he** or up must find and/or catch the others.
[BRISBANE REGION, CENTRAL COAST QLD, FAR NORTH QLD, NORTH COAST QLD, WEST CENTRAL QLD]

up and down like Mark Foy's lift going back and forth repeatedly (indecisive, repetitive activity). Mark Foy's was a large department store in Sydney, and gave rise to the expression: "Just sit still! You're up and down like Mark Foy's lift!" [SYDNEY REGION]

uppers the upper decks (or topside) of a RAN warship. [SYDNEY REGION]

up-time schoolyard shout summoning children back to the classroom at the end of recess. [FAR WEST NSW]

up ya mum's tea pot the mythical location of anything that's lost; as in "Where's my other sock?" Reply "Up ya mum's teapot". [SYDNEY REGION]

urge in to queue jump. [SYDNEY REGION]

USSR acronym for Uninterrupted Sustained Silent Reading – an instruction given by a teacher to a class. Replaced the earlier expression "silent reading" by putting the stress on the "uninterrupted" and "sustained".
[NORTHERN WEST AUSTRALIA, CENTRAL WEST AUSTRALIA, CENTRAL HIGHLANDS VICTORIA, PERTH REGION, BRISBANE REGION]

utility pole telephone and/or power pole. [BRISBANE REGION]

V

var lese an exclamation used to gain respite from the rules during a children's game. See also **bar**[1], **barley**, **barleys** and **bars**.
[PERTH REGION]

Valigrunt a car; a powerful, modified Valiant. [BRISBANE REGION]

Valley, the Fortitude Valley, Brisbane. [BRISBANE REGION]

veeb Victoria Bitter beer. See also **green can**, **mother's milk**, **Victor Bravo**, **vitamin B** and **vomit bomb**. [SYDNEY REGION]

vegemite a student entering into their first year in high school. Abbreviated to "veggie". [BRISBANE REGION]

veggie a stupid person (as in "I've met broccoli brighter than that bloke"). See also **couple of lamingtons short of a CWA meeting, a; dipsticks; doughy; dubbo; gimp; Milo; moonya; munted** and **nuffest.** [SOUTH COAST AND SOUTHERN TABLELANDS]

veggie maths the easiest maths stream at high school.
[SOUTH COAST AND SOUTHERN TABLELANDS, SYDNEY REGION]

veg out hangin' out, doin' nothin'. [PERTH REGION]

veranda bum a spare tyre of fat that goes "all the way around the building". One contributor explains: "A fat backside merging into a fat stomach with overhang". [ADELAIDE REGION]

verge a grassed strip of land between the front boundary of a residential block and the edge of the road; lawn that fringes the street. See also **berm**, **footpath** and **nature strip**.
[PERTH REGION, MELBOURNE REGION]

Victor Bravo Victoria Bitter beer; from the phonetic alphabet used in radio call signs. See also **green can**, **mother's milk**, **veeb**, **vitamin B** and **vomit bomb**. [SYDNEY REGION]

Victorian cursive style of handwriting taught in primary schools. See also **foundation handwriting**.
[WIMMERA AND MALLEE, CENTRAL HIGHLANDS VICTORIA, WESTERN DISTRICT, NORTHERN VICTORIA, GIPPSLAND, MELBOURNE REGION, EYRE AND YORKE PENINSULAS, ADELAIDE REGION, NORTHERN SOUTH AUSTRALIA, BRISBANE REGION, CENTRAL COAST QLD, NORTH COAST QLD, FAR NORTH QLD, WEST CENTRAL QLD, PERTH REGION]

Vic-wit driver of a car with Victorian numberplates (derogatory).
[SOUTH COAST AND SOUTHERN TABLELANDS, FAR WEST NSW, CENTRAL WEST NSW]

Vietnamatta the Sydney suburb of Cabramatta, home of a large Vietnamese population (derogatory). [SYDNEY REGION]

vince an expression uttered by schoolboys after breaking wind to prevent other schoolboys from pummelling the perpetrator for his antisocial offence. For this preventive to work another member of the group must respond with the word "slugs". See also **badger**!
[CENTRAL HIGHLANDS VICTORIA, WIMMERA AND MALLEE, THE RIVERINA]

vino collapso cask wine (so named because the bladder collapses as the wine is drawn off.). See also **bag of death**, **Balga handbag**, **Bellambi handbag**, **boxie**, **box monster**, **Broadmeadows briefcase**, **cardboard handbag**, **Coraki handbag**, **death bag**, **Dubbo handbag**, **gin's handbag**, **goon**, **goonbag**, **goonbox**, **goonie**, **goonsack**, **lady in the boat**, **red handbag** and **sack**. [TASMANIA]

vino vitrio wine in glass bottles. [TASMANIA]

vitamin B Victoria Bitter beer. See also **green can**, **mother's milk**, **veeb**, **Victor Bravo** and **vomit bomb**.
[WIMMERA AND MALLEE, WESTERN DISTRICT]

vitamin P Prozac (or any of its derivatives). [TASMANIA]

vomit bomb a can of Victoria Bitter beer. See also **green can**, **mother's milk**, **veeb**, **Victor Bravo** and **vitamin B**.
[ADELAIDE REGION]

vomitous feeling a need to vomit. [BRISBANE REGION]

W

wadjella (or "wadjula") European Australian; white person. See also **gubba**, **goonya** and **guddiyah** (Aboriginal). [PERTH REGION]

wagga a blanket of several layers (often hessian chaff bags inside two blankets, which were then sewn together). Contributors report them to be widely used during the Depression years and by shearers in times past.
[GIPPSLAND, PERTH REGION, CENTRAL WEST NSW, FAR WEST NSW]

Wallaby Bob's cousin Wallaby Bob's cousin is Roo Ted. So the expression is used by saying, "I'm feeling very Wally Bob's cousin at the moment", or simply "I'm feeling very Wallaby Bobbed".
[SYDNEY REGION]

wallop any alcoholic beverage, particularly beer. (Formerly an English dialect expression that now survives in one Australian linguistic region.) [PERTH REGION]

wankertank a four-wheel drive that never leaves the bitumen. See also **Balmain bulldozer**, **Bronte buggy**, **Burnside bus**, **Kenmore tractor**, **North Shore tank**, **Rose Bay shopping trolley**, **Toorak tractor** and **Turramurra tractor**. [MELBOURNE REGION]

ward eight crazy. From the number of the psychiatric ward at Lismore Base Hospital. See also **Baillie**, **crackadog**, **Richmond Clinic**, **ward twenty** and **womba**.
[HUNTER VALLEY AND NORTH COAST]

ward twenty crazy. From the number of the former psychiatric ward at Wollongong Hospital, now closed. See also **Baillie**, **crackadog**, **Richmond Clinic**, **ward eight** and **womba**.
[SOUTH COAST AND SOUTHERN TABLELANDS]

war rope nickname for Wauchope. [HUNTER VALLEY AND NORTH COAST]

warwicks arms. (Rhyming slang "Warwick Farm", from the Sydney racecourse.) [SYDNEY REGION]

washaway a break in the Alice Springs/Port Augusta railway line. A contributor explained: "Between Port Augusta and Alice Springs the rail lines were laid flat on the ground and crossed many dry creek beds in the Flinders Ranges. When rain fell in the ranges, the creeks came down (flooded), taking the rail line with them." [ADELAIDE REGION]

washer a small towelling or flannel cloth for washing with. See also **face cloth** and **flannel**.

[BRISBANE REGION, NORTH COAST QLD, HUNTER VALLEY AND NORTH COAST, TASMANIA, SOUTH COAST AND SOUTHERN TABLELANDS, MELBOURNE REGION]

wash shed a small school building, separate from the classrooms, often open on one side, with sinks and taps for the children to wash in. [SOUTH COAST AND SOUTHERN TABLELANDS, SYDNEY REGION]

wash trough a sink or trough. See also **laundry trough**, **laundry tub**, **trough**, **trove** and **wash tub**.

[WIMMERA AND MALLEE, CENTRAL HIGHLANDS VICTORIA, WESTERN DISTRICT, NORTHERN VICTORIA, GIPPSLAND, MELBOURNE REGION, TASMANIA, EYRE AND YORKE PENINSULAS, ADELAIDE REGION, PERTH REGION]

wash tub a laundry tub. See also **laundry trough**, **laundry tub**, **trough**, **trove** and **wash trough**.

[SYDNEY REGION, HUNTER VALLEY AND NORTH COAST, NEW ENGLAND DISTRICT, THE RIVERINA, SOUTH COAST AND SOUTHERN TABLELANDS, CENTRAL WEST NSW, BRISBANE REGION, CENTRAL COAST QLD, NORTH COAST QLD]

water boot gumboot. See also **rain boots**.

[ADELAIDE REGION, WIMMERA AND MALLEE, EYRE AND YORKE PENINSULAS]

water bottle hike an informal measurement of distance ("you'll need a water bottle to get there"). See also **cut lunch and a waterbag, a.** [ADELAIDE REGION]

waterfall a girl's hairstyle (the front half of the hair tied up in a hair band, the back hanging loose). See also **half up**, **half down** and **Pollyanna.** [MELBOURNE REGION]

water fountain a source of cool drinking water on a hot day (very necessary in the days before bottled water). Known by many different names. See also **bubbler**, **bubble tap**, **drinking fountain**, **drinking tap**, **drink tap** and **fountain**.

[BRISBANE REGION, CENTRAL COAST QLD, NORTH COAST QLD, FAR NORTH QLD, WEST CENTRAL QLD, WIMMERA AND MALLEE, CENTRAL HIGHLANDS VICTORIA, WESTERN DISTRICT, NORTHERN VICTORIA, GIPPSLAND, MELBOURNE REGION, TASMANIA, EYRE AND YORKE PENINSULAS, ADELAIDE REGION, PERTH REGION]

wawa brother (from the Gumatj dialect of East Arnhem Land).
[DARWIN AND NORTH COAST NT]

wax to share, or take turns (especially in a children's game or sport). Also spelled "whacks".
[CENTRAL HIGHLANDS VICTORIA, ADELAIDE REGION, GIPPSLAND, MELBOURNE REGION, NORTHERN VICTORIA, WESTERN DISTRICT, WIMMERA AND MALLEE, PERTH REGION, THE RIVERINA, HUNTER VALLEY AND NORTH COAST, SOUTH COAST AND SOUTHERN TABLELANDS]

weather shed a shed on school grounds, usually open on one side (and separate from the class rooms), in which children could play in wet weather. See **play shed**, **shelter shed**.
[HUNTER VALLEY AND NORTH COAST, SYDNEY REGION]

wedge[1] to buy yourself a drink between shouts.
[SYDNEY REGION, PERTH REGION]

wedge[2] 1. to try to win a mate's girlfriend from him 2. "a wedge" is the person who does this. [HUNTER VALLEY AND NORTH COAST]

weekender a holiday house or **shack**.
[CENTRAL WEST NSW, FAR WEST NSW, HUNTER VALLEY AND NORTH COAST, NEW ENGLAND DISTRICT, SOUTH COAST AND SOUTHERN TABLELANDS, SYDNEY REGION, THE RIVERINA]

weekend warrior[1] a home handyman (habits include: prowling the aisles of hardware stores on Saturday mornings, then making a mess of the house for the next day and a half). [SYDNEY REGION]

weekend warrior[2] a member of the Defence Force Reserves (derogatory). Largely obsolete; now replaced by "cut-lunch commando". [SYDNEY REGION, CENTRAL HIGHLANDS VICTORIA]

weero crested (mainly grey) parrot. Also called a "cockatiel".
[CENTRAL WEST AUSTRALIA, NORTHERN WEST AUSTRALIA, PERTH REGION]

wees and kees childish expression for emptying the body cavities ("wees" for the bladder and "kees" for the bowels.) Addressed to children during toilet-training (often with duplication of the word). [TASMANIA, NEW ENGLAND DISTRICT, HUNTER VALLEY AND NORTH COAST]

Weldon's a brand of street directory. See also **Gregory's** and **Referdex**. [SYDNEY REGION]

well verbal tag employed as an audible punctuation mark (as in, "I'm going to town, well"). See also **but** and **eh**.
[HUNTER VALLEY AND NORTH COAST]

Wenty abbreviation for the Sydney suburbs Wentworthville and Wentworth Park. [SYDNEY REGION]

were you born in a paddock with the sliprails down? Meaning: "Please shut the door." This indirect appeal to your good breeding and good taste occurs if you enter a room and leave the door open behind you. A common variation is, "Were you born in a tent?" to which the polite reply is, "No, a hospital with swinging doors."
[MELBOURNE REGION]

Werribee trout untreated faecal matter in the waters off ocean beaches. See also **blind mullet**, **blind trout**, **Bondi cigar**, **brown trout**, **King River prawn** and **pollywaffle**. [WESTERN DISTRICT]

westie originally a geographical identifier, indicating a person from the western suburbs of Sydney; now a derogatory term identifying a person as belonging to the burgeoning peasant underclass (indicated by their clothing, tastes, social skills etc.). Although this expression has now spread beyond Sydney, other labels are used in other regions to identify this same group: **bevan**, **bog**[2], **bogan**, **chigger**, **booner**, **boonie**, **feral**. In Sydney the geographical distinction quickly disappeared, due to lack of agreement as to what counted as "western suburbs". Balmain folk called Ryde residents westies; but Ryde said "not us" and labelled Parramatta people westies, they in turn repudiated the title and applied it to people from Penrith … and so on. (In fact, many residents of the eastern suburbs believe the western suburbs start at Anzac Parade.) See also **bennie**, **bethan**, **chookie**, **mocca** and **scozzer**.
[SYDNEY REGION, HUNTER VALLEY AND NORTH COAST, SOUTH COAST AND SOUTHERN TABLELANDS, CENTRAL HIGHLANDS VICTORIA]

westie shirt a flannelette checked shirt. See also **flannie**.
[HUNTER VALLEY AND NORTH COAST]

wet Nellie vanilla slice. See also **phlegm cake**, **pus pie** and **snot-block**. [MELBOURNE REGION, ADELAIDE REGION]

wet week slow, as in "You're as a slow as a wet week". Often addressed to a dawdling child. [THE RIVERINA]

whacko a long (5 to 6 metres) bamboo rod with a fishing line attached directly (no reel). One contributor explained: "The line required a string of corks to allow it to float on the surface of the water. Preferred bait was worms for smaller fish while larger fish were usually taken on moss found in the shallow water of the stream." [BRISBANE REGION]

whacko the chook a sarcastic expression of mock surprise.
[DARWIN AND NORTH COAST NT]

what o a form of general greeting (reportedly common around Devonport); replaces "hello", "g'day" etc. [TASMANIA]

wheel meat yet another name for this pre-cooked, sliced sausage meat (served cold). See also **baron sausage**, **beef Belgium**, **Belgium sausage**, **bung fritz**, **Byron sausage**, **devon**, **Empire sausage**, **fritz**, **German sausage**, **luncheon sausage**, **mystery meat**, **polony**, **pork German**, **Strasburg** and **Windsor sausage**.
[TASMANIA]

Wheelyabarraback mythical remote outback town. (Belongs on the same map as **Bundiwallop**, **Kickastickalong** and **Oodnagalahby**.)
[SYDNEY REGION, TASMANIA]

wheely bin large rubbish bin on wheels. See also **otto bin** and **sulo bin**.
[CENTRAL WEST NSW, FAR WEST NSW, HUNTER VALLEY AND NORTH COAST, NEW ENGLAND DISTRICT, SOUTH COAST AND SOUTHERN TABLELANDS, SYDNEY REGION, THE RIVERINA, BRISBANE REGION, CENTRAL WEST AUSTRALIA, PERTH REGION, WIMMERA AND MALLEE, CENTRAL HIGHLANDS VICTORIA, WESTERN DISTRICT, NORTHERN VICTORIA, GIPPSLAND, MELBOURNE REGION, EYRE AND YORKE PENINSULAS, ADELAIDE REGION, CENTRAL COAST QLD, NORTH COAST QLD]

where at to? meaning "Where did you go?" or "Where have you been?" See also **where is it to?** and **where ya to**? [FAR WEST NSW]

where is it to? meaning "Where is it?" or "Where have you been?" See also **where at to?** and **where ya to?**
[NORTHERN SOUTH AUSTRALIA, EYRE AND YORKE PENINSULAS]

where ya to? meaning "Where are you going?" or "Where have you been?" or "What are you doing now?" See also **where at to?** and **where is it to?** [FAR WEST NSW]

whippy[1] home base in a children's game (the whippy was usually **bar**[1]). [SYDNEY REGION]

whippy[2] a long flexible aerial on a vehicle. [FAR WEST NSW, NEW ENGLAND DISTRICT, CENTRAL WEST NSW]

whirly wind small twisting windstorm (a willy-willy). See also **cockeye bob.** [WEST CENTRAL QLD]

white ant to steal someone's girlfriend. [TASMANIA]

white can 1. a can of Swan Light beer. [DARWIN AND NORTH COAST NT, THE CENTRE] 2. a can of Carlton Draught beer. [MELBOURNE REGION] Also as "can of white". See **blue can, green can, red can, yellow can.**

white hen's chick top of the heap; phrase addressed to someone who is being overly self-congratulatory: "Aren't *you* just the white hen's chick?" [ADELAIDE REGION]

whoa-boy a drain and embankment dug diagonally across a steep farm track designed to divert water and prevent erosion. Also used of large potholes or scours on gravel roads. (Pronounced woo-boy.) [NORTH COAST QLD]

whoopee a work vehicle at a mining operation (e.g. a company ute). Also spelled "whoopy". [NORTHERN SOUTH AUSTRALIA, WEST CENTRAL QLD]

widow's curtain the flabby triceps (upper arms) of an overweight woman. See also **aunty arms, bingo wings, bye nows, good-bye muscle, nannas, piano arms, reverse biceps, ta-ta flaps** and **tuckshop arm.** [MELBOURNE REGION]

wife basher full-strength alcohol beer. (Sometimes known as "wife beater".) [PERTH REGION]

wild cat the quoll or native cat. [HUNTER VALLEY AND NORTH COAST]

wild man of Bungaree a person of wild or uncouth appearance or behaviour. (Often applied as a comic reprimand to children: "You look like the …".) [MELBOURNE REGION]

windcheater 1. a long-sleeved, fleecy-lined jacket or pullover. 2. a wind and water proof jacket.
[WIMMERA AND MALLEE, CENTRAL HIGHLANDS VICTORIA, WESTERN DISTRICT, NORTHERN VICTORIA, GIPPSLAND, MELBOURNE REGION, CENTRAL WEST AUSTRALIA, ADELAIDE REGION, PERTH REGION, CENTRAL COAST QLD, BRISBANE REGION]

windies winding roads (especially in the Adelaide Hills).
[ADELAIDE REGION]

window licker an intellectually disabled person (derogatory; highly offensive). See also **nuff nuff.** [MELBOURNE REGION]

Windsor sausage a large, mild-flavoured, precooked sausage, usually sliced thinly and eaten cold. (This is a patriotic name apparently substituted for earlier German-sounding names during the First World War.) See also **baron sausage, beef Belgium, Belgium sausage, bung fritz, Byron sausage, devon, Empire sausage, fritz, German sausage, luncheon sausage, mystery meat, polony, pork German, wheel meat** and **Strasburg.**
[BRISBANE REGION, CENTRAL COAST QLD, NORTH COAST QLD, FAR NORTH QLD, WEST CENTRAL QLD]

wine gooey a wine shop, often on the road side.
[NEW ENGLAND DISTRICT]

win on to flirt successfully with. [BRISBANE REGION]

wire gate temporary farm gate (fencing wire with steel posts or thin wooden posts). See also **bogan gate, COD gate** and **Methodist gate.** [CENTRAL WEST NSW]

wish the fluffy, airborne seeds of various plants. See also **fairy, Father Christmas, robber** and **Santa Claus.**
[SOUTH COAST AND SOUTHERN TABLELANDS]

with a sentence tag that asks a question. A contributor writes: "'With' is used in the Barossa in a way similar to the German *mit*, being put at the end of a sentence to imply 'with me' or 'with us', as in: 'Are you coming with?' meaning 'Are you coming with me?'"
[ADELAIDE REGION]

wock broken, deformed, incorrect. A contributor writes: "*The Toowoomba Chronicle* a few years ago discussed 'wock' as a regionalism restricted to the Darling Downs. Examples included: 'That table's no good, it's wock in the middle' and 'My dog can't see too well – he's got one wock eye.'" [BRISBANE REGION]

wodgil tall, shrubby vegetation dominated by acacia. Also known as "wodgil scrub". (Possibly from an Aboriginal source word.)
[NORTHERN WEST AUSTRALIA, CENTRAL WEST AUSTRALIA, PERTH REGION]

wog castle a large Italianate mansion, often red-brick with columns, with large expanses of concrete instead of lawn, and cement cherubs or other statuary in the front yard. (Derogatory.) Also as "wog mansion". [SYDNEY REGION]

wog roll a sausage roll in a buttered roll with sauce. Mostly associated with the western suburbs. (Note: does not have the Heart Foundation tick.) [MELBOURNE REGION]

wog shoes suede shoes. (Now obsolete; dates to a period when suede shoes were not widely available in Australia.)
[HUNTER VALLEY AND NORTH COAST]

wog togs see **Speedos**. See also **ballhuggers, boasters, budgie-huggers, budgie-smugglers, cluster busters, cockchokers, cock jocks, codjocks, dick bathers, dick-pointers, dick-pokers, dick stickers, dick togs, dikdaks, dipsticks, fish frighteners, jammers, Jimmy clingers, knobbies, lolly-baggers, lolly bags, meat-hangers, nut huggers, nylon disgusters, racers, racing bathers, scungies[2], sluggers, sluggos, slug huggers, tights, toolies** and **trunks**.
[HUNTER VALLEY AND NORTH COAST]

WOM acronym for Women Over Mates; a male who prefers to spend time with women instead of with his mates. (To the women he's a SNAG, but to the blokes he's a WOM.) [SYDNEY REGION]

womba crazy. (Possibly from an Aboriginal source word.) See also **Baillie, crackadog, Richmond Clinic, ward eight** and **ward twenty**.
[BRISBANE REGION, CENTRAL COAST QLD, NORTH COAST QLD, FAR NORTH QLD, WEST CENTRAL QLD]

wong a small shellfish found in sand. See also **cockle, eugarie** and **pipi**. [BRISBANE REGION]

wongie watermelon; watermelon rind. (For schoolboys, a wongie fight consisted of spitting or throwing chunks of watermelon rind at each other.) [ADELAIDE REGION, PERTH REGION]

wood in the hole, put the shut the door. See also **were you born in a paddock with the sliprails down?** [CENTRAL WEST NSW]

wop to take a day off school; to wag school.
[HUNTER VALLEY AND NORTH COAST]

woppett yet another Australian expression for a drongo, drip, dill or boofhead. See also **drap sack** and **rubbernut.** [MELBOURNE REGION]

worker's crack the cleavage that peeps coyly above the belt as the shorts creep down. See also **builder's smile** and **coin slot**.
[SYDNEY REGION]

working like a drover's pup working very hard. (Sometimes "working like a drover's dog".) [BRISBANE REGION]

wouldn't stop a fat pig in a narrow passage bow-legged or bandy-legged. [MELBOURNE REGION]

wriggly tin corrugated iron. [BRISBANE REGION, NORTHERN SOUTH AUSTRALIA]

wrinkly an elderly person. Also spelled "wrinklie".
[DARWIN AND NORTH COAST NT]

wumps, to get the to die, used only of cows. (Supposedly from the sound a cow makes when it falls over dead.)
[CENTRAL COAST QLD, WEST CENTRAL QLD]

XYZ

XPT express passenger train.

XYZ jam tin a nonsense expression used to replace a series of irrelevant words in a story, or to replace a name you have forgotten. [WEST CENTRAL QLD]

yabbo a member of the peasant underclass; an ill-mannered boor. (Probably a local variation on the British slang term "yob" or "yobbo".)

[BRISBANE REGION, CENTRAL COAST QLD, NORTH COAST QLD, FAR NORTH QLD, WEST CENTRAL QLD]

yabby edible, freshwater crayfish. Also spelled "yabbie". From the Wembawemba Aboriginal language (Victoria/New South Wales) yabij. The activity of catching yabbies is called yabbying. Very small yabbies (obtained on mudflats or sandy beaches using a yabby pump) are used as bait. Yabbies often inhabit farm dams. Yabbies are native to New South Wales, Victoria and South Australia, and were stocked into farm dams in Western Australia in 1932 (where their wide spread now poses a threat to the marron fishery). See also **cherub**, **clawchie**, **crawbob**, **crawchie**, **craybob**, **craydab**, **crayfish**, **jilgie**, **lobby**, **lobster**, **marron** and **pink nipper**.

[ADELAIDE REGION, CENTRAL HIGHLANDS VICTORIA, EYRE AND YORKE PENINSULAS, GIPPSLAND, MELBOURNE REGION, NORTHERN VICTORIA, SOUTH COAST AND SOUTHERN TABLELANDS, TASMANIA, THE RIVERINA, WESTERN DISTRICT, WIMMERA AND MALLEE, NORTH COAST QLD, CENTRAL COAST QLD, SYDNEY REGION, NORTHERN WEST AUSTRALIA, CENTRAL WEST AUSTRALIA, PERTH REGION, BRISBANE REGION]

yacka a grasstree plant.

[EYRE AND YORKE PENINSULAS, ADELAIDE REGION, NORTHERN SOUTH AUSTRALIA]

yaffle empty talk; endless talk; to waffle on; to prattle on.
[TASMANIA]

yalla-bax Darwin Community Night Patrol vehicle (which has yellow canvas on the rear cage section, hence yellow, or yalla, box or bax). [DARWIN AND NORTH COAST NT]

yammagi an Aborigine, especially a male Aborigine. Also spelled "yamidgee". From the Aboriginal language Watjari (Murchison River, Western Australia) word *yamaji* meaning "person, man".
[NORTHERN WEST AUSTRALIA, CENTRAL WEST AUSTRALIA, PERTH REGION]

yang yang wild cattle (also used of wild people). [WEST CENTRAL QLD]

yappa sister (in the Gumatj dialect used in north-east Arnhem Land); used loosely, as Europeans use "mate".
[DARWIN AND NORTH COAST NT]

yard duty rostered time a teacher spends supervising students in a school playground. See also **playground duty**.
[WIMMERA AND MALLEE, CENTRAL HIGHLANDS VICTORIA, WESTERN DISTRICT, NORTHERN VICTORIA, GIPPSLAND, MELBOURNE REGION, TASMANIA, WIMMERA AND MALLEE, EYRE AND YORKE PENINSULAS, ADELAIDE REGION, PERTH REGION, BRISBANE REGION, DARWIN AND NORTH COAST NT]

Yarra banker soapbox orator; one who harangues passers-by from a soapbox on the banks of the Yarra; an agitator.
[WIMMERA AND MALLEE, CENTRAL HIGHLANDS VICTORIA, WESTERN DISTRICT, NORTHERN VICTORIA, GIPPSLAND, MELBOURNE REGION]

Yeah Griff expression of sarcastic disbelief (similar to "Yeah, right!"). [CENTRAL WEST NSW]

yeast any cake or bun containing yeast.
[ADELAIDE REGION, EYRE AND YORKE PENINSULAS, WIMMERA AND MALLEE]

yeast bun a glazed or iced sweet bun (sometimes containing fruit). See **fruit bun**.
[ADELAIDE REGION, EYRE AND YORKE PENINSULAS, NORTHERN SOUTH AUSTRALIA, FAR WEST NSW, MELBOURNE REGION]

yellow belly[1] golden perch.
[CENTRAL COAST QLD, NORTHERN VICTORIA, THE RIVERINA, SYDNEY REGION]

yellow belly[2] the red wattlebird (which has a yellow-tinted underbelly). [MELBOURNE REGION]

yellow belly[3] a fifty dollar note. See also **fiddy, golden drinking voucher, olive leaf, peacemaker, pineapple** and **Uncle David**.
[BRISBANE REGION]

yellow can a can of Castlemaine XXXX beer. Sometimes called "a can of yellow". See also **blue can**, **green can**, **red can** and **white can**. [DARWIN AND NORTH COAST NT]

yellow Monday a type of yellowish cicada. See also **black prince**, **brown baker**, **brown bomber**[2], **cherrynose**, **cicada**, **floury baker**, **greengrocer**[2], **pisswhacker** and **tick tock**. [SYDNEY REGION]

yellow sand bright yellow sand used by brickies (occasionally called "lawn sand"). [PERTH REGION]

yellow sticker a police notice identifying an unroadworthy vehicle (attached to the windscreen of the offending vehicle). See also **canary**[1]. [NORTHERN WEST AUSTRALIA, CENTRAL WEST AUSTRALIA, PERTH REGION]

yes, no expression used as a sentence starter, where only the context can determine if the positive or negative is intended. As in, "Yes, no, I'll come with you." Sometimes in the form of "Yeah, no". [NORTH COAST QLD, FAR NORTH QLD, SYDNEY REGION, WESTERN DISTRICT, MELBOURNE REGION]

yickadee an exclamation of greeting or farewell. (Aboriginal.) [DARWIN AND NORTH COAST NT, THE CENTRE]

yike an argument, disagreement, fight. [ADELAIDE REGION]

yip yip a member of the rodeo crowd (or who dresses like one). [WEST CENTRAL QLD]

yiros (or "yeeros") slices of lamb or mutton, layered with herbs and spices on a vertical spit and roasted as it revolves against a tall narrow grill. As the surface is cooked the meat is sliced thinly downwards and served, often with flat bread. From the Greek word *gyros* (pronounced "year-ross") – related to the English word "gyrate", because the meat turns as it cooks. The regional significance is that in some parts of Australia this is known by the Greek name (yiros) and in others by the Turkish name (Doner Kebab, or simply kebab) and in others by an alternative Greek name (souvlaki). [DARWIN AND NORTH COAST NT, ADELAIDE REGION, SYDNEY REGION]

YMCA dinner leftovers (Yesterday's Muck Cooked Again). [SYDNEY REGION, BRISBANE REGION]

Yogie visitors from the Australian Capital Territory (where car numberplates start with "Y"). Also spelled "Yogi".
[SOUTH COAST AND SOUTHERN TABLELANDS, SYDNEY REGION]

yonnie a stone, especially one for throwing. According to some contributors a yonnie is larger than a **brinnie**. So, is a yonnie no larger than a piece of gravel? Or is it large enough to stop a plough? There was no common agreement among contributors on these technical details. See also **boondie**[2], **brinnie**, **connie**[2], **gibber**, **goolie**, **gonnie** and **ronnie**.
[CENTRAL HIGHLANDS VICTORIA, GIPPSLAND, MELBOURNE REGION, NORTHERN SOUTH AUSTRALIA, NORTHERN VICTORIA, TASMANIA, WESTERN DISTRICT, WIMMERA AND MALLEE]

Yorkie the intellectually stimulating activity of driving a car up and down the main street of Albany, Western Australia. [PERTH REGION]

yourn pronoun: second person singular possessive; as in "Is that dog yourn?" [TASMANIA]

yukka no, not, no-way. [DARWIN AND NORTH COAST NT]

yukka worries no worries. (From the Yolngu word for "no".)
[DARWIN AND NORTH COAST NT]

Z car a NSW government car (numberplates of which begin with "Z"). See also **red plate** and **QG**.
[BRISBANE REGION, CENTRAL COAST QLD, FAR NORTH QLD, NORTH COAST QLD, WEST CENTRAL QLD]

zivagating the movement patterns of a drunk whose feet are firmly placed on the ground but whose body is describing circular motions. [TASMANIA]

zonkerpede an all-purpose name for an unidentified insect of vaguely sinister appearance. [MELBOURNE REGION, BRISBANE REGION]

zots pimples. See also **acker** and **gumby**. [CENTRAL COAST QLD]